# ❧ Limits of horror ❧

D1568298

MANCHESTER
1824

Manchester University Press

# Limits of horror
## Technology, bodies, Gothic

Fred Botting

Manchester University Press
Manchester and New York
*distributed in the United States exclusively
by Palgrave Macmillan*

Published by Manchester University Press
Oxford Road, Manchester M13 9NR, UK
and Room 400, 175 Fifth Avenue, New York, NY 10010, USA
www.manchesteruniversitypress.co.uk

Distributed in the United States exclusively by
Palgrave Macmillan, 175 Fifth Avenue,
New York, NY 10010, USA

Distributed in Canada exclusively by
UBC Press, University of British Columbia, 2029 West Mall,
Vancouver, BC, Canada V6T 1Z2

British Library Cataloguing-in-Publication Data is available

Library of Congress Cataloging-in-Publication Data is available

ISBN 978 0 7190 8365 5 paperback

First published by Manchester University Press in hardback 2008

This paperback edition first published 20011

Printed by Lightning Source

# Contents

# Acknowledgements

Many people have helped in the process of writing this book, too many to mention by name. Colleagues in the Department of English at Keele University were particularly supportive and constructive in their criticisms as were numerous colleagues across several departments at Lancaster University. That august body of scholars, the International Gothic Association, offered a highly productive environment for developing ideas on the topic and many of its members provided much stimulating conversation. Parts of the work have previously appeared in different forms and I would like to thank the editors of the following presses and journals for allowing revised versions to be reprinted here: the English Association, *Gothic Studies*, Cambridge University Press, *Romantic Circles Praxis*. I would also like to acknowledge the role of the Arts and Humanities Research Council in granting much-needed research leave to aid in the completion of this project.

# Introduction
# Horror now and then

## Making love to a vampire with a monkey on my knee

'WHOOAH BITE! WHOOAH BITE!' An impassioned howl fights its way through a rumbling screech of metal, skins and amplified wire. 'Sex bat horror vampire sex ...' The singer writhes and flails, tall and skinny in a second-hand suit, head topped with a mess of back-combed black hair. 'Sex bat horror vampire sex ...' The frame of reference is Gothic, heavily inflected with an early 1980s Goth chic suturing of punk and metal (but let's not get too new romantic) in a dark swathe of leather, dye and make-up. Not that there are many Goths on stage: drummer and guitarist have sensible haircuts and the bassist, cropped under a ten-gallon hat, wears a tight bodybuilder's t-shirt! 'Sex vampire, cool machine ...' The audience, despite some body-crashing revels, is none the less beginning to look distinctly gloomy. 'Bauhaus', with a pared-down, posed, art school glamour gloom, have already won cult status for a celebration of the undeath of Bela Lugosi. There is more, much more, yet to crawl from the cave, more singles and albums to be released, more press releases, more leather and dye. 'Release the Bats' howls in anticipation – and dark mockery. 'Release the Goths', it seems to say, and mysteriously the machine of popular culture complies.

'Horror Vampire ...' The ventriloquised exchange between the song's speaker and his vampire-loving lover does not look particularly favourably on the emerging world of Goth. Dolled up, one imagines, to resemble a late twentieth-century idea of the vampiric femme fatale, she yearns for something more than the masquerade: 'Horror Vampire/ How I wish those bats would bite!' Her wish implies that 'those bats' are toothless, another masquerade devoid of the very dangers and horrors with which they are associated. 'Bite!' The exclamation is an incantation, a demand for action: 'She doesn't mind a bit of dirt'. But she doesn't get bitten by those horror sex vampire bats. Like any self-respecting femme fatale, she registers disappointment: 'She says damn that horror bat/ Sex vampire, cool machine'. She has been let down. All she wants is a little bite from the real thing, but all she gets is a 'cool machine'. Promising so much intensity, so much sexhorrorjoy, the bats have no bite. Those bats, like her, are sex vampire cool machine: 'my baby is a cool machine'. It's all fabrication, coolly machined. Her pose acknowledges theirs and the mirroring exposes the artifice accompanying all Gothic productions from Walpole's fake original and fabricated castle, Twain's dismissal of southern Gothic shams to *Rocky Horror* camp, and beyond.

'Release the Bats', then, is far from a call to unleash the wolverine children of the night. A song of disillusion and mockery: a scruffy band of Australians arrive in early 1980s London expecting a vibrant and anarchic music scene. However, the bright-burning negativities of punk have guttered in the made-up face of Goth's plundering of an all-too familiar wardrobe. *The Birthday Party*'s repertoire, littered with songs of degradation, sexual horror and quasi-sacred abjection, does little to dispel their assimilation as a 'crucial proto-Goth' group (Reynolds, 433). But the comedy is not lost on everyone: 'Release the Bats' 'rocks so rabidly it just can't help being as funny as fuck' (Mulholland, 164). The havoc wreaked by the song is wreaked on the very expectations embedded in the Goth masquerade of darkness and horror. If she, as cool sex horror vampire machine, is disappointed in her demand for some serious bloody tooth action (bite me!), the song sets out the illusions in which she and her dark kind cloak themselves. It is not a call for a release of some primordial energy or for an expression of some dark truth but bitterly and energetically mocks the masquerade as itself a mockery. 'Bite!' the injunction vainly exclaims in Goth's gaping fangless maw. But if it is no more than mockery, the song nonetheless acknowledges an appeal that operates at the level of fantasy: an imagined thrill of sex horror vampire stuff remains in her wish to be bitten. It is a fantasy that, though everywhere realised only in cool machine mockery, sustains and harbours the possibility of some dark and intense actualisation. The disjunction, doomed to remain on the side of wish rather than fulfilment even as its masquerade endlessly replays itself, may require a different kind of release: a release from rather than of the bats. Just let them go; unchain them from the tired cycle of fantasy and vain masquerade.

## Disneygothic

Reports of turmoil in Transylvania reached the British press in March 2002. UNESCO heritage experts were sent to Sighisoara, Europe's only inhabited citadel and a world heritage site. With the support of 85 per cent of the local population, the Romanian government was preparing to open a Dracula terror park on the basis that the fifteenth-century Count Vlad Tepes ('Vlad the Impaler') may have been born there. A ghost castle, Dracula hotels and a 'vampirology' centre had been designed; snack bars serving blood red candy-floss, plates of brains, garlic-flavoured ice cream and blood pudding were planned. The exclusive rights to soft drinks sales had already been sold to Coca-Cola (for £330,000) and negotiations with the Austrian beer company, Brau Union, and the hotel chain, Best Western, were well in hand. Before you book your holidays, the row between the government and UNESCO resulted in plans being shelved. Historical heritage, perhaps only temporarily, won out over the more commercial myth market. Don't be disappointed, however. The Castel Hotel Dracula is open. Located in Bistrita-Nasaud, Romania, at an altitude of 3,600 feet in the Carpathian mountains, it is a mock-Gothic edifice with a turret nightclub built between 1983 and 1985. It has been refurbished and rebranded since then. At the time of building no references to Dracula were permitted: it was built for Nicolae Caeusescu.

Disneygothic, of course, has already happened. The Romanian government were only trying to cash in on a lucrative market long since opened up by Hollywood studios. The terror park need not have been located in Romania, but a tiny touch of the real always helps heritage marketing: Vlad the Impaler, a possible historical model for Dracula *may* have been born in Sighisoara, and the Castel Hotel boasts a Carpathian setting. Not that reality really matters when it comes to the Gothic heritage business. Disney, as Baudrillard notes in his account of the end of history, already includes Gothic. As a place 'where all past and present forms meet in playful promiscuity, where all cultures recur in mosaic', Disneyworld presents 'a prefiguration of the real trend of things'. 'Magic Country, Future World, Gothic, Hollywood itself' are sites where 'the whole of the past and the future [are] revisited as living simulation' (Baudrillard, 1994: 115). Gothic, curiously, is prominent, a tacit acknowledgement, perhaps, of its enduring involvement in history's fabrication. It is an appropriate inclusion none the less, providing an image of dead simulations living on vampirically, freezing all culture and history in their immortal bite. But simulations have another function: they work differentially and retrospectively in the play of imaginary and real. Disneyland, supposedly imaginary, maintains the illusion that America is real even though it is already given over to the unreal. So, too, with Gothic: it preserves the illusion of darkness, death, and sexuality in a world given over to the omnipresence of virtual light and life on screens. Its trajectory is double, however: Gothic versions of mortality and the sexual body emphasise bloody corpses, ripped flesh and oozing wounds. Its imagined return to the pulsing reality of the body evokes re-pulsion, a pulsion to the body and of the body, but also away from the body, a repulsion that accelerates the career of images within further simulations and idealised bodily forms.

Gothic forms, though celebrated for their subcultural and subversive status, for their fantastic disclosure of another, 'realer' if darker reality are inextricably entangled in webs of simulation. Discussing the way that ideas of reality change in respect of the conventions of visual communication, Teresa de Lauretis draws numerous examples from horror cinema to illustrate the paradoxes of live TV and mediated reality. If 'reality is only accessible as televised', then 'the paradox of current Hollywood cinema is that reality must surpass in visual fascination the horrors of say, Carpenter's *Halloween* or Romero's *Dawn of the Dead*, must be fantasm-agoria, revelation, apocalypse here and now'(45). Horror cinema frames reality, demands that reality (distinguished from simulation by the stain of horror and shock of violence) must be more fascinating and horrible. But neither fiction nor actuality, neither reality nor illusion, remain in fixed opposition. The terms have been displaced: 'it is not by chance that all the nature-culture thresholds are being thematized and transgressed in recent movies: incest, life/death (vampires, zombies, and other living dead), human/non-human (aliens, clones, demon seeds, pods, fogs, etc), and sexual difference (androgyns, transsexuals, transvestites, or Transylvanians)' (45). Made in 1984, de Lauretis's observation is only reinforced by the succession of often high-profile re-makes undertaken in subsequent years. Reality, she concludes, is superseded by hyperreality as it assumes the power to simulate all aspects of nature, from Edenic plenitude to horrifying decomposition: reality finds itself '*absolutely* coded', 'not merely artificial, artful, made-up, masqueraded, transvested or perverted, but permanently so, like the vision of its viewers, irreversibly transformed'(6). Even that little bit of the real, the darkness or pulsing, slimy excess of horror, say, cannot, it seems, escape the absolute coding of simulation.

## Simulating abjection

A teenager in Anglesey cuts out the heart of an old age pensioner. His computer reveals extensive interest in vampirism websites. North American students go on high school shooting sprees: horror films, Goth music and violent videogames are cited as their hobbies. 'Scream' killings occur across Europe, the killer wearing a mask popularised by the stalking villain of Wes Craven's movie. In Germany a notoriously bloody case unfolds: a Goth couple, Daniel and Manuela Ruda, are sentenced for murder. They hammered, stabbed and carved their 33-year-old male victim with a pentagram, drinking his blood.

'Pitch black vampire seeks princess of darkness who hates everything and everyone.' Daniel and Manuela met through small ads placed in a heavy metal magazine. They enjoyed visits to graveyards and ruins; they practiced devil worship; at home they slept in silk-lined coffins. He had animal fangs implanted and filed down; she became a vampire during visits to London Goth clubs, clubs where, according to Ruda, one can 'have a perfectly normal chat and drink some blood'.

Where do simulations begin or end? Does horror or abjection counter their thrust or feed the cool machine with a fleeting bite? These horrors seem to defy hyperreality and simulation with bloody, violent and all-too real acts. But simulations have effects. The world of these killers is, or is presented as, one suffused with Gothic images and myths. The Rudas' lifestyle takes its bearings from fictions; their act interpreted as a 'Gothic horror' (McGowan, 5). Boundaries between fiction and reality blur, to the extent that each interpenetrates and shapes the other, dismantling conventional patterns of differentiation. For the Rudas, vampirism entered everyday life, perfectly normal chats and the drinking of blood rendered familiar and routine activities. At the same time, ascriptions of 'Gothic horror' attempt to register repulsion at the enormity and excess of their act: its horror lies beyond reality or hyperreality even as it is rendered almost palatable (palatable enough, at least, for the prurient) in fictional and generic terms. Normal and excessive, routine and repugnant, attributions of horror retroactively confirm the act as both a simulation and irruption of the (simulated) real. Vampires, of course, have only ever been unreal beings: to live as a vampire makes the unreal of familiar horror images real. In taking its bearing from fiction, in violently realising scenes from page and screen, it simultaneously rejects and returns to a world of simulations: desire and fantasy, coordinated by image and text, seek out the horrifying plenitude of a reality displayed and deferred in simulation. Hence the paradox (or what in modernity's terms would appear as paradox – or psychosis): to simulate vampirism (to the extent of turning it into an everyday lifestyle) is undertaken with the aim of breaking through sanitised screens of hyperreality, of finding something real in blood and horror. But bloody, violent, horrifying reality – shaped by Gothic figures and horror fictions – is returned as Gothic horror by the media. Artifice, conformism, convention remain at work, despite the efforts to break through their frames in acts of violent realisation. 'Horror bat. Bite!'

Violence, horror, abjection, in being rendered figures of excess, are opposed to or cast out of hyperreality only to the extent that their excision gives simulations some bite.

What appear as counters to heritage or disneygothic, horror and abjection, remain tied to simulation. Spectacular and very real enactments of vampirism, in pursuing a nostalgia for modernity defined by distinctions of reality and fantasy, nature or culture, to the extent of murderously mimicking a creature that never was, intensify the spin of simulations. A violent consumption looks back to darkly idealised times, rendered hygienic by heritage and screen visions; it re-pulses from the sanitisation to search for a fantasised reality of blood and death. A vicious, repetitive short-circuit. Media, too, look for realer images to anchor their spin of simulations, feeding upon horrors that cannot be fully expelled by the reactive condemnations of moral judgement and social panic. Simulations, it seems, come too close to home: in 1993 in Liverpool a very young child, James Bulger, was killed by two slightly older boys. The disturbing case of child child-murderers brought out an unbearable proximity between screens and social realities. A horror movie – from the *Child's Play* series – apparently inspired the impressionable young killers to terrible mimicry. Social control, censorship, parental (and communal) responsibility, were cited in the anxious aftermath, attempts to understand, explain, blame. Other than an automatic identification of the evil nature of the killers, unequivocal judgements were difficult to make. Perhaps the act, and the circumstances that surrounded it, were symptoms of the critical nature of the times. Much later, reviewing the case and its reverberations, Blake Morrison commented: 'it is the age of the Bad Boys. And we're the Frankensteins who made them. From the spring of 1993 can be dated this new horror, of the monsters to whom we've given birth – dwarf killers …' (Morrison, 12). A deed, apparently inspired by horror video, finds another explanation in different Gothic terms. As Frankensteins responsible for creating the new horror of dwarf killers, every member of society is found to be at fault. The new horror demands a broader Gothic frame: fiction and film cross into everyday life, displaying the permeable, shifting boundaries between reality and fantasy and enveloping every social position. We are all Frankensteins, or monsters. The collapse of boundaries separating reality and fantasy, fiction and life, a psychological condition associated by Freud with the uncanny, has become generalised. No one, its seems, is immune from its effects: Morrison's account of 'dwarf killers', monsters whose deeds return on those who made them, suggests that evil, otherness and the fictional figures which give them familiar form, cannot be simply excluded or expelled.

## A general uncanny

The Enlightenment did away with ghosts and supernatural beings. Reason and empiricism bestowed a scientific order on the world and condemned spirits and spectres to a bygone barbaric age of superstitious credulity, a primitive, immature stage of culture akin to childhood (Addison, Scott). Curiously, however, ghosts and spectres kept on returning in Gothic romances, popular dramas and spectacular entertainments. These remnants of a superseded era, like the ruins, old and new, that littered country estates, haunted an enlightened present. Like Horace Walpole's 'Gothic story' and his fake 'Gothic' mansion, these remnants were inventions, fabricated leftovers distinguishing past from present and delineating cultural and historical differences that testified to the newness of modernity. As much productions as anything else in the eighteenth century, the signs of its past functioned as significant markers of cultural, scientific, commercial, political and economic transformation.

The uncanny, too, assumed modern form in the eighteenth century. In premodern times, the uncanny had a religious and social place and retained sacred and untouchable associations: super-natural, it lay outside the mundane world. The 'specific historical conjuncture' named as the Enlightenment introduces a '*specific dimension of the uncanny that emerges with modernity*': the uncanny 'constantly haunts' modernity 'from the inside' (Dolar, 1991: 7). As a register of social and political transformations, the uncanny, with its psychological focus, its manifestation of shifting boundaries, is an effect of the physical and ideological disturbances attendant on a move to commercial and industrial economic organisation, middle-class society, democratic politics and bourgeois individualism. It is no accident, Dolar notes, that Gothic fictions reached the height of their popularity in the period of the French Revolution:

> There was an irruption of the uncanny strictly parallel with bourgeois (and industrial) revolutions and the rise of scientific rationality – and, one might add, with the Kantian establishment of transcendental subjectivity, of which the uncanny presents the surprising counterpart. Ghosts, vampires, monsters, the undead, etc., flourish in an era when you might expect them to be dead and buried, without a place. They are something brought about by modernity itself. (7)

The uncanny, less a return from the past, becomes an effect of a disturbed present, a present affected by massive upheaval and transformation. It is less the revenance of a lost or suppressed human nature (against the artifices of modern culture) and more a product of scientific and technical innovation (Castle). Like the ruins that remain in an eighteenth-century (literary) landscape, the uncanny marks dis-continuity: situated in a gap between epochs, a gap carved out by the developments a nascent modernity has still to fill, it simultaneously signals the breakdown of older social formations and values (feudal, religious, aristocratic, agricultural) and acknowledges the institution of modern arrangements (enlightened, secular, scientific, bourgeois, commercial).

The uncanny, an effect of the emergence of modernity, participates as much in its constitution as its decomposition. Crossing boundaries, it marks out differences; its displacements signalling relocations. Slavoj Zizek offers an instructive way of understanding the ghosts of modernity: 'perhaps the best way of encapsulating the gist of an epoch is to focus not on the explicit features that define its social and ideological edifices but on the disavowed ghosts that haunt it, dwelling in a mysterious region of nonexistent entities which none the less *persist*, continue to exert their efficacy' (Zizek, 2000: 3). The spectres, rather than spirit, of an age define it. As a gap in which excluded or suppressed figures arise, the uncanny announces the doubleness of modernity: fantasy irrupts into reality, ghosts, death, darkness and monstrosity crossing lines of exclusion, otherness returning upon the same. At the same time, in giving form to the disturbing locus of otherness, dressing it up as monster or vampire, modernity partially stabilises anxiety with objects of fear, exclusion or repugnance. Modernity thus constitutes and polices its boundaries on the basis of the exceptions, the others or monsters, it excludes: workers, women, deviants, criminals, 'orientals' etc. are produced as the antitheses fantasmatically and ideologically establishing modern norms of bourgeois rationality, heteronormative sexuality, racial integrity, social and cultural cohesion (see Hogle, 2002). For all attempts to contain and define otherness, the relation remains ambivalent, haunted by a monstrosity that cannot be recognised or countenanced.

In his account of the discursive formation of modernity, Michel Foucault comments upon the function of monsters in processes of biological classification. Unnatural but of nature, monsters are necessary figures in the taxonomic systems through which species are identified and associated. Monsters are both necessary and excluded, exceptional figures crucial in the process of furnishing the natural world with systematic scientific knowledge: they serve as the 'backward projection of those differences and identities that provide *taxonomia* first with structure, then with character' (Foucault, 1970: 157). Monstrous exceptions allow structures to be identified and instituted, difference providing the prior condition for identity to emerge. As exceptions to the norm, monsters make visible, in their transgression, the limits separating proper from improper, self from other. For Jacques Derrida, 'faced with a monster, one may become aware of what the norm is and when the norm has a history'. In this way, monsters are not merely sites of expulsion and otherness, but figures who serve in 'an analysis of the history of norms' (Derrida, 1992a: 385–6). As exceptions to historically specific and artificially constructed norms, monsters define the limits of a particular formation. Yet, constantly invoked in the policing of norms, they retain a curious position on the margins of cultural formations, the negatives to an enlightened self-image. While remaining projections, figures designed to screen the lack of systematic foundations in nature, their exclusion also serves to legitimate, naturalise and solidify those boundaries. Doubleness clings to modernity: if it invents the liberties, it also produces an array of disciplinary mechanisms; if it seeks to enlighten, it also conjures up realms of darkness to penetrate and illuminate; if it realises a spirit of human progress, it also imagines spectres of regression. Gothic fictions, in Anne Williams's phrase, disclose the 'mysteries of Enlightenment', the internal differences and limits and darkness on which modernity's systems of knowledge depend. Light and dark, good and evil, knowledge and mystery, self and monster, are paired productions of the same cultural system rather than natural or universal characteristics. Reiterations of persistent and hackneyed dualities in (human) nature as explanations of Gothic phenomena as, say, the dark or evil side of the mind, avoid examining their systematic entanglement in a modernity that invents the human figure and is itself doubly constructed.

## Pervasion

'Frank N Stein' was a comic monster who served in the privatisation of national electricity utilities in Britain in the 1990s. 'Count Duckula' and 'Count Chocula' were, respectively, cartoon characters and cereal icons, Gothic figures for children in a period full of little monsters and friendly ghosts. Buffy slays vampires with ease but finds it harder to lay teen angst to rest. Lost boys roam near dark boulevards; Hollywood remakes old and new horrors, so many nocturnal returns of the dawn of living dead shopping their way across screens and malls. Clothes, puppets, masks, lifestyles, dolls, sweets, locate Gothic images in a thoroughly commodified context in which horror is rendered familiar. No longer exceptions, the monsters of and on technical screens are no different from the norms they once negatively defined.

The doublets defining modernity have become disentangled and the uncanny, barely frightening, crosses boundaries in overly familiar repetitions, a hint of disturbing transformations, perhaps, but also an indication that modern systems of normalisation, exclusion and differentiation have become increasingly difficult to sustain, legitimate or police. The condition is, as Lyotard has diagnosed it, postmodern: metanarratives fragment, boundaries collapse, systems of difference unravel. Ghosts become ordinary figures for the operations of new technologies and their hallucinatory, virtual effects (Kittler 1990; Virilio 1995a). Monsters of modernity, once the exceptions giving shape, difference and substance to the systems that excluded them, become normal. No longer monstrous, these figures, recognisable, reiterated, familiar, are 'normal monstrosities' (Derrida, 1990: 80). Identity and difference, norm and monster become indistinguishable in a proliferation of differentiations and hybrids. Charting a shift in relationships and representation, Foucault notes the move in modern painting from an articulation of resemblances and affirmation which sustain a hierarchy of identities and differences to an order in which similitude alone comes to the fore: 'a day will come when, by means of similitude relayed indefinitely along the length of a series, the image itself, along with the name it bears, will lose its identity. Campbell. Campbell. Campbell. Campbell' (Foucault, 1982: 54). Warhol's Pop Art serves as the destiny of a move from artistic and mechanical reproduction to an order of similitude based on endless reiterations of the same. Difference and otherness, too, are absorbed in the serial circulations of the same, a flat plane of indifference, the monstrosity of norms.

Difference evaporates into the in-difference of simulations; otherness collapses on the same. Boundaries between inside and outside become redundant. A persistence of Gothic forms and figures becomes a 'per-vasion' (Seltzer, 1995: 145; Punter, 1998: 168). Unlike the more familiar 'invasion', through which bodies or minds are taken over by external, alien or supernatural forces, pervasion describes a more thoroughgoing dislocation of spatial, physical and fantasmatic coordinates. Embodied and bounded experience, it seems, fades in the face of technical mediations that manifest their own ghostly force. In a discussion of the phenomenal changes wrought by new visual technologies like television, videogame and computer screens, Vivian Sobchack suggests that interiority is opened to the scrutiny of pervasive screens transforming culture and consciousness (Sobchack, 1987: 229–32). The pervasion of new technologies eclipses modern notions of difference that sustain a hierarchical and humanist sense of self and body. Invoking Foucault's discussion of resemblance and difference, otherness (in this case science fiction's representations of aliens) shifts from rendering the other 'like us', thereby maintaining a system of resemblance and differentiation in which modern oppositional hierarchies are preserved, to making the other the same as us in 'reversible and non-hierarchical relations of similitude'. The effect is to displace otherness from marking 'the difference that makes a difference' to 'the difference that makes a sameness' (Sobchack, 1987: 297). Pervasion thus describes the everyday effects of hyperreality as it takes its leave from a modern framework: 'no more black magic of the forbidden, alienation and transgression, but the white magic of ecstasy, fascination, transparency' (Baudrillard, 1990a: 71). Beyond transgression and limits lies terroristic homogeneity.

Beyond transgression all the paraphernalia of Gothic modernity change: the uncanny is not where it used to be, nor are ghosts, doubles, monsters and vampires. Nor are the systems which produce them. Pervasion, however, ensures ghostly reanimations: 'our entire culture is full of this haunting of the separated double' (Baudrillard, 1993a: 142). Ghosts, however, are no longer the negatives of a real world: 'in denouncing the ghostliness of those technologies – and of the media – one implies that there is somewhere an original form of lived existence. Whereas, if the rate of reality is falling every day, this is because the medium itself has passed into life, has become the ordinary ritual of transparency' (1996: 27–8). Transgression, in modernity, did not function as a celebratory subversion of tyrannical laws: in crossing limits, it gave them form. Foucault, discussing the glib notion of sexual liberation, outlines the complex 'play' of transgression and limit where one is defined in terms of the other as part of a single network (Foucault, 1977). Now, however, with a postmodern incredulity towards paternal metanarratives, metaphor cedes to metonymy, transgression to transversalism:

> economics becomes transeconomics, aesthetics becomes transaesthetics, sex becomes transsexuality – all converge in a transversal and universal process wherein no discourse may have a metaphorical relationship to another, because for there to be metaphor differential fields and distinct objects must exist. But they cannot exist where contamination is possible between any discipline and any other. Total metonymy, then – viral by definition (or lack of definition). (Baudrillard, 1993b: 7–8)

Monsters, the uncanny, ghosts, all Gothic forms tied to modern metanarratives and bound up with metaphor, are transformed in a viral play that generalises and assimilates all categories … without limit, otherness, or difference.

## Gothicise

Modern culture produced Gothic forms and figures that served in the negative definition of its limits so that the genre occupied a shadowy place in the context in which it circulated. There it, if not entirely overlooked, could reflect critically and culturally on modernity. When otherness and differences roam freely, like transnational capital, across all borders, Gothic becomes both more visible and more difficult to locate. The genre, appropriately enough, begins to eat itself: consuming its own conventions in a highly reflexive play of recycled features. Wes Craven's *Scream* offers a good example of horror's 'devouring and regurgitating' of its own history (Kermode). Even as it implodes as a genre, it continues to expand in a pulsive movement across cultures, screens, texts, and criticism. Collecting a long list of 'gothics', Maurice Lévy identifies a proliferation that threatens to gothicise the entirety of human experience: 'if Gothic is not just a literary *genre* … if Gothic has become our surrounding culture, if Gothic is history and not myth, if Gothic is for real, then our lives are much more gothic than the gothicest novel one could think of' (Lévy, 34). Modern Gothic, Postmodern Gothic, Female Gothic … Queer Gothic, Imperial Gothic, Postcolonial Gothic … Scottish, Irish, Welsh Gothic, Gothic bodies, Gothic technologies, Gothic culture, digital Gothic … Southern Gothic, American Gothic, Indiana Gothic, Minnesota Gothic, *The American Gothic Cookbook*. Gothic proliferations in culture and criticism are typically hybrid, thoroughly monstrous and co-dependently vampiric, each coupling operating according to the logic of capitalism's inexhaustible plus. Derrida, writing of the hybrid forms of literary theory – the various 'isms' and 'posts' that conjoin so freely – asks his audience to imagine 'what kinds of monsters these combinatory operations give birth [to]' and notes the heterogeneous serialisation of 'contaminating and teratological coincorporation' linking 'psychoanalysis, poststructuralism, postmodernism, feminism, Marxism, etc. This teratology is our normality' (Derrida, 1990: 67). In reducing monstrosity, homogenising difference, rendering it familiar and yet, curiously hybrid, critical monstrosities produce yet more normal monstrosities, all with an increasingly fleeting status: 'as soon as one perceives a monster in a monster, one begins to domesticate it' (Derrida, 1992a: 386). Always at the limit of normality, monsters point to the future, opening a space for something other, 'that for which we are not prepared'. 'A future that would not be monstrous', he continues, 'would not be a future; it would already be predictable, calculable, and programmable tomorrow' (1992: 386). Without monsters, no future. But in welcoming the monster, what arrives may neither be a future nor a monster.

Monsters no longer render norms visible; they are the norm. Derrida's untenable but no less important distinction between an oxymoronic 'normal monstrosity' and a tautological 'monstrous monstrosity' discloses the problematic. The former involves critically and culturally homogenising monstrosity. 'Monstrous monstrosities' retain an older aspect, having a 'formless form' beyond recognition, presentation and legitimacy: 'Monsters cannot be announced. One cannot say: "Here are our monsters", without immediately turning the monsters into pets'(1990: 80). Our monsters, ourselves; our selves, our pets: the arena of indifference leaves only a predictable and programmed – digitally and genetically – future, one, perhaps, already marked out by those fish from Taiwan that glow in the dark: 'Frankenstein pets'.

## Expressive hypothesis

Foucault, who repeatedly emphasised the doubleness of modernity, also drew attention to the productive function of repression in respect of sexuality. In addition, repression sustains critical fantasies and their ideals of subversion and liberation. To speak of sexuality in a context that assumes repression, that assumes power simply silences and prohibits, has, Foucault comments, 'the appearance of a deliberate transgression' (Foucault, 1981: 6–7). A repressive hypothesis is affirmed in critical denunciations of repression: power guarantees the critic's illusion of subversion and radicalism since to condemn repression is to condemn power. Such a position, Foucault notes, remains, 'part of the same historical network as the thing it denounces' (1981: 10). A similar structure applies to Gothic and its criticism, particularly in the shift towards sympathising with monsters. The suffering, curiously humanised monster, presents a humanity defined, not as the support of the cold and normative mechanisms of bourgeois modernity, but as its exception, unrecognised, excluded, silenced. Instead of being repulsive, monsters attract; instead of being destroyed, they must be loved. Repression is relocated: in identifying with outcasts and victims, those 'othered' and 'monstered' by repressive state apparatuses, they become charged with romantic rebelliousness. Speaking for themselves, telling of their pain and suffering, their status as victims preserves both the system that oppresses them and a critical fantasy of radical liberation.

The 'repressive hypothesis', which in the name of silence and discipline veiled so many injunctions to speak and define sexuality, has ceded to an 'expressive hypothesis' in which sexuality – and Gothic – is overexposed. Reviewing changes in vampire films in the late 1970s, Robin Wood writes: 'it is time for our culture to abandon Dracula and pass beyond him'. He goes on to argue that 'if the "return of the repressed" is to be welcomed, then we must learn to represent it in forms other than that of an undead vampire-aristocrat'(Wood, 328). To welcome the return of the repressed, in Wood's terms, signals the obsolescence of Gothic and its Victorian sexual baggage. In being everywhere expressed, sexuality moves beyond the dark, violent and Victorian associations of vampirism. But Dracula does not die. He does, however, turn into something different. One account of Coppola's *Bram Stoker's Dracula* claims it has taken a novel, 'one steeped in the mystification of defilement for the sin of sexual desire and the fear of sexual difference, and transformed it into a work of innovative and affirmative exultation. Never before has a horror film embodied such hope in the conquering power of love beyond death'(Dika, 399). A ringing endorsement of the film's poster slogan, 'love never dies', it reads vampiric undeath as a joyful condition, one well beyond Gothic horror: 'affirmative exultation'? 'Hope'? 'Love'? What is affirmed is not horror, nor any return of the repressed, but romance.

The move to expression and affirmation abandons the couplets of silence and speech, repression and disciplinary injunction: in expressing the private interior of being, human contents are squeezed out, like the juice of an orange, onto screens, into the digital coding of images and genes. Monsters, ghosts and vampires become figures of transitional states representing the positive potential of posthuman transformation: they participate in a fantastic flight from a humanised world and towards an inhuman technological dimension, figures for developments in genetic and information science, cyborgs, mutants, clones. With technology become pervasive, however, such technological monstrosity is seen as no more than an everyday condition. There is nothing special about monstrosity in an age of cybernetics and Frankenstein pets. The future, once so monstrous, has already collapsed on an indifferent present. Gothic cedes to 'cybergothic': cloaked in reassuringly familiar images, technology envelops humanity in a resolutely inhuman system. Unlike Frankenstein's monster, however, cyborgs do not expect the father-creator to save them or return a shocked and threatened humanity to itself (Haraway, 1990: 192). Where 'monsters have always defined the limits of community in Western imaginations', cyborgs 'define quite different political possibilities'(Haraway, 1990: 213) Anne Rice's vampire-hero, Lestat, 'exemplifies a style of cyborg existence' by evincing the 'pain and complexity' of adapting to a society, lifestyle, language, culture (and species) that is not one's own (Stone, 178). The identification of and with Gothic and cyborg figures renders both increasingly familiar: outsiders and monsters move within the culture they have redefined. At the same time, cybergothic shapes appear as no more than the surface effect of a thoroughgoing transformation of all the relationships and differences of modernity, a transvaluation in which life is lived in post-human or transhuman terms.

## ✵ 1 ✵

# Daddy's dead

### Gun of the father

A YOUNG WOMAN'S PASSION beats in time with the steam engine that hurries her to the ancestral bed of her husband. She pauses to reflect on the mother and the girlhood that her marriage leaves behind. Her imagination flares: ahead is romance, magic and the fairy castle that will be her home. A poor, fatherless girl, she has become a Marquise, lavished with jewels and fine dresses. There are greater luxuries and riches to be enjoyed in the castle itself.

But this is only the beginning of a mock Gothic romance by Angela Carter, the short story entitled 'The Bloody Chamber'. The husband, of course, will turn out villainous, that much is clear from his three previous wives, his waxen, ageless skin, the 'carnal avarice' of his gaze; the fairy castle will be a place of dark secrets and horrible chambers, as well as her prison, her place of execution and her tomb. A Radcliffean heroine whisked away to persecution in an enchanted palace by an evil aristocrat, an ingénue, like Jonathan Harker at the mercy of powers beyond his control in Dracula's castle, her story spans the entirety of Gothic romance: the death of one of the wives in a boating accident and the disconcerting presence of a house-keeper include Daphne Du Maurier's Rebecca in the list of the genre hero-ines. Another wife, an operatic diva, recalls the Phantom, while the last, a Romanian princess, was named Carmilla. The Marquis, a Sadean figure, owns a library of pornography and a working torture museum: this, the 'bloody chamber', is the forbidden place entered by the heroine when her husband is conveniently called away on business. There she finds the re-mains of her predecessors and discovers her fate.

In this world all women are objects, objects to be looked at, to be dis-played, to be collected, exchanged and possessed symbolically and physi-cally in marriage, to be enjoyed – and to be disposed of – in sexual and fatal consummation. The gifts of marriage, the exchange of rings and the taking of a new name see a girl transferred into womanhood and from one man to another, a father to a husband. Memories prompted by the smell of smoke from her husband's fat Romeo y Julietta, readily elide the Marquis and a father who used to embrace her amid the fug of his own Havana cigar. Romantic ideals about love and marriage quickly turn Gothic in the story: Carter's vampiric, Sadean villain, with his collection of antiquarian pornography and implements of torture, turns romantic dreaming into nightmare, his wealth, refinement and gourmand's tastes are the luxurious excesses that find their baser counterpart in comparisons with a horse dealer examining new flesh and the housewife prodding goods at the market. The heroine, so she observes, is the fourth to be invited 'to join this gallery of beautiful women' (Carter, 1981: 11). She may not be the last Marquise: as the Marquis, on the point of raising the executioner's axe, reclaims her opal engagement ring, he notes that 'it will serve me for a dozen more fiancées' (49). For a serial husband, wives are to be collected and put away like any other valuable items of property.

Even before the heroine discovers his secret, the magic wears off quickly as she finds she has been made an exile through marriage. Carter's story, however, is not content with disillusioning the romance of marriage by exposing its darker side and turning a critical feminist eye on the patriarchal cruelties underpinning the Gothic tradition. That this tradition involves the exchange, expropriation, exile and execution of women is the given, signalled in the many Gothic allusions of the story. Its ending, however, presents a subversive twist, a telling reversal of expectations and conventions that discloses and opposes the normal symbolic investments of Gothic plots and formulas. With only a blind piano-tuner as company, the helpless heroine is summoned to her death. Then, from her turret window, she glimpses a figure in the distance desperately speeding to her aid. 'Like a miracle' a properly romantic ending awaits. However, despite the scene, the urgency and mode of arrival, the figure is not suitably attired:

> a horse and rider galloping at a vertiginous speed along the causeway, though the waves crashed, now, high as the horse's fetlocks. A rider, her black skirts tucked up around her waist so she could ride hard and fast, a crazy, magnificent horsewoman in widow's weeds. (48)

This should be a shining knight on a white charger rather than an old woman dressed in black. A more significant reversal of conventions becomes apparent as the figure, almost too late to stop the fall of the axe, bursts through the castle gates:

You never saw such a wild thing as my mother, her hat seized by the winds and blown out to sea so that her hair was her white mane, her black lisle legs exposed to the thigh, her skirts tucked round her waist, one hand on the reins of the rearing horse while the other clasped my father's service revolver and, behind her, the breakers of the savage, indifferent sea, like the witnesses of a furious justice. (50–1)

Thoroughly romantic in setting, timing and posture, the conventional heroism of the rescue is only slightly at odds with the person of the rescuer. The incongruity barely leaves time for a smile, the gap between scene and actor quickly filled as the latter lives up to her demanding heroic responsibilities and unerringly completes her role: 'Now, without a moment's hesitation, she raised my father's gun, took aim and put a single, irreproachable bullet through my husband's head' (51). As cool and determined as the happy band of adventurers who storm Dracula's castle to exact righteous punishment on the object of evil, the heroine's mother, as right and just as the irreproachable bullet she fires with such accuracy, brings the murderous career of the husband to an end: monsters must die.

Drastic and violent romantic conclusions of this kind sit comfortably with the conventions of Gothic romance. It is only the sex and age of the person who delivers them that has changed. Indeed, the mother impersonates romantic heroism so effectively – particularly in the dispatch of the villain – as to leave romanticism's conventions intact. Almost. A banal explanation is quickly offered to account for the overblown arrival: having taken a train and reached the isolated station near the castle to find no taxi waiting, she was forced to borrow an 'old Dobbin' from a local farmer. Realism undercuts romance. The heroine does not live happily ever after to enjoy her riches and castle and her new, less ideally romantic, love: most of the wealth is given away and she returns to Paris to set up a small music school with her mother and the piano-tuner. A taint of romance remains: a heart-shaped bloodstain is indelibly imprinted on her forehead as a reminder of deluded aspirations to love, social status and wealth.

The return to simple domesticity, recommended in the Gothic romance since Radcliffe, seems to banish the spectres of romantic fancy. With the exposure and expulsion of those fictional spectres comes a more sustained interrogation of the assumptions and illusions supporting familial and social relations. Women become active in the home and in the world, no longer subject to the rule of male exchange. That, painted in Gothic extremes, has become a cruel and insupportable tyranny. The return of the mother, so often absent from the plots of Gothic novels, a return in a heroic role conventionally allotted to males, initiates a reversal of positions allotted to different genders in family and society. The reversal,

moreover, which places an unexpected figure at the centre of conventionally male romantic action, divorces gendered person from convention so
that ascribed characteristics and attributes no longer appear fixed as natural and unchanging biological features. Anyone can play the role of the
hero because it is simply a role. The story's knowing engagement with and
subversion of fictional conventions draws attention to their formality and
artifice. Its reversals extend from sexual and marital conventions to social
habits and mores, as conventional, artificial and contrived as anything else
in the story and thereby as subject to critique, subversion and transformation.

While it exhumes the mother from her early Gothic grave and places
her in a determining position at the beginning and end of the narrative,
the story does not simply replace a paternal principle with a maternal one.
All the mother does is act out a conventionally male role with all its heroic
and violent trappings: she impersonates the father, or one of his paternal
surrogates (an agent of justice, an officer of the law, a lover, a son-in-law
etc.), as an active defender, protector, even saviour, of 'his' women. Paternal roles, of course, as the Marquis dramatically demonstrates, extend to
darker counterparts: owner, abuser, murderer. In playing roles, however,
she discloses paternal artifice, exposing and severing its purely formal association with a male figure. The father becomes just another role, an
ideal, a metaphor or figure that is impersonated in turn. Neither form nor
structure is identical with the person who takes his or her place, name and
bearings within it. The story does not so much celebrate, in place of a
dead father and a killed husband, the triumph of the mother and maternal
domesticity, for that would merely replicate the same structure with different players: its reversals and substitutions open that structure itself up
to scrutiny and disclose the impersonations and impostures of all roles
within it. Any figure of paternal authority is ultimately an 'impostor' oc-
cupying the space vacated by the M/Other (Lacan, 1977a: 310–11). Perhaps this is where, beyond the story's playful subversion of convention,
the strangeness of its effects comes to the fore.

The return of the mother, though something of a miracle and formula-
ically fortuitous, is not in itself uncanny; nor, in the heroine's musings, is
the recollection of the dead father in the memories evoked by certain spousal
habits. Strangeness arises in the appearance of figures where they ought
not to be, conventionally and generically speaking: in Gothic fiction the
mother is more often than not dead, while the father, for a time at least,
remains alive. The reversal and substitution of roles is what engenders
reversals in significance, opening up a play of figures in a supposedly closed
form. Here, a Derridean play, a dissemination of (gendered) differences, is

produced, one that discloses the loss of final truth or fixed meaning: 'far from presupposing that a virgin substance thus precedes or oversees it, dispersing or withholding itself in a negative second moment, dissemination *affirms* the already divided generation of meaning'(Derrida, 1981: 268). This affirmation of an originary absence to meaning or truth, sketched in terms of sexuality and reproduction by Derrida ('virgin substance', 'generation', 'dis*semination*') is linked to the play of the uncanny in Freud, a play in which the meaning of the word '*unheimlich*' crosses from familiar to strange, homely to unhomely, canny to uncanny. But disseminaton does more than undermine opposed terms within psychoanalysis: it opens the fundamentals of gender division, a difference based on castration and genitalia, to an originary nonorigin:

> No more than can castration, dissemination – which entails, entrains, 'inscribes', and relaunches castration—can never become an originary, central, or ultimate signified, the place proper to truth. On the contrary, dissemination represents the affirmation of this nonorigin, the remarkable empty locus of a hundred blanks no meaning can be ascribed to, in which mark supplements and substitution games are multiplied *ad infinitum*. In *The Uncanny*, Freud – here more than ever attentive to undecidable ambivalence, to the play of the double, to the endless exchange between fantastic and real, the 'symbolized' and the 'symbolizer', to the process of interminable substitution – can without contradicting this play, have recourse both to castration anxiety, behind which no deeper secret (*kein tieferes Geheimnis*), no other meaning (*kein andere Bedeutung*) would lie hidden, and to the substitutive relation (*Ersatzbeziehung*) itself, for example between the eye and the male member. Castration is that nonsecret of seminal division that breaks into substitution. (268 n. 67)

Castration, which calls up paternal identification and fear in the conferral of sexed identity, which cuts off undecidability with the imposition of a phallic signifier, does not, in the uncanny encounter, secure a single, original meaning. Instead, it discloses an anterior space, an 'empty locus' for 'interminable' substitutions, multiplying signification beyond the finality of one meaning. A maternal locus shadows the paternal impostures, thwarting phallic authority: the 'empty locus of a hundred blanks' is a space of improper metaphorical substitutions; the blanks are shells fired without effect, impostors in the gun disarming the single bullet of meaning. For Hélène Cixous, the absence of any deeper secret in Freud's 'Uncanny' discloses the feeling 'of resistance to the threat of castration': nothing lies on the 'other side' of castration, '"no meaning" other than the fear (resistance) of castration'. This fear re-presents itself repeatedly 'in the infinite game of substitutions', a double of castration, acknowledging and screening it off: 'castration and fear at the blank it discloses'; horror and a hole; resistance and substitution, a host of impostures (Cixous, 536).

That the chosen method of execution in Carter's story is decapitation, or that the heroine's lover is blind, are not accidental features, but again point to the questions of sexuality at the heart of the tale, features that implicate Freudian psychoanalysis and its reliance on castration in the structuring of sexual relations and identities in the tradition of Gothic (family) romance. In this respect, and in relation to the issues of uncanniness in the story, the paternal and maternal positions are crucial: their reversal renders the familiarity of family relations strange and opens the absence structuring those relations to view. Where castration stresses the lack of the penis, that is the absence of something and a substitute already projected in its place, dissemination emphasises the priority of absence itself, a blank space resistant to meaning that none the less facilitates and engenders its production, albeit temporarily. Castration and the fear it engenders places an inaugural gap over a prior absence, thereby directing the path of meaning away from the empty locus and its interminable substitutions.

What the uncanny discloses, then, is a locus that gives rise to substitution, symbols, meaning, while refusing fixity and stability. It remains undecidable and ambivalent. Its absence generates an endless process of games of symbolisation, substitution and exchange, one which assumes a Gothic aspect with the appearance of the double and the anxiety-provoking glimpse of the secret absence or absent secret at the centre and origin of systems of meaning. 'The Bloody Chamber', in staging its reversals and substitutions touches upon the uncanny in this sense. In filling the space of the father, who previously established his position on the basis of maternal absence, the mother neither closes the gap nor returns to the priority of an originary absence. What is uncanny results from the interplay of the absence of what should be present (the father) and the presence of what should be absent (the mother), an interplay that opens a chasm in the structure of relations whereby the imposture of both figures appear in relation to a double gap.

Ambivalence and undecidability persist, as do the two figures, as figures. In the case of the mother, she has a determining influence in the choices made by her daughter. The latter from the start is marked out for not being overly enamoured of the illusions of romance: she refuses to answer her mother's question as to whether she is sure she loves her husband. Her subsequent observations suggest two, related motives in which her mother's past is implicated: she notes her mother's sigh, 'as if it was with reluctance that she might at last banish the spectre of poverty from its habitual place at our meagre table' and goes on to comment that her mother 'had gladly, scandalously, defiantly beggared herself for love' and suffered the consequences of impoverished widowhood (Carter, 1981: 8). In not repeating her mother's mistakes, the daughter rejects romantic notions of marriage for more practical (monetary) reasons. But there is a sense of reluctance, too, that implies her sacrifice of romance is not made out of anything like liberated, selfish desire for wealth and status: it is performed out of filial duty. Her choice of husband, while informed by a refusal of her mother's romantic attitude (which, of course, saves her at the end), is also shaped by paternal similarity. Though dead, the (ghostly) figure of the father continues to exert effects. The paternal function, moreover, is passed on to the son-in-law in his exercise of unspeakable sovereignty over his bride. It is employed most fully in the trap set for the heroine. On the point of departure, he shows the heroine the keys to the house and itemises the various riches they will unlock. He also singles out one key as that which opens his most private and secret chamber at the same time as he absolutely forbids entry. Obviously, no other or more effective encouragement is required to instil her desire to discover what it contains. Prohibition, the story makes all-too plain, leads inexorably to transgression. While the heroine only belatedly realises the logic, its inevitability has already been heavily marked by the tale. It is, however, a false prohibition in that the villain wants her, counts on her, to transgress. Not only will she, in horror, discover her fate, her transgression will permit, perversely legitimate even, his punishment, thereby allowing him to act on his desire to murder her like the others. Prohibition leads to transgression which, in turn, lets the paternal law enforce its rule and thereby consummate the paternal figure's most sovereign desire: the power over life and death. Law, then, maintains its limit through excess.

Though the heroism of the mother interrupts the completion of this perverse paternal circuit and exposes its artifice, the story never sets out to entirely escape the bounds of paternal structures, symbols or functions: it remains neither fully trapped nor utterly free, neither inside nor out, sustaining an interstitial position in relation to the empty locus of the uncanny. Written in the 1970s, the story holds to a critical feminism that refuses to advocate easy models of liberation which would overlook the external and internalised power and persistence of prevailing, if weakened, structures and unwittingly repeat their patterns. Perhaps the story's return to familiarly mundane domesticity is not to be fully embraced as anything resembling a radical challenge to prevailing norms and fictional conventions. For all her heroism and its disruption of conventional assumptions, the actions of the mother replicate the violence of a romantic closure, in many ways a simple assumption of a paternal role. Indeed, as the story underlines through repetition, it is the father's gun, instrument and symbol of power and violence, that is used in the execution of the paternal surrogate. Even though person is separated from structural position in the disruption of gendered conventions, the structure remains; even though the father is already dead, the paternal principle – and the gun – lives on in its numerous effects: the power of the figure persists though the person that once embodied it is gone. While the space of the father is emptied and nobody seems adequate to the task of filling it, the story does not bemoan this loss, nor is it concerned with anyone ever living up to a paternal ideal. The glorious action of the mother only mocks it, mimicking and parodying its function. In keeping the anoriginal space of substitution open to the end, the story provokes a critical examination of the persistence of paternal, and Gothic, effects.

The father is dead. But that does not matter. It is the principle that counts. It lives, a ghostly paternal figure, in myths, ritual, symbols and signs. Not necessarily embodied by but embedded in the circulation of signs, images, totems constituting cultures, the father remains as metaphor. The father, indeed, is long dead, his death the precondition for metaphorical afterlife, the basis for law and morality. While many Gothic villains, the Lords, Marquis, Counts that assume sovereign sexual and supernatural powers, evoke an archaic paternal position, their inevitable and necessary deaths form the basis for a restoration of law and a renewal of the values temporarily interrupted by an insurgence of untamed energies. The father's death allows the foundation of the laws, bonds and rituals of culture to be formed: crime gives birth to law, guilt to morality, symbolic repetition of the act of murder becoming the basis of communal rites. In *Totem and Taboo*, the father of psychoanalysis turns to Darwin for a picture of the first father: humans once lived in small groups presided over by the strongest male who kept all the females to himself and expelled the sons as they approached maturity. This is the father of the 'primal horde'. The male offspring, of course, were far from happy with the situation. So, speculates Freud,

> one day the brothers who had been driven out came together, killed and devoured their father and so made an end of the patriarchal horde. United, they had the courage to do and succeeded in doing what would have been impossible for them individually. (Some cultural advance, perhaps, command over some new weapon, had given them a sense of superior strength.) (Freud, 1984: 203)

Gothic villains, in the eyes of heroines at least, often manifest the terrifying return of such a primal father. *Dracula*, with the 'crew of light' uniting to drive the vampire away from their women, and using various technological aids to chart his downfall, fits this pattern well. In 'The Bloody Chamber', the father's gun is the 'advance' that evens the odds between mother and villain.

Freud's account of the father does not end with his murder. The psychological and cultural consequences of the act are extensive. Having killed and eaten the object of fear and envy, the sons' identification with him is complete. They, however, repeat the act symbolically: a totem meal, 'mankind's earliest festival', commemorates the crime and constitutes the beginnings 'of social organisation, of moral restriction and of religion' (203). To unravel the subsequent developments of the process Freud alludes to Oedipus and the father-complexes of the young in which hate for a person blocking their path to power and sexual satisfaction is mixed with the love and admiration that underpins their identification with him. As a result, the murder induces feelings of guilt to the extent that 'the dead father became stronger than the living one had been' (204). Belatedly, through the prohibitions introduced by the sons, the father's rule is instituted as law: the killing of the totem is forbidden along with sexual promiscuity. Father still rules: the enjoyment which prompted the act remains prohibited after its completion. Laws against murder and incest emerge from committing the former with the intent to commit the latter. In the rituals that commemorate the murder, the father figure lives on to be killed and eaten again in order that both triumph and guilt reinforce the laws binding communal organization, thus preventing what happened to the father happening to the sons. In these rituals, Freud suggests, one finds the basis of what becomes generalised as the founding principle of morality and law: 'thou shalt not kill' (207–8). 'Society,' Freud continues, 'was now based on complicity in the common crime; religion was based on the sense of guilt and the remorse attaching to it; while morality was based partly on the exigencies of this society and partly on the penance demanded by the sense of guilt' (208). In myth, then, the father lives on with greater power. But myth, and murder, gives rise to law. For Lacan,

> the myth of the origin of the Law is incarnated in the murder of the father; it is out of that that the prototypes emerged, which we call successively the animal totem, then a more-or-less powerful and jealous god, and, finally, the single God, God the Father. The myth of the murder of the father is the myth of a time for which God is dead.
>
> But if for us God is dead, it is because he always has been dead, and that's what Freud says. He has never been the father except in the mythology of the son, or, in other words, in that of the commandment which commands that he, the father, be loved, and in the drama of the passion which reveals

that there is resurrection after death. That is to say, the man who made
incarnate the death of God still exists. He still exists with the commandment
which orders him to love God. (Lacan, 1992: 177)

From the father of the primal horde to the single paternal divinity, the
already dead figure who exerts his authority in the myth of the sons forms
the basis of external and internalised law. The order which commands
obedience also requires emotional investment; the imperative which orders social bonds also shapes psychological investments: the paternal law
is both without and within.

'The Bloody Chamber', in distinguishing between gendered person and
structural position, not only interrogates the assumed naturalness of conventional sexual and social relations: in disclosing an uncanny gap which
no impersonation can fill and which reveals the imposture of any paternal
figure, the text opens itself to the absence at the heart of all metaphorical
substitutions. In the process the function of metaphor is placed under
scrutiny: all paternal institutions become suspect. Carter's story was written in a context of challenges to political, social and sexual institutions,
mores and assumptions: to make the paternal figure visible and subject to
scrutiny constitutes a disavowal of its authority, a weakening of belief in
its powers. It is part of the process associated with postmodernity and the
'incredulity towards metanarratives' (Lyotard, 1984: xxiv). Metanarratives,
moreover, call up the spectre of a metanarrator, and this figure, too, is
rendered suspect: it is 'no accident', writes Jean-Joseph Goux, that 'imaginary signifiers of paternity are called into question at a time when the
sociohistorical meaning of "creativity" is overturned, when metasocial
guarantees, now defunct, yield to a new mode of historicity' (Goux, 1990a:
194). With feminism's challenge to male institutions, including an assault
on the patriarchal foundations of psychoanalysis, all signifiers of paternal
power find themselves subject to stringent criticism: in the attack on psychoanalytical constructions of femininity as castrated or lacking, in the
frontal assault on Oedipus and the paternal signifier, postmodern and
postoedipal theory are allied (Cixous; Irigaray; Deleuze and Guattari,
1983).

Economic transformations, moreover, shadow political and social
changes. Again the function of the paternal metaphor is threatened. Economic and social regulation used to operate according to 'the *paternal
metaphor* (money, phallus, language, monarch), the central and centralising
metaphor that anchors all other metaphors, the fulcrum of all symbolic
legislation, the locus of *standard* and unity' (Goux, 1990a: 21). The standard was that of gold, the measure that held signifiers of value – monetary
tokens – in place in respect of the reality of treasury reserves. Without it,

both money and signification become free-floating, 'no longer anchored by a fixed standard' (113). Human creativity and agency, along with paternal metaphors, are replaced by a mechanical system in which questions of meaning and agency matter less and less (131). Everything once outside economy – sacred values, transcendent meaning, even desire, is absorbed in the market's flow (202). Flow opens onto the 'viral', transversal realm of Baudrillardian hyperreality, a realm of incessant metonymic associations without a presiding, unifying or organising metaphor. There is no longer any 'invisible hand' guiding the market. Nor is it regulated according to human need, usefulness or rational or moral principles. All distinctions, Goux argues, collapse. Even desire, once organised in respect of paternal signification, is transformed. The postmodern capitalist economy is founded not on demand preceding supply, but the reverse, 'on a metaphysical uncertainty regarding the object of human desire'. Hence desire must be created by entrepreneurs 'through the invention of the new' (Goux, 1990b: 212). New goods make new desires and increase sales and profits. Such is the logic of an economy oriented towards consumption rather than production. Zizek, commenting on commodity culture and the market's freedoms of choice links the frenzy of consuming desires to a weakening of the paternal figure:

> The decline in the function of the Master in contemporary Western societies exposes the subject to radical ambiguity in the face of his desire. The media constantly bombard him with requests to choose, addressing him as the subject *supposed to know what he really wants* (which book, clothes, TV programme, holiday destination) … At a more fundamental level, however, the new media deprive the subject radically of a knowledge of what he wants: they address a constantly malleable subject who has constantly to be told what he wants – that is, the very evacuation of a choice to be made performatively creates the need for an object of choice. (Zizek, 1997: 153, original emphasis)

Empty spaces appear where there used to be figures and subjects. The free play of postmodern aesthetics and economics coheres in its incredulity towards and evacuation of the paternal metaphor.

There are at least two responses to this condition: a mourning of the father, a call for the restoration of political, religious, or family values, for instance, or a continued, even accelerating, repudiation of anything resembling a paternal institution or authority. One, in the manner of mourning and psychosis articulated by Lacan, follows the pattern of bereavement: rituals of burial and grieving allow the tear in the symbolic fabric (metanarratives or metasocial guarantees) to be repaired. The other process forecloses the possibility of paternal organisation: it does not fill the absence with a credible metaphor that binds social and structures together but allows any figure or image (that of a commodity, brand name, or celebrity, say) to circulate unstably in the space. 'The Bloody Chamber' is situated between mourning and psychosis: it discloses the tear in symbolic structures and conventions but leaves the gap open. While impeaching paternal institutions and assumptions, it offers no new image or figure to restore order, psychotic or otherwise.

Postmodernity, however, does not only appear after modernity but also, Lyotard claims, 'in its nascent state' (Lyotard, 1984: 79). Economic, social and political upheavals tear holes in the ordering of the world, holes in which Gothic spectres are wont to transport themselves. At this point the uncanny in its modern form appears. Where, in premodern societies, the uncanny had a place in religious frameworks under the auspices of sacred and untouchable elements, in the Enlightenment it became 'unplaceable', that is, uncanny in its Freudian sense (Dolar, 1991: 7). Gothic fictions throughout modernity, in loosing monsters and terrifying images for the titillation and abhorrence of audiences, generally manifested a conservative or restorative function: the destruction of threatening, unsanctioned otherness allowed cultural anxieties (the apprehension of a gap, a rupture or hole in the fabric of ordered reality) to be expunged and limits and values to be pleasurably reasserted. Imagined losses of social, familial and psychological order ultimately reinforced its necessity. Mourning an imagined loss enabled the bourgeois values emerging in the eighteenth century (democratic freedom, individuality, family responsibility, enlightened progress) to be defined against, and surpass, those of a feudal and aristocratic era. Increasingly in recent Gothic fictions, however, monsters, vampires in particular, come to assume a positive, and pseudo paternal, role in the identifications they engender, in the images, imitations, desires and lifestyles they give rise to, in the identities they celebrate. Gothic figures swarm beyond fiction to give the entirety of western culture an uncanny sensation. Though daddy's dead, he lives on as ghostly figure and image, a curiously Gothic figure haunting modernity's crises and anxieties from the start.

Post-modernity signals a crisis, a tear in the symbolic fabric of modernity and a consequent incredulity in respect of the paternal metaphor. Reactions to the empty space it makes visible differ, split along modern and postmodern lines in terms that calibrate well with mourning and psychosis. For Lyotard, the sublime brings forth a sense of the unpresentable, something, some Thing, even, that cannot be reduced to form, meaning or order while providing the formless basis for an idea of community or culture. The sublime, though dating back to classical aesthetic theory, became a crucial topic in eighteenth-century aesthetic debates. In Edmund Burke's *Enquiry* it is contrasted with the harmony and uniformity of beauty in which aesthetic objects are seen to accord with the gaze of the viewer and evoke gentle feelings of pleasure and love. Beauty, for Burke, is associated with femininity. The sublime, in contrast, is gendered masculine: it marks an encounter with wildness, immensity, objects whose scale cannot be readily grasped; it evokes sensations of horror and terror intermingled with pleasure. Causing feelings of wonder and awe in the viewer, the sublime experience has religious connotations: a sense of divine infinity and power is glimpsed. The complex emotions evoked – 'a sort of tranquillity tinged with terror', a 'delightful horror' – indicate the dynamism of the experience. Initially the viewer is overwhelmed by immensity: reason and sense fail to comprehend what is seen; the self, even, is threatened by dissolution. At this point, the sublime activates the strongest of passions, that of 'self-preservation', and, under the emotional stimulus of terror, the viewing subject actively and imaginatively apprehends, in awe, the magnificence of the scene in a movement experienced as uplifting, invigorating and thrilling: from an imagined threat to the activation of an imaginative response, the subject, at first overcome, participates in the power of the sublime, recovering a heightened sense of self in the process.

The aesthetics of the sublime, as the popularity of the topic in the eighteenth century suggests, are important in the development and conservation of the values of an emergent bourgeois, commercial society and helped consolidate a new sense of individuality in a world in which change was occurring at every level. A 'solution to the defects of a commercial society' (Clery, 104), the sublime offers an experience that temporarily allows the private individual to glimpse something other than commercial imperatives and gain a sense of values in the threat and dissolution it poses: immensity, wonder, incomprehension testify to a quasi-sacred space beyond individual self-interest, returning the subject to the world of commerce with a stronger sense of self and social duty. The sublime, of course, informs the dynamics and devices of many Gothic fictions in which the loss of reason, morality, reputation, self are repeatedly threatened by objects of terror and mystery. These imagined threats invigorate the emotions of protagonists and readers, the basis of the sensations and thrills defining the genre, and, despite all their violence and immediacy, serving as preludes to recuperation. In the Radcliffean novel, the losses of position, protection, family, rational and moral sense, the horrifying threat, moreover, of losing a young woman's greatest asset – her virginity – are the conditions for the return to paternal values of reason, morality, duty, moderation and virtue. Lost, or threatened, at least in the imagination, values return and the threat of individual and social dissolution is imaginatively overcome. In this way the sublime operates recuperatively, conservatively: the relation sustained to that which is unpresentable, like the hole torn in the fabric of social and symbolic structures in periods of crisis and transformation, is one of limitation, an absence marking the restored borders of sense, subjectivity and system.

The experience of the sublime, its thrills, novelties, surprise and excitement, though without its recuperative resolution, sustains another trajectory, one that, in dispensing with form and values, aligns itself with the imperatives of free-floating capitalism. In this case, so Lyotard argues, the sublime 'proceeds "directly" out of market economics', manifesting a 'collusion between capital and the avant-garde' that is 'ambiguous, even perverse' (Lyotard, 1991: 104–5). The postmodern sublime, he writes,

> would be that which, in the modern, puts forward the unpresentable in presentation itself; that which denies itself the solace of good forms, the consensus of a taste which would make it possible to share collectively the nostalgia for the unattainable; that which searches for new presentations, not in order to enjoy them but in order to impart a new sense of the unpresentable. (1984: 81)

In modernity, the sublime involves a contradictory oscillation of pleasure and pain to open a conflict between the faculties of conception and presentation, Idea and object: 'the empty "abstraction" which the imagination experiences ... itself is like a presentation of the infinite, a "negative presentation"' (Lyotard, 1984: 78; 1991: 98; 1994). Modernity's sublime is nostalgic, conceiving the unpresentable as the 'missing contents' of presentation and providing a form that 'because of its recognizable consistency, continues to offer to the reader or viewer a matter for solace and pleasure' (Lyotard, 1984: 81). The postmodern refusal of good forms, taste, consensus does not testify to the unpresentable, but, under the loose imperative of 'anything goes', capitalises on emptiness to project an eclectic mixing of styles and images selected only for their capacity to thrill, shock and surprise, a generation and satisfaction of desires for novelty and difference. Innovation in this sense is not concerned with aesthetic experimentation in the manner of the modern avant-garde: it is bound up with recent developments of technoscience and the consumer economy, with pressures on performance enhancement and indicators, optimised efficiency, and the profitable creation of desires.

Art and aesthetics are no longer concerned in the definition or interrogation of cultural values, but tied to the pursuit of profitable innovation just like any other department of a corporate research and development division: the aim 'is less to embody the Idea of community, and it is more turned towards the management of infinite research for knowledge, know-how and wealth' (Lyotard, 1991: 124). Like the sublime, the place and role of Gothic fictions changes, subject to different cultural and economic conditions. Once articulating sublimity's apprehension of the unpresentable with terror's popular excitements, shadowing modernity with figures of otherness and objects of fear that occlude or ward off an otherness beyond itself and at its core, Gothic styles and figures, as they spread across aesthetic and cultural boundaries, now seem indifferent, perfectly presentable, all-too palatable and pre-packaged. There may, however, remain some Thing Other lurking in Gothic's cultural per-vasion, some trace of what made Gothic fictions and figures both an index of cultural anxieties and a mode of giving them forms and objects. Perhaps the proliferation and rapid circulation of Gothic styles evinces a nostalgia for objects terrifying enough to testify to the unpresentable, sublime enough to stimulate the recuperation of a sense of a self become dissipated and fragmented, intense enough to ensure the restoration of symbolic structures that are cracked if not already in ruins: here monsters and horrors would call for institutions and figures of authority strong enough to expel them. Alternatively, anxiety and apprehension may only serve as a resource of innovation, surprise, profit, desire: the faint Gothic frisson, its historical association with vice, sex and death, forms a highly marketable source of novelty, thrills and excitement.

## Beyond the paternal principle

Gothic fiction is bound up with the function of the paternal figure, an effect of and an engagement with a crisis in its legitimacy and authority, with tremors in its orchestration of symbolic boundaries and distinctions, with disruptions to its heterogeneous maintenance of cultural values and mores, with challenges to the way it presides unseen over the structured circulation of social exchanges and meanings. More precisely, Gothic fiction can be defined as a transgression of the paternal metaphor. Transgression, however, operates in a complex manner: it is not a celebratory breaking of laws and taboos considered unjust or repressive, not a straightforward liberation from rules and conventions binding individuals within strict frameworks of duty or normative identity. Transgression, as an act that is both constructive and disruptive, forms a strangely integral process in the definition and preservation of limits. As a transgression of the paternal principle, then, Gothic fiction constitutes a game of loss and recovery, a play of forces in which it interrupts and invigorates the circulations over which it presides.

Foucault, discussing the glib notion of sexual liberation, outlines the complex 'play' that relates transgression and limits, where the former 'incessantly crosses and recrosses a line in a wave of extremely short duration, and thus it is made to return once more right to the horizon of the uncrossable' (Foucault, 1977: 34). There is no transgression without a prior limit, the pulse traversing the line bringing it into relief as much as erasing it. But the reverse is also the case: 'the limit and transgression depend on each other for whatever density of being they possess; a limit could not exist if it were absolutely uncrossable and, reciprocally, transgression would be pointless if it merely crossed a limit composed of illusions and shadows'. It is transgression, then, that gives the limit its power, while the latter serves to mark out a zone of attraction providing transgression with its force. Hence 'transgression carries the limit right to the limit of its being', forcing 'the limit to face the fact of its imminent disappearance, to find itself in what it excludes' (34). Without absolute boundaries, the play of limit and transgression establishes and maintains the divisions, borders, oppositions of inside and outside structuring social and subjective existence.

The key figure in the structure is the father who, Foucault glosses, 'separates, that is, he is the one who protects when, in his proclamation of Law, he links spaces, rules, and language within a single and major experience. At a stroke, he creates the distance along which will develop the scansion of presences and absences, the speech whose initial form is based on constraints and finally, the relationship of the signifier to the signified which not only gives us to the structure of language but also to the exclusion and symbolic transformation of repressed material' (81–2). Foucault's rendering of a psychoanalytic account of the father stresses the role of division and decision, the paternal no and paternal name central to structures of language and the world of experience. A figure of prohibition, the man who says No!, the paternal role decides and polices the boundaries of legitimacy in meaning, behaviour and identity; as one who names, however, the paternal figure produces identity: the figure simultaneously maintains injunctions against unsanctioned utterances and actions while enjoining subjects to speak, act and desire in proscribed ways.

In Lacanian terms, the paternal figure or metaphor forms the apex of symbolic relationships: the father's name is passed to the child, thereby positioning him or her from birth in a structured set of relationships defining a place in terms of social and sexual identity and directing their subsequent development. The symbolic register of language provides the

structure for subjectivity to emerge, 'a form into which the subject is inserted at the level of his being' (Lacan, 1993: 179). The insertion, however, necessitates a loss: in accepting the law of the father through identification, an acceptance of social, moral and familial rules or conventions,
the child must sacrifice something of his/her prior existence, that is, must
renounce the satisfactions initially associated with the mother as 'Other',
or 'primordial subject of demand' (Lacan, 1977c: 12). This renunciation,
of course, is part and parcel of what Freud discusses in terms of oedipal
and castration complexes. The movement from a being absorbed by infantile demands and instinctual gratification to a subject of language and
culture thus introduces a gap or division in the subject, subordinating him
or her to the functions of language: 'the phallus is our term for the signifier of his alienation in signification' (28). The Other now takes the form
of the 'locus of the signifier', the chain of signification in which subjective
identity and desire is given shape and direction (Lacan, 1977a: 310). The
phallus or paternal metaphor, then, is not a substantial entity: different
figures can assume its function (God, father, king, president, teacher, priest,
doctor etc.), but it remains a function and, as such, any claim to incarnate
him discloses an act of imposture; 'the fact that the father may be regarded
as the original representative of this authority of the Law requires us to
specify by privileged mode of his presence he is sustained beyond the subject who is actually led to occupy the place of the Other, namely, the
Mother' (310–11). Filling the gap left by the alienation in signification,
by the transfer and deferral of desire from an object of immediate satisfaction to a structure of conventions, a gap negated and conserved in language, the phallus is the 'signifier of this *Aufhebung* itself, which it inaugurates by its disappearance' (288). The paternal metaphor is thus 'negativity in its place in the secular image', that which embodies '*jouissance* in the
dialectic of desire' (319). The structure depends on the projections or identifications of those positioned within it and is underpinned, not by any
positive substance, but by a fundamental absence, an underlying negativity whose emptiness is focused on the lost object, the gap connoted by the
term *objet petit a*, the locus of projection and subjective fantasy. The paternal metaphor, then, exists as a signifier projected into the gap hollowed
out in the process of enculturation, a substitute, a figure veiling an intensely charged absence, a spectral non-present articulation of the shared
structure of experience which, in everyday exchanges, remains unseen. The
phallus is, Lacan notes, 'a ghost' (1977c: 50).

From its beginnings, Gothic fiction takes the form of a family romance
in which paternal figures assume a variety of guises: tyrants, impostors,
murderous, rapacious villains, ghostly revenants. Manfred, in *The Castle*

*of Otranto*, encompasses nearly all these roles, as well as underlining his villainy with incestuous ambitions. His illegitimate lordship is brought to an end, however, with the return of the rightful heir and, with the aid of some supernatural machinations, a proper lineage is restored. Though Radcliffe's villains are revealed to be less colourful in their vicious traits, their designs on the heroines' virtue or life more often motivated by materialistic intentions, malevolent postures are glossed with a diabolical energy. Montoni, in *Udolpho*, has an eye on Emily's inheritance; Montalt, the fratricidal uncle (and suspected father) of Adeline in *The Romance of the Forest*, has only the satisfaction of his own selfish interests at heart. Matthew Lewis's ambitious villain, Ambrosio, conceals his violent passions behind a veil of vanity and pious respectability, but, as Michelle Masse notes, is an 'oedipal figure':

> Although he is an orphan (a textual erasure of the past that supports the 'family romance' of the individual as self-created), he enacts the mandates of the oedipal struggle through the most lofty of surrogates, the parental arms of the Catholic church. In his ambitious virtue, he supplants all other 'Fathers', and nothing less than the Madonna excites his lust. (Masse, 236–7)

Ambrosio's desire manifests the most exorbitant of paternal identifications. In a different way, Victor Frankenstein exhibits ambition on an equally fantastic scale. In mastering the secrets of maternal nature and assuming the ability to create life from death, his presumptions to divinity aspire to the apex of paternal roles. As he hastens to implement his discovery, he makes his paternal identification explicit, saying that 'a new species would bless me as its creator and source; many happy and excellent natures would owe their being to me. No father could claim the gratitude of his child so completely as I should deserve theirs' (Shelley, 1969: 54). Later in the nineteenth century, a truly diabolical evil father appears in the undead anamorphotic figure of Dracula: his bloodlust and sovereign command of natural and supernatural forces make him an archaic father of the primal horde, beyond law and able to enjoy as many female victims as he wants; his viciously parodic rituals, feeding Mina with the blood of his breast, for instance, usurp the properly paternal orders of religion. In the homosocial late Victorian world that Dracula attacks, it is masculinity and virility that is seen to be in crisis, threatened by decadent circulations and exchanges of bodily fluids. In the twentieth century, moreover, the paternal metaphor remains at stake. As Steven Bruhm notes of Stephen King's *The Shining*, queer elements in Gothic fiction disclose concerns with the paternal figure, concerns that are, at least, less consumed with Victorian anxieties: 'no longer the source of panic, male interpenetration becomes a means of restoring (at least partially) the phallus lost at individuation, one's own phallus, the phallus of another man' (Bruhm, 278). As much the desire of another as his body, the phallus here is imagined to fill the gap of alienation and affirm identity, rather than threaten it.

There are good paternal surrogates, but far fewer than the figures of evil littering Gothic pages and screens; their function as positive models of paternity, moreover, emanates as a direct response to the threat of bad, depraved or criminal fathers. In *The Romance of the Forest*, La Luc, counterposed to Montalt, offers an example of a caring, responsible and morally upright father; in *Dracula*, Van Helsing is set up as the good, priestly, scientific and professorial counterpoint to vampiric decadence. But these good surrogates are themselves paternal substitutes, slight attempts to fulfil what, in the fiction, seems an impossible ideal. All the negative images, the figures of failure, egotism, crime and vice that masquerade, in familial, legal or religious ways, as fathers seem to emphasise the lack of either suitably strong moral frameworks or characters who have internalised the requisite fibre. The villainous paternal figures remain no more than impostors, usurpers of power and position, opportunistic adventurers capitalising on a general collapse of defined symbolic parameters. Indeed, the negative figures, in association with the delusional or hallucinatory projections, present a world in which all boundaries become spectral and immaterial, a world in which fears and anxieties conjure up only the most threatening and destructive of figures from a past of paternal sin and guilt in which law is overshadowed by violence, irresponsibility and crime. For critics, moreover, Gothic fiction itself performs a similar function to the villainy represented in it. Rather than restoring paternal order, they exacerbate its decline: Robertson's *An Essay on Education* (1798) makes the common case that fiction leads young readers astray to cause an 'abjuration of all parental authority' (de Bolla, 272). A reviewer of *The Monk* offers a similar cautionary judgement: 'Not without reluctance then, but in full conviction that we are performing a duty, we declare it to be our opinion, that the Monk is a romance, which if a parent saw in the hands of a son or daughter, he might reasonably turn pale' (Anon., 1797c: 197). Fiction not only presents seductive examples of transgression, in doing so it perpetuates those transgressions of paternal authority on another level.

Not only is the paternal figure, as regulative ideal, repeatedly transgressed, it is often absent. There are few families in Gothic fiction. Mothers are long dead, often before the start of a novel, and fathers rarely stay the course. Parentless children are left to roam the wild, gloomy landscapes without protection or property and often without the secure sense of themselves that comes with proper name and position. So it is for Adeline as she flees through the forest; so, too, for Emily, imprisoned in *Udolpho*, after her remaining parent has died. She has, moreover, failed to observe his dying wishes and began to suspect his honour and the legitimacy of her own family origins. Her doubts, indeed, impeach paternal authority and provide the occasion for terrible speculations. Similarly, the whole narrative of Regina Maria Roche's *Clermont* turns on suspected paternal guilt: the motherless heroine, though she has a living father, has been deprived of a figure entitled to social position and economic status. Orphans, or children dispossessed of inheritance and due identity, like the heroine of Eleanor Sleath's *The Orphan of the Rhine* (1798) become prevalent, even emblematic figures of the revolutionary decade, cast adrift in a world bereft of social and familial security. The threats to paternal order disclose an underlying instability, an absence at the heart of any symbolic structure.

The absence of a stable paternal order constitutes the space for the projection of both ideal and terrifying figures of authority and power, gaps which can be readily filled by transgressive as well as proper images. That fatherly authority can be assumed by rapacious aristocrats, ambitious monks, impassioned bandits suggests that what is at stake is the symbolic function, the formal framework which orders identities and social roles: the paternal substitutes, good or bad, distinguish the familial, religious and social institutions threatened by paternal decline, a decline sustained by the superstitious credulity and lack of rational and moral good sense manifested by heroines. The transgressions so evident in the fictions thus mark out the limits of symbolic boundaries, displaying both the underlying insubstantiality of any symbolic structure and the necessity of maintaining some kind of credible order. Marriage serves as the knot between religious, familial and social orders: the symbolic exchange of women as objects passed between men situates the paternal figure at the juncture of naming, circulation and reproduction. To transgress this circulation, as the many threats of forced marriages, stolen virtue and bodily violation suffered by heroines indicate, raises the spectre of a world out of joint. Only through proper marriage and the recovery of a secure symbolic structure can the demons of the fiction be cast out. Indeed, only after learning to temper her superstitious fancy and overindulged imagination can *Udolpho's* heroine return to the security of a symbolically regulated world of sense, position and property, a world, for her, represented by a good marriage. The end of *Dracula*, too, is marked by the birth of a son to Jonathan and Mina Harker: a novel full of good and bad parental substitutes finally renders paternity actual thereby restoring the previously fractured symbolic order, an order whose existence was only made possible negatively, imagined throughout as the antithesis to vampiric transgression.

Loss or absence leads to recovery; that which has gone returns on another level, a projection realised in the gaps and negative spaces so vividly presented in the fiction. The losses pictured repeatedly in violent terrifying threats thus serve as a prelude to recovery: the shocks intimating imminent ruin and destruction invigorate a sublime recuperation of order. The sublime works, of course, to activate the imagination and overcome an imaginary threat. The ending of *Udolpho*, for all its emphasis on a providentially ordered cosmos where virtue is rewarded and vice is punished, presents the matrimonial celebrations in magical terms, as enchantments and fairytales (Radcliffe, 1980: 671). Order has been restored on a symbolic level through marriage: though more pleasant than the imaginings and terrors dominating the course of novel, it remains, it seems, just as fantastic. The terrifying loss and absence overwhelming the narrative is magically filled. A fantasy, acceptable though it may be, has been projected into the disordered physical and mental spaces of a Gothic environment. Nothing real, then, is returned to: a symbolically sanctioned reality is instituted in place of its imagined opposite, a reality whose empty basis is supplemented by the attractive fullness of fantasy rather than the destructive chaos of nightmare. Loss and recovery operate on an imaginary level, the movement between them uncovering and veiling a hollow at the heart of symbolic systems, a gap which the projections, identifications and rituals of readers must fill. Loss and recovery, on another level, are also linked to mourning, an activity which Gothic fiction's depictions of death, ruin and the past encourage. In death, the loss of the loved one causes a tear in the symbolic fabric of everyday life to be evinced. The secure boundaries of the paternal order are impeached. Mourning, however, serves to repair the breach through ritual, retying threads, bonds and meanings in symbolic activity so that signification fills the hole in the real.

In the movement of loss and recovery structuring Gothic fiction, mourning occurs on a cultural as well as individual and familial level. As a mode of fiction produced in the eighteenth century depicting a feudal past, its deployment of loss involves two cultures. Indeed, replaying eighteenth-century anxieties in feudal costumes and settings, far from expressing a nostalgic wish for an age of knights and fairies, mourns an absence or symbolic rupture in present rather than past orders. The sublime alternation of loss and recovery, even as it distinguishes and interrelates a Gothic past from an enlightened present, hollows out a space for projection and fantasy in which the past is rendered both proximate and distanced: the gap in the eighteenth-century present forms the transitional space between feudal and bourgeois modes of social organisation. An eighteenth-century fantasy of the past is projected backwards in order to establish the coordinates for reimagining its own phantasmatic frameworks: the figures of vice, of paternal failure and evil, form the negative projections that allow for the appearance of new symbolic models. Gothic fiction, with its depictions of paternal transgression, articulates a shift in symbolic orders from a feudal economy based on land ownership, patrilinear property rights and aristocratic rule and privilege to a bourgeois economy maintained through commercial contracts, mobile, monetary wealth and the production and exchange of commodities. The provenance of Horace Walpole's own country house offers a good example of the symbolic effects of the economic shift from feudal to bourgeois orders:

> The house at Strawberry Hill was acquired from the proprietor of a London toyshop, and the happy coincidence was not lost on the new owner as he systematically transformed the building into what we call today a 'theme park' treatment of aristocratic ascendancy. As the feudal origins of the aristocratic order were turned into the plaything of a whimsical hobbyist, its present legitimacy was symbolically diminished. (Clery, 76)

As commercial power comes to dominate social organisation, the remnants of feudalism are decoratively reconstructed in an idle aesthetic fashion. Lost, they are recovered in another form, subject to a different arrangement of economic practices, given a new meaning as the phantasmatic antithesis, the heritage history, of the present. In hollowing out, negating the reality of the feudal past, the Gothic play with history also charts a movement forward, a bourgeois fantasy of self-possession, reason, merit and mastery filling the symbolic tear its emergence has created. Back and forth, cultural continuity-in-difference is maintained, transgression enabling the supercession, recuperation (with a difference) and production of the paternal figure.

There may be a limit to the momentum of disappearance and return in which the figure of the father is lost and recovered, to the point that loss alone takes over: losses of power, of credibility, of control become increasingly evident in cinematic representations. In the late 1970s, with the revival of popular horror cinema, 'the genre begins to overtly interrogate paternal commitment and its relations to paternal power'. *The Fury* (1978) presented the father as feeble and inadequate. *The Amityville Horror* (1979) showed the middle-class father to be 'weak, economically beleaguered, and under pressure from his corrupt and demanding dream house in a period of economic recession' (Sobchack, 1996: 152). Father no longer functions as a point of resolution but becomes a figure of violence and an

object of fear. *The Shining* (1980) dramatically displays his psychotic breakdown. Unable to live up to his ideal or his responsibilities, unable to keep
a lid on the tensions and pressures of work and family, the father explodes
in uncontrollable violence. Control and repression no longer seem possible. On the one hand males crumble under the weight of social demands
and structures to take out their inadequacy on those closest to them; on
the other hand, however, their failure impeaches the authority and solid-
ity of the social and psychic systems they are supposed to embody; their
violent eruptions come to symbolise the violence and corruption of family values and structures themselves: horror movies' presentation of terrifying relations between children and parental figures discloses 'a crisis in
the belief in the Oedipal model' (Sobchack, 1996: 156). Thematically and
structurally, as both a failure of the paternal figure and in the structures
like the family over which it presides and maintains, horror films interrogate the paternal position. The very mechanisms of horror film, moreover,
also shatter the security of a male and paternal gaze since films are shot
with no aim of bolstering any sense of mastery in the viewer. On the
contrary, they assault the eyes, refusing comfort and security by sudden
shifts and shocks in order to stimulate emotions and unreflective sensation. The gaze sustained by horror film is not designed to promote a secure subject looking at objects presented to him for his pleasure (Mulvey).
In being assaulted by the structure, editing and shooting of scenes, in
literally attacking the eyes of the viewer, the conventional 'he' of the cinematic gaze is violently disrupted. Indeed, in being made subject to, rather
a subject of, filmic assaults, a recipient of visual blows, the position of the
viewer is made passive, feminised by cinematic technique itself (Clover).
Given the Freudian associations of eye and phallus, of looking and power,
this technique constitutes a very literal form of emasculation, a castration
in which technology supplants or appropriates the mastery associated with
masculinity and paternity.

## Gothic times

'We live in Gothic times', Angela Carter commented in 1974, in an account of the way that genres once consigned to cultural margins have
begun to prevail over their canonised counterparts, emerging as standard,
if not dominant, forms of aesthetic expression (Carter, 1974: 122; see
Neumeier). That Gothic styles have become acceptable as norms of cultural production and consumption rather than provocations or disturbances of systems of aesthetic and moral value, suggests not only a change

in taste whereby the repetitious, attritional reproduction of formulas of terror has worn away the defences and resistances of a more discriminating palate: it implies and occurs within a wider cultural transformation. Far from excluded, Gothic figures and fictions circulate with greater visibility manifesting the absence of strict, prohibitive mechanisms. The lack of strong exclusionary force itself announces a change in cultural values, while the proliferation of figures of fear, desire, taboo and horror suggests that the display of once negative images and associations serves a different function: where the restoration of symbolic boundaries was celebrated in the climax to tales of terror, order reasserted in acts of counterviolence and righteous expulsion against abnormal threats, only the frisson of fear seems to remain, the legacy of enjoyable expenditures of terrifying energy. Threatening figures are less and less objects of animosity to be ab-jected in the return to equilibrium. Instead, they retain the fascinating, attractive appeal emanating from a cathexis that is neither expended nor transferred: no longer unequivocal objects of intense emotional expenditures of hate, rage or fear, monstrous others become sites of identification, sympathy, desire and self-recognition.

As identifications shift, channels of desire are redirected from the proper, normative social and symbolic (and patriarchal) order of work, reason and family and towards darker forces of passion, violence and death. The world of darkness is, in the process, lightened. The excluded figures once represented as malevolent, disturbed or deviant are rendered more humane while the systems that exclude them assume terrifying, persecutory and inhuman shapes. The reversal, with its residual Romantic identification with outcast and rebel, with its feeling for liberation and individual freedom, not only displays a re-evaluation of social attitudes but, in making transgression a positive force, a sign of heroism in anguished suffering, strength of character and intensely personal resistance, simultaneously diffuses its power by undoing the hold of prohibition and the cathectic charge of the negative. Transgression, without regimes of prohibition and limit to maintain its ambivalent energy, becomes the norm, no longer able to fix upon a threatening enough object of terror. Celebrating transgressive energy, in repeating gestures that simulate its charge in ever-decreasing spirals of reversal and counter-valence paradoxically diminishes its power. Without a symbolic framework to direct, suppress, exclude and prohibit, without the spectre of a terrifying paternal limit giving forceful legitimacy to imperative acts of expenditure, the cultural field is levelled, its energies intensified and dispersed, its boundaries uncertain and desires deregulated. In the absence of prohibition, transgression seeks out limits that become less and less visible; with the decline of the paternal figure, transgression finds itself to be incited, reproduced, encouraged, repeated as if to conjure up a spectre fast vanishing. In the process, as with the fate of sexuality to which it was once tied, transgression becomes just another social activity; permitted and thus barely transgressive any more, its residual charge of energy can be readily capitalised upon.

In her fiction, Carter powerfully, and often critically, demonstrates the reversal of values and identifications that occurs via the Gothic genre. Otherness takes centre stage; sexual transgression, dark desire and fantastic deviance wonderfully subvert the regimented and restrictive orders of reason, utility and morality. There is an energy of rebellion and liberation evoked in the challenges to aesthetic conventions and social norms, an energy associated with the political and sexual movements of the 1960s, the period in which Carter began writing. The pastiche Gothic of 'The Bloody Chamber' has a feminine figure replace the father figure, but the reversal of normal hierarchy does not institute a new regime of the mother as the inverted replica of the old order: while feminist issues and concerns with sexuality and gender achieve increasing cultural prominence, dominance is not on the agenda. In turning over expectations and conventions, the reversal exposes the artifice and constructedness of social and symbolic meanings, to refuse fictional credulity and disrupt the credibility of the ideological frame in which the tale is given meaning. As in the rhetoric of the social and sexual revolutions of the 1960s, an established order is not overthrown and replaced with its mirror equivalent, but an opening up of boundaries and possibilities is effected, a challenge to forms of authority introducing new norms and quietly insistent imperatives, to be sure, without announcing the arrival of a solitary and sublime new centre of social and political cohesion. With its spectral power demystified, the space of a single credible, forceful paternal figure is left vacant, a space that finds itself filled with a host of fleeting spectres of power – governmental, conspiratorial, military, corporate, criminal, alien.

In Gothic times, margins may become the norm and occupy a more central cultural place, but that centre is characterised by dispersal, evacuated of core and apex. The Gothic times of the present, then, though defining a world of innumerable real and imagined terrors and horrors do not simply signify the actualities of a physical or psychological condition, a new dark, barbaric age or a life spent in fear. Inured to everyday horrors through repetition in stories, or framing terror in fictional form, reality and fantasy feed on each other, disclosing pervasive and generalised patterns of production, simulation and consumption in which, unanchored by the historical weight of taboo, desire and anxiety float freely to ghost the high-speed circulation of information and commodities. To live in

Gothic times means that the genre loses its specific intensity, shedding the allure of darkness, danger and mystery. A matter of lifestyle, consumer choice or personal taste, Gothic exists in domains of fashion, entertainment and aesthetics as one genre among many, normalised, commodified, with a hint of the delicatessen about its taste for blood, the macabre lifted by camp flavourings. A report on the recent World Dracula Congress in Poiana Brasov, Romania, a convention for vampire enthusiasts and researchers, offers an example of the diverse tones, meanings and lifestyles associated with the genre. For Ingrid Pitt, a star of Hammer Horror films who continues to make a living out of the vampire entertainment industry, the conveniences of the event leave much to be desired: the toilets, she comments, are 'bloody disgusting and the paper's scratchy as hell'. While the superficial celluloid attractions of vampirism remain good for business, there is certainly no wholehearted indulgence in a life of degradation and defilement. The report details some of the 'other horrors' besetting the delegates: Arlene Russo, for example, an editor of a vampire magazine, 'is shocked at eastern Europe's lack of vegetarian food, and at having to walk back from the restaurant through an unlit pine forest after midnight'. Vegetarianism and a disinclination for midnight darkness seem utterly out of place at an event celebrating a nocturnal bloodsucker. The congress presents other examples of contemporary vampirism: participants in search of ancestral connections to Vlad the Impaler; a German forensic scientist studying New York's vampire youth detailing how 'they puncture their bodies and drink each other's blood and consider it as normal as you guys going to conferences on Dracula'; a psychologist outlining 'the positive aspect of psychic vampirism' to argue that 'becoming a vampire should be a conscious process; you need to work closely with a psychologist. You can't just wake up one day and be a cool, cute, sexy vampire and lose yourself' (Connolly, 19). Screen image, social practice and psychic therapy assemble at a convention embracing academics, fans, tourists – vampirism diversely embracing entertainment, leisure, heritage and educational industries.

Everyday life in Western culture is, of course, dominated by commodities, by goods, images or information. Vampires, delivered of their fearful form become familiar and consumable figures: 'the vampire's domestication accompanies its dilution as vampire signifiers are appropriated and sold', writes Judith Roof, noting how Dracula became a Dell comic book superhero in 1962 and, more comically in the 1980s, turned into the children's cartoon character 'Count Duckula'. Far from cult appropriation, the vampire is assimilated on a mass scale so that 'candy stores sold wax teeth' (Roof, 169). Vampires saturate consumer culture – a figure of

consumption in the sense of a destructive using up of energies and resources and a model for its processes and consumers – and assume a
strangely normative character. Commenting on Poppy Z. Brite's *Lost Souls*,
Jan Gordon observes how America is populated by alienated youths abandoned by their families: 'these vampire teens leave their soulless broken
homes ... searching for kindred vampire spirits: other black-garbed, hol-
low-eyed, amoral, abandoned teens, vampiric here, in fact, as so many are
by wish and by fashion in our world' (Gordon, 46). Vampires cease to be
threats to individual and social identity and curiously give shape to the
unformed mass of desires, cravings and appetites called the consumer.
Anne Rice's fiction comes to the fore in this respect: her vampires exist in
a world of luxurious consumption, voracious, hollow, wasted images of
attenuated desire beyond an end of history consigned to be spent spending. Hollywood finalises the assimilation, enabling Rice's vampires to assume the glitzy celebrity glossing consumer culture and orientating its
desires: 'with Cruise playing Lestat ... the vampire has ceased to be unrec-
ognizable. Once a menace to the conclaves of average America, he was
now an honorary resident' (Tomc, 96). For Tomc, Rice's vampires are
concoctions of 1970s liberation politics and liberalism. They are symptomatic effects of the conjunction between feminist freedoms and myths
of beauty demanding that bodies be defined in terms of powerful cultural
images, the pressures of consumption manifesting themselves in pathological restraint or excessive satisfaction: 'Rice's manipulation of appetite
illuminates the trajectory of the vampire from tortured anorexic to guilt-
less consumer' (Tomc, 106). Vampires are thus recognised, mirrors of contemporary identity and sympathetic identification, strangely human, if
not more than human: 'we love and honor our monsters for bringing us to
that place in ourselves, the place from which we continually create humanity in a brutal fearful world' (Charnas, 67). The vampire is warmly
embraced, included, naturalised, humanised in an appropriative liberal
gesture that is scarcely tenable given the vampire's historical construction
as that which is both most proximate and alien to human identity, the
necessary internal antithesis cultures and subjects have to expel in order to
survive. But the other, technologically transformed into virtually pure image
sheds, along with any negative intensity, any fearful weight it might, historically, have possessed, and casts off, too, any illusion of substance that
the human subject may once have imagined for its self. The trajectory
allies itself with the flight towards a disembodied and decontextualised
posthumanity (Hayles).

Contemporary identifications with the vampire, consolidating a
recognisable image of consumerist humanity, also extend beyond the

mirrors and screens of the present and towards a future reverberating with posthuman promise. The future, of course, is already present in the form of virtual systems and digital technologies. For Stone, Rice's vampire fantastically absorbs a range of posthuman possibilities; Lestat is a liminal, boundary, cyborg figure:

> he nicely exemplifies a style of cyborg existence, capturing the pain and complexity of attempting to adapt to a society, a lifestyle, a language, a culture, our epistemology, even in Lestat's case a species, that is not one's own. Lestat is a vampire for our seasons, struggling with the swiftly changing meanings of what it is to be human, or, for that matter, inhuman. (Stone, 178)

The reciprocal fascination flickering between undead vampires and humans touched by mortality discloses the mobility and instability of identity, confronting humans with what Stone calls a 'new Dark Gift': 'the passing on of the newly transformed vampire gaze, the visual knowledge which makes the machineries of subjectivity visible and the nuts and bolts that hold the surface of reality together stand out from the background' (Stone, 182). An artificial, boundary figure, the vampire's liminal cultural presence enables the mechanics of selfhood to be exposed so that it can be dismantled and reassembled: no one is securely ensconced in carefully delimited or stable subject positions: 'the vampire subjectivity sees the play of identity from the metalevel, sees the fragrant possibilities of multiple voices and subject position, the endless refraction of desire, with a visual apparatus that has become irreducibly and fatally different'(182). In its conjunction with technologies of vision, this version of the vampire looks back at a modern world of illusory human securities, not as an archaic remnant of a barbaric prehistory, but as an uncanny harbinger of what is to come, glimpsing a fatal difference possessed by apparatuses and machines rather than humans. There is a challenge and promise held out by the emergence of virtual systems: 'the war of desire and technology is a war of transformation, in which, if we look deeply enough, we can make out the lineaments of our own vampire future' (183).

The 'gaze of the vampire' with which Stone renders technology gothic and promotes the shifting, plural possibilities of cyborg identity is quite different from the gaze that horrifies Jonathan Harker as he prepares to strike Dracula, asleep in his coffin. Harker meets his limit, paralysed in the middle of his brutal but righteous act, his powers drained by a look that reduces him to an anxious, impotent wretch. The vampire's gaze hollows out the secure identity of the middle-class Englishman, devastating illusions of rectitude and virility. The novel refuses to celebrate this crisis as a space for innovation, pluralisation or new possibility: it remains a threat to be apprehended and expelled so that English identity can be reasserted as singular, superior and secure. The destabilisation caused by the vampire, the uncertainty it provokes and gap it exposes in identity is something to be filled. The vampire is given form by mystical as well as technological media and executed by an eager band of victims turned hunters: rendered visible and reversing the direction of an objectifying gaze, Harker's act can be completed, a single order re-established through the sacrificial murder of the singular Thing. The vampire becomes the means to solve the crisis that, as cultural symptom, it represents as well as provokes: with the energy of righteous expenditure, a paternal symbolic order restores itself, realigning circuits of desire and identity in an act of closure and expulsion. In contrast, Stone's liminal vampire remains open to possibilities: it marks a refusal to fill the gap with an overriding and restrictive paternal figure. The horrifying sight of the vampiric eye becomes a place of attraction rather than repulsion, the site of new, plural projections, a space defined by the waning power of prohibition, within and beyond limited symbolic borders: it offers 'fragrant possibilities of multiple voices and subject position' (182). The transformation of vampirism is doubled: not only does the vampire undergo a re-evaluation, it serves as a metaphor of transformation itself, its liminality articulating a space of transition, a symptom of a cultural, economic and technological shifts.

It is not only virtual technologies that materialise the decline and transformation of a paternally regulated symbolic order. Noting the impact of the move from analogue to digital patterns of encoding, recording and transmission, Judith Roof's discussion of biological and medical advances argues that new methods of reproduction and genetic manipulation directly, and often quite literally, threaten the ideological reproduction of paternal formations. Her case for a paternal crisis draws heavily on examples from Gothic fiction, *Frankenstein* and *Dracula* in particular, to contend that the continued circulation of historical figures of terror and horror gives form to contemporary fears about technological, scientific and biological innovations. While *Frankenstein* and *Dracula* have extensive associations with science and technology (Wicke; Kittler, 1997), Roof claims that 'vampires, aliens, and feminist heroics, all represent anxieties about an unauthorized reproduction that challenges proper (i.e., paternal) reproductive order and human aegis' (Roof, 10). Vampire fiction and films, in the 1970s, 'all followed the Stoker story with its particular threat to the order of property and patrimony', their representations serving 'as a specifically reproductive threat impinging on a patriarchal order that has allied itself with the very technology whose system has already spelled its transmogrification' (144; 149). Technology, once seen as merely a tool for patriarchal production and dominance, becomes threatening when it emerges as a dangerous supplement that supplants and exceeds its control. Like the vampire, once the excluded support of paternal order, technology monstrously undoes the system which designed it.

The feminism Roof links to anxieties about vampires and aliens is also strangely supplementary in the way it overturns and opens up gendered hierarchies. In feminist accounts of new technology and cyborg identity, this logic of supplementarity is brought to the fore. Sadie Plant's 'cyberfeminism' combines writing and sexual identity in a new weave or network of identities that are fluid, multiple, changing and, significantly, beyond masculine control. Destroying human identity, mapping the transcendent soul of enlightened man, the digital matrix that was 'the culmination of his machinic erections' surpasses his power: 'man confronts the system he built for his own protection and finds it is female and dangerous' (Plant, 183; Haraway, 1990). Computer code and genetic code allow everything from identity to bodies to be rewritten according to different, supplementary logic. If the future is vampiric, it is also female and machinic.

Embracing anxieties about technological, corporeal and sexual changes, the figure of the vampire marks the space of transition, a metaphor for the absence of the paternal metaphor, for the 'viral loss of determinacy' of a culture given over to the flows of 'trans': transsexuality, transeconomics, transaesthetics ... It marks the fate of the body subjected to a new, unstable system of relationships and forces: once a metaphor for the soul or sex, the body 'is no longer a metaphor for anything at all, merely the locus of metastasis, of the machine-like connections between all its processes, of an endless programming devoid of any symbolic organization or overarching purpose'; it participates in 'the same promiscuity that characterizes networks and integrated circuits' (Baudrillard, 1993b: 7). Cloning, for Baudrillard, materialises the viral revision of reproduction according to a matrix in which digital and biological code combine to erase the chance and difference of 'natural' human creation:

> Father and mother are gone, but their disappearance, far from widening an aleatory freedom for the subject, instead leaves the way clear for a *matrix known as a code*. No more mother, no more father: just a matrix. And it is this matrix, this genetic code, which is destined to 'give birth', from now till eternity, in an operational mode from which all chance sexual elements have been expunged (115, original emphasis).

This 'hell of the same' also destroys the individual: 'the subject, too, is gone, because identical duplication ends the division that constitutes him. The mirror stage is abolished by the cloning process – or, perhaps more accurately is monstrously parodied therein' (113–15). Like the vampire, who subverts the mirrors of identity and the patterns of reproduction, the rewriting of bodies and practices enabled by biological and digital code inaugurates a posthuman system of reproduction, one that, though presented in gendered terms as a 'matrix', far exceeds the conventional notions of femininity.

Postmodern, postoedipal, the human figure, along with the monsters and vampires that, negatively, gave it form, are rewired. If the human becomes posthuman then perhaps the monster becomes 'post-monstrous'. Like the vampire, invoked as a positive representative of the transition to a new order of existence, *Frankenstein*, too, makes repeated returns as a metaphor for current identities and relationships. Informed by experiments into the power of electricity and speculating on the creation of life beyond death, a production and reproduction that supersedes (feminine) nature, *Frankenstein*, of course, has regularly been invoked throughout modernity as a text concerned with human and scientific power over nature and the unleashing of uncontrollable and monstrous energies. The story combines romantic promise of discovery with nightmarish realisation; it also unleashed a metaphor on the world which shaped popular responses to scientific innovation. Despite the sympathies for the monster's plight elicited by *Frankenstein*'s first-person narratives, it is the scientist who remained the determining figure: the monster, as his creation and sign of the dangers he irresponsibly lets loose, forms the dramatic and cautionary embodiment of his own monstrous project. Monsters must die, while humans live on, excited by fears of a 'race of devils' threatening – and constituting – their imaginary existence. Now, however, it seems that the idea of humanity has already been overcome, even absorbed, by that race of devils. Rather than highlighting the fantastic failings of the would-be father of the 'new species', current invocations of Shelley's text focus on the monster as a prototype of a new biological and technological alignment: sire of 'every robot, every android, every sentient computer', the novel's monster is also the 'first cyborg' (Russ, 126; Gray, Mentor, Figueroa-Sarriera, 5). Where fears of Frankenstein as 'mad scientist' concentrated anxieties on a moral and social ambivalence regarding the progress and benefits of experimentation, the focus on the monster opens up concerns with identity and corporeal integrity that tacitly yet readily accept the arrival of a new biotechnological order.

From being a figure of curious sympathy in Shelley's text, the monster becomes a site of projection and identification in which human and monster merge in a posthuman configuration. Eliding creator and creation, Mark Poster proposes a 'high-tech Frankenstein' as 'a figure for the relation of humans online to machines' (Poster, 29–30). The boundaries which allowed human and monster to define each other by their difference are erased. Humans are made monsters, technologically altered, prosthetically enhanced beyond human specifications. A reversal occurs in this process of identifying with a monster become cyborg: 'the Gothic tale of technology as the being from the dark lagoon is perhaps, then, narrativised otherwise as a romance with an alien cyborg, a monster who is already none other than ourselves' (29). The fear and horror of monsters that underpinned Gothic fiction's cautionary project returns to a romantic investment in otherness. While romance draws humans towards monster, alien and cyborg, the allure of otherness does not restore a transcendent sense of self: otherness is merely the desire for novelty that leads only to the indifference and multiplicity of posthumanity.

Gothic figures facilitate flights towards new identities, an expansion into the new and virtual realms of a technocorporate order. The monster, then, is no longer a figure of fear but metaphor of change and possibility, a model to be imitated and affirmed rather than abhorred. Like any other identity, that of monster is simply a position one can freely choose for oneself, off the peg:

> to be perceived as monstrous, or consciously to construct oneself as monstrous, is to have an affinity with disorder, chaos, mutation and transformation, in an attempt to work against logic, rationality, normality, purity and science. It can often be seen as a way of both undoing and resurrecting the past and its fiction in order to create some new forms, connections, leakages and abstractions. (Clarke, 36)

Looking backwards to move forwards, the recovery of Gothic fictions and figures resurrects the past only to leave it behind. In the process, polarities are reversed, with older negative associations of monsters turned into positive evaluations and affiliations.

Looking back while flying into the future, however, reiterates the historical momentum of modernity as presented by Walter Benjamin's 'angel of history' (Benjamin, 1973: 259–60). Poster offers a posthuman version in which 'high-tech Frankenstein ... functions as an opening to globalized, machinic post-humanity, one who will stare backwards at us, his/her historical ancestors, like Benjamin's angel, as if observing a monster' (Potter, 30). In retrospection, a posthuman gaze looks on humans as monsters. Poster's angel is thus machinic, taking a line of flight away from the monstrous excrescence that is humanity. Leaving human-monsters behind, though tracing a line of flight they might wish to follow, monsters are things of the past. But they are also, as cyborgs, signs of future identities, monsters to come, new hybrids and harbingers of unthinkable configurations. Monsters, returning from the past or the future, collapse on a present that has itself become monstrous. Virilio's version of the 'angel of history' sees Benjamin's 'theological vision' break down and 'become the vision of each and every one of us'(Virilio, 2000: xiii). The divine vision finds itself replaced by the vision machines of everyday life, consumed by the ever-present screens that define western existence in real-time relays. Both the future and history disappear on receding horizons: neither is credible as a source of hope in a present defined by a 'retreat of knowledge, the retirement of progress' (xii).

Monstrosity becomes a general condition rather than an exception. When monsters become, rather than mark out the limits of, humanity, it is difficult to see why the name 'monster' needs apply at all. Monsters are the norm. Bruce Sterling's cyberpunk version of *Frankenstein* sketches out the extent of their current indifference. No longer the creation of a romantic mad scientist, the cyberpunk rewrite has its monsters developed by the Research and Development department of a global corporation. They are 'already loose on the streets': 'quite likely WE are them'. Their genetic composition patented and mass-produced in the thousands, these monsters are employed in the most mundane of occupations, such as night-shift cleaners in fast-food outlets. There is nothing special or exceptional about them. On the contrary, 'jump-starting corpses', so inventive in Shelley's time, now 'happens in intensive care wards every day' (Sterling, 1991). Monstrosity spreads with biotechnology to normalise itself in every day practices and relations: prosthetic devices and enhancements, cosmetic surgery, genetic screening and engineering, and, even, the strange figures of celebrity – ideal, airbrushed, outlandish, remarkable or not – that flicker across screens, all testify to an indifference. If the identification with the monster is complete in this curiously excessive normalisation, then the obliteration of any discernible difference between human and monsters has also rewritten the rules governing the distinctions of self and other: the humanisation of the monster tends in opposite, equivalent and reversible direction as the monstering of humanity.

## Candygothic

Pleasure and pain; horror and joy; candy bars and razorblades. Candyman is the son of a slave who became a wealthy manufacturer. Educated and talented, he practiced his profession as portrait artist to the rich until, falling in love with one of his subjects, he fell foul of her father. A mob was set upon him, hounding him to Cabrini Green where they hacked off his right hand with a rusty saw, smashed some nearby hives and smeared him with honey. He was stung to death by frightened bees. Romance and death;

sweetness and agony: candygothic.

Candyman becomes an urban legend, a ghost returning to haunt the decaying urban spaces built in the place of his fatal suffering. As a spectre of past crimes, injustice and horrifying communal violence, his figural and supernatural reappearances call for retribution and vengeance, for a law outside law. He is a figure of guilt, kept alive in the whispered tones of a culture that continues to be defined by racial divisions and violence, a spectral projection in excess of liberal reason and a site of passions that cannot be contained. Past crimes, painful guilt, supernatural figures of terror and passion are conventional features in a fictional genre associated with the liberation of the darker impulses of violence and sexuality. But these features, in the late twentieth century, became all-too familiar as the daily diet of popular culture, items on news reports and in commercials as much as fantasies on screen. On the street, in the schoolyard and in the home, violence and fear pervade everyday existence. The repetitive reiteration of familiar formulas, moreover, paints sexuality in the same familiar colours.

Repetition, automation, pleasure, pain are discussed in Sylvère Lotringer's supplement to a history of sexuality – a book of interviews with sex clinicians in the US. The argument notes the disappearance of anything resembling prohibition, taboo or repression when it comes to sexuality. This is not a victory for sexual liberation, for personal freedom or, even, for a 'right to orgasm', but a banal occurrence underlined by reports that sex 'is fast becoming America's dominant social activity' (Lotringer, 8). Relentless sexpression ironically mimics a treatment devised in sex clinics and recorded by Lotringer:

> '… the treatment consists of giving him [the patient] everything he wants.'
>
> 'We certainly try to get him to use the best possible and most deviant sexual fantasy he's ever had. If it's a rapist, I specially want him to use the most aggressive rape possible: lack of concern for the victim, using her as an object …'
>
> 'You really go out of your way to satisfy your customers.'
>
> 'Yeah, we *satiate* them. Think "extinction".'
>
> (Lotringer, 1988, original emphasis)

This technique of 'masturbatory satiation' is also called 'boredom therapy' (122–3). It operates according to a principle of more, of stimulating fantasy to death. Its underlying premiss bears strong resemblance to a late eighteenth-century attack on 'terrorist novel writing' in which the anonymous critic lists the formulaic mechanisms of popular fiction and hopes that 'the insipid repetition of the same bugbears will at length work a cure'. For Lotringer, however, 'boredom therapy highlights the curious dilemma of our postmodernity: pleasure not pain, consumption, not prohibition, have become our punishment. Repetition is the norm, and the cure' (177). The norm underwriting the repetitive circulation of sexual images is economic. Writing on the 'sexual fix', on the 'fabrication' that goes under the name of 'sexuality', Stephen Heath criticises the triumphant association of sexuality with liberation or revolution and argues that what emerges is no more than a new myth or ideology, 'a new mode of conformity' coming into existence 'in relation to the capitalist system': 'the production of a commodity "sexuality"' (Heath, 3). The sexual revolution does not engender a massive social transformation but reinforces 'multi-million pound or dollar industry' spreading sex 'like butter on all its products' (149). Tasty. Spread over everything, sexuality loses its associations of liberation and transgression to become just another commodity in a cycle of (boring) consumption.

'Candygothic' – another tentative generic subcategorisation – signifies an attempt to reassess the function of horror in a (western) culture in which transgressions, repressions, taboos, prohibitions no longer mark an absolute limit in unbearable excess and thus no longer contain the intensity of a desire for something other, something that satisfyingly disturbs – and defines – social and moral boundaries. Though numerous figures of horror are thrown up by contemporary fiction and film, Krugers, Chuckies, Pinheads, Lecters, their shelf-life seems limited in the face of a demand for more thrilling horrors, their terror index-linked to the novelties provided by special effects, visual techniques and stylised killing. Predictable and acceptable, figures of horror function as 'titillating exercises in reassurance' which become 'highly marketable commodities' (Grixti, 18–19). The market for horror since the 1970s is primarily composed, Carol Clover notes, of the children of a more liberated and consumerist generation, the post-war baby boomers. Roger Dadoun's speculation that, through fetishisation, the culture industry 'takes over from the faltering economic system' offers a suggestive account of the manner in which popular aesthetics become inextricably entangled in the operation of a consumer economy (Dadoun, 46). Fetishism, of course, brings the question of desire to the fore. For Dana Polan, late capitalism, as 'a society of services and information, of a flow of desire', constitutes 'a capitalism that encourages excessive expenditure, that desires a desire that is not sublimated or organized within the frame of the Oedipalised family' (Polan, 178). The family romance, so important to gothic fiction and cinema alike, along with rational subjectivity and the reproductive apparatuses of bourgeois ideology, is rendered powerless in the face of the rapid circulations of postmodern economy. Aesthetic categories and distinctions between high and low culture are also confounded by the consumerist dynamics of terror and pleasure (Modleski). In horror as in kitsch, then, one finds a certain contemporary veracity, evidence of the condition that Jean-Francois Lyotard calls 'postmodern', a condition in which judgements – aesthetic, rational, moral or legal – are subsumed by the flows of monetary exchange and performance optimisation.

In Gothic terms, however, there is nothing new in the relationship between culture and economy, nor in the blurring of sexual boundaries and disturbing aesthetic and moral categories. Since the eighteenth century, popular fictions have been associated with wasteful expenditures of energy, overstepping the boundaries of reason, taste and propriety and unleashing the spectre of a voracious, libidinal – and feminised – market of undiscriminating consumers (see Ioan Williams). Andrea Henderson's account of Gothic fiction and economy identifies, in the move from gold to paper currency and in the slippage of use and exchange values, a spectralisation of identity linked to commodities. The shifting base of Gothic fiction, between landed and commercial wealth, is integral to Gothic texts themselves, as Clery's analysis of Ann Radcliffe's *The Mysteries of Udolpho* has shown: the heroine's propriety and virtue are not values in themselves but markers of her worth as a commodity in the marriage market. Fantasy and the supernatural nonetheless shape processes of exchange: the horror of losing oneself and one's virtue to superstition, passion and vice is turned, through terror, into the sublime recovery of position, propriety and property and the expulsion of all threatening excesses. The fantastic fairytale ending to *Udolpho* returns to an order presided over by a providential and paternal figure: material and symbolic economies are realigned, excess expelled and desire properly regulated by morality. The paternal figure, with its superegoic and symbolic power, becomes the crucial feature of all Gothic fiction, central to its desires and transgressions. In *Dracula*, for instance, the absence of a unifying moral order releases vampiric circulations of blood, desire and money dissolving social and familial bonds: the sacrificial violence of the ending serves, through an excessive expenditure of male energy, to restore the bourgeois fantasy of paternity and family and the symbolic framework in which goods and desires can be exchanged properly.

Figures of excess, of immorality and monstrosity, are strangely integral to the establishment and maintenance of symbolic and social structures, simultaneously included and expelled as the threats that underwrite the promise of identity and order, the formless, abjected basis of paternal frameworks of desire and exchange. The disturbance of sexual, social and moral categories is thus not simply the effect but also the unseen locus of symbolic economies. Susan Sontag's account of the 'extreme moral simplification' in science fiction and horror films identifies a 'morally acceptable fantasy where one can give outlet to cruel or at least amoral feelings'. 'This,' she continues, 'is the undeniable pleasure we derive from looking at freaks, beings excluded from the category of the human. The sense of superiority over the freak conjoined in varying proportions with the titillation of fear and aversion makes it possible for moral scruples to be lifted, for cruelty to be enjoyed'(Sontag, 427–8). Enjoyment and cruelty are, it seems, integral to morality. Sontag's position accords with the psychoanalytic registers of Lacan and Kristeva. Law, in its paternal, prohibitive sense organises enjoyment and identity in language through the exclusion of some Thing – a void, a 'vacuole' – that is inassimilable, unbearable and yet intimately exterior to the subject. An object fills the void of subjectivity to shield it from the intensity of an extreme pleasure, *jouissance*, which tears open the 'inaugural loss' founding subjective being (Kristeva, 1982: 5). It is a locus of constitution and dissolution, pleasure and pain, attraction and repulsion, limit and transgression. A site of what Bataille calls an 'imperative act of exclusion' 'founding community and morality', the abject is thus associated with the accursed share, that element of sacred or profane excess heterogeneous to social, rational and productive functioning. Kristeva, observing how 'the logic of prohibition' 'founds the abject', cites Bataille as the only thinker 'who has linked the production of the abject to *the weakness of that prohibition*, which, in other respects, necessarily constitutes each social order' (64, original emphasis).

Gothic figures have much to say about the fragmentation and instabilities that form the constitutive features (rather than the aberrant exceptions) of normal subjectivity (Donald, 234). Objects of horror are necessary in the anxious, cultural dynamic of subjectivity and otherness (Twitchell, 1988: 41–2). Given form and apprehended, the object can then be violently expelled: 'the pleasure of the [horror] text is', notes Philip Brophy, 'getting the shit scared out of you – and loving it' (Brophy, 5). Such expenditure describes the discharge of intensity that allows the pleasure principle of signifying circulation to regain equilibrium: pleasure arises as an effect of intensity, at the moment of release, from it and of it. Barbara Creed, in her Kristevan reading of the monstrous-feminine, identifies a 'confrontation' that serves 'to eject the abject' and 'redraw' boundaries of humanity according to 'paternal law' (Creed, 72). The conservatism and moral violence of earlier, traditional Gothic fictions seems to be replayed in contemporary horror, while presenting new objects of cultural anxiety on which to expend righteous rage. This contradicts, at least in diegetic terms, queer and posthuman readings of horror which exploit the ambiguity of cinematic identifications to valorise 'the monster queer as sexual outlaw, a counter-hegemonic figure who forcefully smashes the binary oppositions of gender and sexuality and race' or to urge 'the need to recognize and celebrate our own monstrosities' (Benshoff, 231; Halberstam, 27). In contrast, Clover's account of slasher films concludes that, despite their problematisation and confusion of gender identifications and representations, they ultimately restore a masculine order. The 'Final Girl' overcomes the abjection, threats of violence and violation, by killing her male attacker. Abjection turns into sovereignty and allows the (male, teen) audience a vicarious enjoyment of female persecution on two levels: by identifying with her and her attacker and also enjoying the thrilling release of legitimate killing. The heroine is thus both terrorised woman and male surrogate and the audience are consequently '"masculinized" by and through the very figure by and through whom we were earlier "feminized"' (Clover, 123). The effect also operates by and through the cinematic apparatus which 'succeeds in incorporating its spectators as "feminine" and then violating that body – which recoils, shudders, cries out collectively' (118). The camera assaults the eyes and enacts a kind of feminisation. At the level of the cinematic apparatus, cross-identifications problematise the 'hypostatization of the gaze as male' (Fletcher, 343). The gaze on the screen fragments, looks proliferate. Spectators, in horror, are forced to avert their threatened eyes as voyeuristic pleasure turns into pain and punishment: they must 'look away, to not-look, to look anywhere but at the screen'. The effect is that 'strategies of identification are temporarily broken, as the spectator is constructed in the place of horror, the place where the sight/site can longer be endured' (Creed, 81). Spectators are thus moved from a position of visual mastery and pleasure to assaulted, passive and reactive bodies forced to move, conduits of cinematic sensation.

In expending sense and subject, repetitive formulas and cinematic devices come to the fore: a technical production of intense effects and sensations transforms identification into spectatorial subjection to and abjection by the apparatus itself. The mechanics of horror generates the insecurity associated with the fantastic: the uncertainty and anxiety regarding I and other, man and woman, good and bad occurs as much in the relation between eye and image as between spectator and character. The formulas, superficial knowingness of horror films and their playful manipulation of audience expectations provide the predictable pattern against which the moments of excess, the visual shocks and violent shifts in angle, can be staged: anxiety and anticipatory desire are heightened so that the emotional discharge can be intensified. The expenditure, the sensation, thrill, scream, forms the end in itself. In the escalating demand for more and more intense thrills, the subject attains an illusory plenitude at the point of subjective evacuation and expenditure, a degraded and devalued intensity in which the interest of a dramatic story is superseded by 'an effacement of pleasure and bliss'. Instead, as Roland Barthes notes, 'in mass culture, there is an enormous consumption of "dramatics" and little bliss' (Barthes, 1976: 48). Repeatedly circulating as a commodity to be consumed, the intensities of a jouissance associated with text and writing are downgraded as a 'little jouissance', a cheap thrill.

Horror, in the formulas and narrative apparatus it depends upon and in the effects it produces, begins to manifest the popular emergence of a different kind of subject, a subject that while always shadowing the higher forms of cultural being as an appetitive, sensation-seeking creature without rational or moral discrimination, testifies to the recent prevalence of ideas of luxurious or wasteful consumption over an order of production regulated by a work-ethic and values of sobriety and conservatism. Noting the 'incoherence' which dominates popular cultural fictions and films as a norm, Polan suggests that economy no longer operates through repression but through the inciting of excess, 'an invitation for individuals to exceed previous boundaries, to be in excess of an analytic, literally conservative control of productivity' (Polan, 178). The individual, in this model, is no longer a useful, productive member of society, but a being who enjoys his/ her loss of will, a being given up to the flows of exchange and desire and giving up on the rational imperative to meaning or sense: 'flow involves the transcendence of meaningful units by a system whose only meaning is the fact of its global non-meaning' (183). Like the spectator of a horror film, possessed by the flows of images across the screen and affected by the flows of sensation it evokes, the consumer is another channel of consumption, expenditure and desire, an evacuated site of economic motility. For Rhonda Lieberman, the consumer is not defined or directed by reason or utility but oscillates between alienated identity and fantasised fulfilment, between insatiable demand and frustrated desire so that he or she 'behaves like an ambulatory kidney faced with the task of purifying and expelling the irreconcilable and heterogeneous semiotic flows dumped on the person from the body of capital' (Lieberman, 246–7). Gender does not matter, only the flows of desire and their hollow subject: 'under consumer culture, "lack" is not only circulated but is actively sought out and produced by any body, masculine or feminine identified' (245). An uncertain space is disclosed at the unseen articulation of lack and desire: 'commodity interpellation' hysterrorises the abject consumer with an imperative to enjoy whatever she wants but without answering the question of what she really wants. Zizek's account of a superegoic capitalism applies: without a master figure to prohibit and regulate excessive desire there is no stabilising point to prevent the subject trailing in the wake of its commodities and signs and no anchor to establish meaning, value or identity. The absence of an organising figure or framework defines, for Goux, the shift from modern to postmodern economy. Bourgeois rules of rational, useful and moral consumption no longer operate when the distinction between need and luxury, useful and superfluous expenditure are erased. Conspicuous, but privatised, consumption replaces the sacrificial, symbolic rituals that established communities. Supply precedes and constitutes demand, capitalising on 'a metaphysical uncertainty regarding the object of human desire' 'through the invention of the new, the production of the unpredictable' (Goux, 1990b: 212).

A general sense of uncanniness or spectrality, a general abjection and perversity, define a normal condition. For Zizek, the dematerialisation caused by electronic money evokes 'an invisible, and for that reason all-powerful, spectral frame which dominates our lives' (Zizek, 1997: 102). Paternal regulation cedes to abjection and perversion, 'in a world', Kristeva notes, 'in which the Other has collapsed' (Kristeva, 1982: 18). 'The abject is perverse because it neither gives up nor assumes a prohibition, a rule, or a law; but turns them aside, mis-leads, corrupts; uses them, takes advantage of them, the better to deny them' (15–16). Perversion turns towards a paternal principle that operates only insofar as it is spectral, superegoic, commanding enjoyment, liberating desire from prohibition and simultaneously rendering its object impalpable and unsatisfactory. The perversity of horror film hysterrorises the subject: the violent shocks and discharges it produces only increase the demand for more thrills and sensation, a demand for technical stimulation to deliver something like full subjective experience, a demand gratified only to the extent that it lasts no longer than the instant of the shock. In the very uselessness and luxuriously irrational expenditures of the horror film, then, not only are the antagonisms and contradictions inherent in social and symbolic systems violently staged and restaged: the impossible satisfactions of an all-too liberal consumer culture are simultaneously replayed and accelerated.

## Repetition-consumption

*Candyman*, directed by Bernard Rose, took $25,000,000 at the US box office by January 1993. Though first shown in 1992, the film is riven with the concerns and contradictions of Reagan's and Thatcher's 1980s. Based on Clive Barker's story, 'The Forbidden' (1985) and scripted by the English director, the film contrasts the world of inner-city housing projects with the comfortable lifestyle of white academics: yuppie consumption, expensive apartments, chic restaurants, set opulence and luxury against urban decay, violence and misery. Moved from a Liverpool housing estate (in Barker's story) to the Cabrini Green Projects in Chicago, the setting of the film brings out two extremes of consumption: it is associated not only with liberal expenditures on commodities and property but also with the wasting of communities. Wasteful expenditure, urban wastelands and wasted lives result from the funding cuts and privatisation policies of governments fixated on the freedoms of the market economy, and the minimisation of state responsibility linked to economic deregulation and tax reductions.

'There is no such thing as society', Margaret Thatcher famously commented to *Woman's Weekly*. Only individuals. Social space disappears as a communal form, to be replaced by a global system in which individuals circulate in the flows of money, information and desire as consumers of property and commodities. With consumption comes fear, personified in the 1980s slasher genre as a single diabolical figure, a figure condensing anxieties in order to give generalised social insecurity a face. In *Candyman*, of course, it is a black face. In Briefel and Ngai's reading of the film, fear is understood as another commodity enjoyed by white America, a form of an 'emotional property' linked to home ownership and security that justifies the cohesion of a community against the threat of dangerous social others (Briefel and Ngai, 71). Even the film's demon is imbued with the economic spirit of the times as 'a blackman for hire, at the beck and call of consumers in a service economy' (77). The fear which accompanies consumption – to the point that it functions as its check in identifying a limit and object and its blank cheque in allowing the projection of more expensive objects of fear to be consumed – concerns the boundaries separating the consumer from social and economic incursions: the freedom with which Candyman can be called to any location displays their permeability. If the limits of propriety used to be the overt concern of Gothic fiction, placing a symbolic frame over a system of property and exchange, the cultural and economic context of *Candyman* subsumes propriety and traditional symbolic relations with an overriding investment in property and commodity exchange, and accompanied by a pervasive delocalisation of anxiety.

Anxiety is fuelled by the ease with which walls and fences can be crossed. No one, in their expensive apartments or, even, in secure psychiatric units, seems to be safe. The '"gothic" rapport between persons and places' has turned into a 'per-vasion' of all symbolic and social spaces by terror and horror (Seltzer, 1995: 145): no longer is the rapport localised in a house or castle; it extends across all social and subjective relations. A Gothic tone spreads to the most unexpected areas, the well-lit and luxurious bathrooms of white yuppie apartments being the most unlikely in the film. The gothicisation of the most banal and apparently innocuous social spaces remains tied to the circulation of anxiety and fear in a consumer society so that even the acceptable and mundane enclaves of middle-class life, the suburbs, resort to Gothic patterns. Kim Michasiw argues that the 'gated community' resuscitates a gothic mood in 'disneyfied' terms: the community itself becomes 'the avatar of the threatened maiden' (Michasiw, 248). Significantly, the image reduces a community to a single threatened body. In this model, the gated community both condenses all threatening features in a single egotistical individual and, at the same time, recognises that such a model has expanded to cover the evacuated terrain once called 'society'. The imaginary, once a model of subjective development and symbolic integration, substitutes itself for all social relations. In Lacan, identity is an effect of identification, the inverted image of the body in the mirror being recognised as oneself: the reflection of bodily integrity allows for the projection of psychological unity and, in turn, the assumption of social identity. An effect, then, of external appearance that unifies corporeal fragmentation, the image in the mirror, is translated in dreams in the form of fortified buildings. As it is opened up and expanded to cover all social relations, this version of the imaginary is simultaneously more exposed and in greater and constant need of protection and fortification against the forces that would dissipate its integrity. Imaginary boundaries, however, remain hard to police: look into the mirror and utter his name five times. Candyman … Candyman … Candyman … Candyman …

Shutting out a world imaginarily full of threatening figures, the suburban community uses fear to attempt to restore its (corporeal) boundaries. Fear generates serious material as well as emotional expenditures on security, from fencing and alarms to electronic surveillance and armed patrols. The threat, however, does not only demand protection and defence from the (imagined) assaults: 'the surbanites are permitted by their constant state of siege and the knowledge of their cause's justice to abrogate any law and countervail any principle' (Michasiw, 249). Through fear and anxiety these gated communities not only reconstitute their borders, but become a law unto themselves, ever ready to lash out, a Gothic variant of law determined only by fear: they are 'panicked, hystericized beings given over entirely not to mere growth but to the instinct for self-preservation, Hobbists who know no bodily sensation but fear' (249). Fear, excited to a sublime pitch, leaves no place for anything but the instinct for self-preservation: on the basis of self's imagined loss, a heightened sense of its value is recuperated. The evacuation and restoration of self leaves no room for any social values like tolerance or respect for others: in its openness to a pervasive anxiety, self closes itself up in fear. The milieu of *Candyman*, though located in the centre of a fragile, separated city rather its outskirts, is informed by the same principle, an internalisation and quotidian reiteration of the sublime terror that evacuates all other principles in the face of an imagined and overwhelming threat to bodily integrity. 'I am fear', Candyman repeats in the course of the film. As the mirror and embodiment of fears, he is both an object to be protected against, attacked, excluded and, since his spectral appearances refuse to remain in a single place, the cause around which anxiety continues to circulate and, against whom, more fortifications have to be vainly erected in a process of serial commodification.

The equation of a subjective imaginary with social identities and borders, an extension of individuality at the expense of modern notions of society, cannot finally restore the boundaries that are threatened. Indeed, because the underlying anxiety constantly requires new objects of fear to maintain borders (opening up to shut them down in an accelerating dynamic) that are as much imaginary as real, fear becomes an infinitely exploitable and marketable resource, one that both demands more and more commodities from the home and personal security industry. Immaterial, imaginary, the threat redoubles itself in the objects purchased to stave it off. Reflecting on the 1980s in Britain and on Thatcher's infamous dictum that 'there is no such thing as society', Peter York notes how wealth creation in the period caused enormous economic disenfranchisement, creating an underclass that incarnated a sense of general (social) insecurity. A 'fear of outsiders' led to an 'arms race' in which *they* with 'their knives, guns and bits of lead piping' prompted *us* to buy

> full-function, infra-red, domestic intruder alarms in those buttery-yellow-interior Edwardian fastnesses, the code-activated/ speakeasy electric door lock systems on our blocks of flats and offices, to the hysterical *Alex*-cartoon car alarms, the autocameras peering out over everything from the corner greengrocer to the square-mile shopping malls. We get *wired* to protect us from the Underclass. We may eventually get moated and walled-up, American style. (York and Jennings, 170)

Lavish expenditures on ever more sophisticated hardware engenders another level of anxiety bound up with the technology itself: the presence of security devices is itself threatening since it 'reminds us what a very slender thread our consumerisms and desires and pretensions hang by'. Two-edged, security technology leaves us double-bound: that 'which keeps us safe tells us how endangered we are' (170).

Fear redoubles itself; it multiplies, announcing a continuing gap between subjective and social being, no matter how hard Thatcherite ideology tried to replace one with the other. Moreover, the market depends on the gap: without fear, a fear that precisely haunts products whose spectral presence forms a constant reminder of imagined and real threats, there would be no demand for the goods the security industry has to sell. In closing the individual off from society, fear opens him or her up to the economy. It manifests the logic of privatisation in which state responsibilities and expenditures are diminished in order to expose individuals to the heady freedoms of the market: the Thatcherite policy to sell off publicly-owned low rental housing stock freed individuals from state interference to take possession of their own homes. To buy a home, of course, requires a mortgage, the rates of which depend on fluctuations in the stock market. Separated from society, individuals were plugged directly into an unstable economic nexus of share values and property speculation: the home became a most precious and expensive asset; it, and the individuals within, were directly exposed to the laws of the market. This practical application of free-market ideology demonstrates one of the key features of the period's neoliberal individualism: it dissolves traditional bonds and unravelled the social texture of modern life (Hobsbawn, 334). Untied from any social fabric, individuals, their property, aspirations and relations, find themselves plugged straight into the fluctuating circuits of transnational capitalism. Anxiety and desire pervade the home. The process discloses an individual whose constitution is quite different from that promoted by bourgeois modernity: reason, morality, responsibility, duty are evacuated by the heightened sense of self given over to instincts of self-preservation and sensations of fear. These baser elements, always shadowing modern constructions, become visible and exploitable as higher values and principles are disposed of, no longer required by the new economy whose networked market has little time for the borders of state or nation. Though older features of ideologically-constructed individuality are retained, they serve as the basis for a redefinition in a new context: hollowed out and made redundant, as economic parameters and imperatives change from stability, regular employment, organised and planned production to the flexibility of networks, consumption and responsive client services, the workforce must become more mobile, with transferable skills and short-term contracts. This is the 'economic horror' that, for Viviane Forrester, means the loss of traditional models of self, esteem, and social identity tied to productive labour.

Fear articulates the porous relationship between its internal and external causes. It does not simply provide the psychological conditions for closing off threats, but keeps them alive, opens subjectivity up to them in a dynamic that ultimately refuses security and equilibrium. Lines of division are crossed and have to be redrawn. Fear, it seems, respects neither fences nor walls. An underlying dynamic, confounding internal and external causes, is disclosed: Seltzer, discussing the 'claustrophobic, thick, saturated' *noir* environments, sees them as exteriorisations of interior settings, 'interiors exteriorized' (Seltzer, 1998: 165). If interiors are externalised, they are also emptied, evacuated, opened to a play that disregards or disavows private space and the security it is supposed to afford. What emerges is a site, a hollow, intimate and external at the same time, an 'extimate' point around which subjective and social space is articulated. In *Candyman*, the same architectural structures are inhabited by poor blacks and white yuppies, the renovation of the latter's domiciles barely concealing the spaces behind the thin walls. The surfaces separating classes and races point to the fragility of social relations and psychological make-ups: the hollows behind the dividing surfaces are sites of fear and sites of exploitation. Social spaces and psychological spaces, through fear, can be opened up and hollowed out so that newer and more expensive walls can be erected. Intimate, private, hidden away, the hollow space (hidden behind the bathroom mirror in the film), is also the site that connects internal projections to the porous boundaries articulating social space (Helen, for example, discovering the space behind the mirror, assumes she has found the actual point of entry for the murderer). Psychological and architectural, the space is neither solely physical nor solely imaginary.

Even as an object, Candyman, is presented to fill the space, that object, his hook specifically, is capable of opening up the insides of any building or body. Fear remains an exploitable resource, and a technical effect. In this respect, the Gothic disruption of boundaries regulating personal and social space serves as a significant register of the extent of the transformation engendered by new economic imperatives. Rather than closing off threats to body and community, the imaginary fears about the security of individual and social boundaries work in the opposite direction, opening both to economic fluctuations. To be secure, physical spaces require constant modification and improvement to keep at bay intruders who may be only imaginary; but peace of mind is afforded and disturbed by security gadgets. The confounding of imaginary and real limits is central to Gothic effects. Early reviewers of the Gothic romances make this plain when comparing Radcliffe's technique to the relationship between locksmith and housebreaker: the one improves his mechanisms in accordance with the skills of the other. But the process does not end: it escalates, demanding better mechanisms and more cunning tricks and better mechanisms, etc.

Ultimately, the reader is exhausted, worn out in the successive emotions of
fear and relief. With horror film, technical and special effects exacerbate
the process. Fear is a luxurious commodity, to be enjoyed, consumed, and
used up. Then the process must start again on a bigger scale.

Fear, despite the many objects on which it can focus, is underpinned by
an anxiety-provoking objectlessness that demands newer objects on which
it can expend itself. *Candyman* exemplifies the process. Its central villain
condenses a range of social fears: sexual and racial discrimination and violence, poverty, crime, drugs, psychopathology, cluster around him. Social
institutions, the media, medical, educational establishments, the family,
the police, the law, all become absorbed in the dynamic. There is no separation, it seems, between repressive and ideological state apparatuses. All
institutions become associated with the figure of terror. But no one object
or institution becomes the focus as the film shifts from the black male
slasher to the white female academic. Only fear persists. 'I am fear',
Candyman repeats. Fear, it seems, provides the glue articulating object,
individuals and institutions. This is not surprising, given the context. Fear
and desire, so readily, if all-too often inchoately, are associated, despite
their apparent opposition: the one repulses, the other attracts. They are,
however, linked in terms of their dynamic: as in Radcliffe's definition of
terror and horror, the former causing expansion and the latter contraction
(like the pupil of an eye) the relation is established in respect of the (par-
tial) presence or absence of an object. Fear, once provided with an object,
can be expelled; desire, too, finds direction and satisfaction in a similar
relation. Underlying both, however, is an absence that can be intensified
and exploited. Goods, in late capitalism, are bought and sold according to
feelings, fantasies, desires: in an age of branding use and practicality seem
of secondary importance. Postmodern capitalism, indeed, works on the
marketing and consumption of imaginary or intangible entities like images, values, meanings. It is part of a shift in the relationship between
production and consumption in which differentiation between moral,
rational and useful work and useless, wasteful, unproductive spending no
longer has any relevance (Goux, 1990b). Things are produced for no reason other than that they might be bought, objects on which money can be
expended: it does not matter whether they are useful or not. Entrepreneurs become benefactors as much as exploitative manipulators: they create what people want to buy. For Goux, the crucial aspect of the shift lies
in the reversal of the laws of supply and demand: instead of the former
following the latter, it precedes it, the creation of new commodities itself
stimulating new desires. A 'metaphysical uncertainty regarding the object
of human desire' is brought to the fore: human needs and wants are not

limited and finite; they cannot be satisfied since desire forms an inexhaustible resource. The reversal thus opens out the human figure as the site for an incessant expansion of markets. It turns human identity inside out: its centre, now an empty space of desiring to be stimulated and incompletely filled by more and more commodities, is opened to the movements of an unregulated market.

Opening up, hollowing out, the dynamics of fear and desire operate in a postmodern context over which no authoritative figure, metanarrative, or unifying institution presides. Contemporary consumption occurs, as Zizek notes, in the absence of a master to regulate excess, to arrest or channel flows of desire within an organising structure. Absence or lack provides the occasion, not for the emergence of a unifying figure, but for the repeated production of newer objects to be consumed, incorporated and used up in incessant expenditures of energy and money. There is no framework operating dialectically, taking these energies and, through sublimation or the triangular structure of Oedipus, say, giving them useful social purpose, outlet or meaning: at the level of subjective existence all that remains is a 'vicious cycle' of superegoic consumption encouraging guilt and expenditure at the same time. The more one feeds it, the more it wants; the more one consumes the guiltier one feels and thus the more one needs to consume to vainly assuage the guilt that requires more consumption. On a social level everything is given over to a consumerist relationship, values deposed by commodities and financial transactions. A dynamic of production and consumption, exhaustion and recreation fuels a demand for more. In a social context without authoritative or legitimate figures and narratives, any image will do: brand names, aliens, cults, celebrities, offer delusional alternatives to explaining the world or making it meaningful. Figures of horror – terrorists, slashers, child abusers or serial killers – serve as objects around which fear and desire, only temporarily, it seems, cohere, signifiers of the absence of social and communal bonds. These figures, as in *Se7en*, function as demonstrations of degradation, ruin, dissolution and, at the same time, serve as places from where horrifying and violent calls for moral authority emanate. They, too, are subject to prevailing consumerist logic. Serial killers, Seltzer notes, duplicate a bureaucratic, statistical and mechanistic process dominated by repetition and seriality: the killers imitate social and corporate processes, their acts governed by acts of compulsion and consumption that have evacuated any humanist conception of subjectivity. The pleasure-killer, for Seltzer, manifests an emptiness in which both pleasure and humanity are evacuated: 'the "devoided" and predead subject, for whom pleasure has become bound to the endless persecution of pleasure and to the endless emptying

and voiding of interiors, in himself and others' (Seltzer, 1998: 109). Economic activity and media practices have the same effect: the self-made
man displays the 'empty circularity' of the liberal subject and the voices
and images from the media, imperative, confessional, sensational, demand
a constant expression, an exteriorisation and evacuation, across airwaves
and screens (115–17). Media, indeed, manufacture as much as expose
monsters, to the extent that the screen itself becomes demonic: 'as a blank
incomprehensibility, the serial killer thus serves as a convenient vessel for
the articulation of what American society finds truly monstrous in the late
twentieth-century – the "TV people", or the authorless but authority-
filled killer screen that drives fantasies, reaches out and snatches kids from
their homes, and transforms them into demons' (Nixon, 233). Media feed
fears and feed off them, make monsters and occlude their own monstrosity, screening being a process that provides a locus both for the projection
of and protection from horror.

Screens, of course, dominate the home, impenetrable windows through
which images of fear and desire are allowed free entry. *Candyman*, with its
representations of various media and representational apparatuses,
emphasises the association. Horror, on screens in the home, returns to one
of its favourite haunts. But with a difference: the Reagan-Bush era 'with its
return to family values, saw the horror film developing into its most grotesque forms – the greater the social repression, the more monstrous the
repressed ...' (Tony Williams, 170). Exacerbation of monstrous returns,
however, also entails a reversal in which notions and figures of repression
change. In the 1970s, as Sobchack observes, horror films like *The Fury*,
*The Amityville Horror*, *The Shining* present fathers who are impotent, economically and politically disenfranchised, even repressed themselves: their
violence stems not from power but from weakness, not figures of identification but husks of horror. Fathers, and the families that they are supposed to provide for and protect, over which they are supposed to preside,
are no longer able to live up to modern or Victorian ideals. They embody
the failure of paternal metaphors and principles, incarnating a symbolic
crisis affecting social, familial and psychological structures alike. Hence,
something more like a lifting or failure of repression seems to be in evidence, but with no less excessive consequences. The political twist, however, is that such failure provides an opportunity: in the absence of repressive father figures and functions, like the state or the nation, economic
markets can free themselves from restraints of morality or reason or, even,
social responsibility. The return to family values, in this context, does not
serve to restore social values but occludes social and state responsibilities
by establishing a morality which, in the name of individual effort and

enterprise, is that of the free market alone: services like education, health, housing must be paid for in the manner of any other economic exchange.

The family, the home, the individual bears the brunt of this political ideology and is opened up to the vicissitudes and in-securities of its economic practices: welfare, education, health and flexible and uncertain employment become familial and individual concerns. Under Thatcherism a rhetoric of 'good housekeeping', of Victorian productivity and prudence, veils policies designed to open up national borders to global markets, corporations and practices: its systematic 'privatisation' of state utilities and monopolies handed public companies over to investors, stockholders and corporations. At the same time domestic economy became an increasingly public issue: plugged directly into the global market, the home no longer offered any, even imaginary, refuge from the world of work and money. Domestic values were thus turned outside in, inside out, in the interplay of politics and economics, the boundaries of private and public space erased by the incursions of free market imperatives. Private vice became public necessity: 'greed is good'. Behind the figure held up as exemplar of free market economics and its accompanying morality – Adam Smith – lay another early economic theorist: Bernard de Mandeville.

*The Fable of the Bees,* first published in 1714 and revised in subsequent years, scandalised eighteenth-century England with its analysis of wealth. In contrast to prevailing values of virtue and moderation in moral, political and economic life, Mandeville argued that the vices were crucial to the production of wealth with man's 'vilest and most hateful Qualities' being 'the most necessary Accomplishments to fit him for the largest, and according to the World, the happiest and most flourishing Societies' (Mandeville, 53). Vices 'are inseparable from great and potent Societies ... it is impossible their Wealth and Grandeur should subsist without' (57). World trade depends on vice: exporting corn and cloth pays for the importation of wines and brandies, a cycle dependent on drunkenness. Theft pays for the drinks bought by thieves and thus keeps landlords in business. Where frugality is unproductive, 'prodigality has a thousand Inventions to keep People from sitting still' (135). Vanity keeps dressmakers in business; prostitution maintains chastity and honour by 'sacrificing one part of Womankind to preserve the other' (130). In Mandeville's argument the strict lines between virtue and vice disappear in a new taxonomy which separates 'agreeable good natur'd' vices, like prodigality, from less productive ones like avarice. His argument, moreover, renders meaningless distinctions between useful and useless, necessary and luxurious objects of consumption. Instead, desire comes to fore: 'if the wants of Man are innumerable, then what ought to supply them has no bounds; what is call'd superfluous to some degree of People will be thought requisite to those of higher Quality' (137). Desire, moreover, becomes the fuel of trade and national wealth: 'Man never exerts himself but when he is rous'd by his Desires: Whilst they lie dormant, and there is nothing to raise them, his Excellence and Abilities will be for ever undiscover'd, and the lumpish Machine, without the Influence of his Passions, may be justly compar'd to a huge Windmill without a breath of Air' (200). Passion, repeatedly suppressed or excluded from eighteenth-century rational and moral discourse, is made visible as an essential element of economic success.

Mandeville's book caused a scandal: he was a 'Man-Devil', his book a 'public nuisance'. He was demonised by John Dennis in 1724, as a 'Champion for Vice and Luxury' (Mandeville, 8–15). In the name of reason and morality, virtue again tries to cut itself off from vice. Mandeville's improper conjugations offer a less than noble conception of humanity in an age of reason and morality, emphasising the interdependence of wealth and vice. The scandal of Mandeville's argument perhaps lay in making visible and public what should have remained occluded, thereby contaminating the purity of moral and political discourse. Indeed, what Mandeville makes plain is the doubleness of productive and consumerist activity: humans are creatures defined by both virtue and vice while goods are not aligned with the Good in a moral sense, but cavort with desires and passions. His beehive is not one governed by a single figure at the apex of a carefully ordered and harmonious hierarchy: the hive is 'grumbling', a restless, desiring but productive model of the relationship between individuals, society and economy. Greed is good.

While Mandeville's demonstration of the contribution by vice, passion, desire and greed to national wealth and prosperity brought too much out in the open and brought on the weight of public censure, Gordon Gecko's unabashed promotion of the goodness of greed became the slogan defining both the mood and ethos of a decade. For one of the vices to be good, however, required more than a simple reversal of hierarchies in which the underside of economic functioning becomes visible: greed is not merely associated with beneficial effects as in Mandeville, it *is* good. What was tacit, the unspoken obverse of early bourgeois commercial activity in *The Fable of the Bees*, becomes the rule of a new conception of social and economic order, a supplanting and transformation of prior conditions. In *Candyman*, the ambivalence of images and uses of bees similarly announces a doubleness in which pleasure and pain, virtue and vice, good and bad are rendered indistinguishable: modernity, as an organised and harmonious whole, becomes a postmodern nightmare of conflicting zones, sweetness and pleasure entwined with fear: there is no land of milk and honey without stings and pain. The entanglement, which brings passions, fears and desires to the fore, sees society turning from hive to swarm and alludes to another figure thrown up by the 1980s: yuppies were often WASP (White Anglo-Saxon Protestant) in aspiration if not origin. Horror fiction, too, has its wasps. Jack Torrance, the failed father and writer, tries to use the wasp's nest as a metaphor for reality. It reminds him of unwittingly putting his hand into a nest and being turned from 'a creature of the mind' into 'a creature of nerve endings', from 'college-educated man' to 'wailing ape' (King, 110). For Joseph Grixti, the shift signals the novel's acknowledgement of the arbitrariness and increasing obsolescence of modern notions of civilised behaviour (Grixti, 65). In a context of horror and consumption, however, it marks the emergence of a new economic being, one subjected to effects and affects that evacuate reason and agency with emotional reactions, asubject of fears and desires.

## Expenditure, sacrifice

*Candyman* tells the story of a married white female graduate (Helen) researching urban legends with a black colleague (Bernadette) in competition with the former's husband (Trevor) and an aloof anthropology professor. The attempt to prove the social origin of the Candyman myth leads to the investigation of a series of murders. After being knocked unconscious by a gang leader who styles himself as the Candyman by carrying a hook, Helen encounters the real, that is, phantasmatic, figure and finds herself accused of kidnapping, imprisoned for murder, abandoned by her husband and forced into a bargain with Candyman: she must become his lover in return for the life of a baby. There are the usual Gothic and horror themes alongside the familiar focus on the persecuted/insane heroine: Candyman is a slasher figure, ever ready to disembowel his victims with a hook; a Faustian tempter drawing the heroine into his diabolical web; a vampiric bloodletter feeding off social fears (Hutchings). Helen is a wronged woman wreaking justified revenge, a psychotic killer with a hallucinatory alter-ego. Including teenage ghost stories, urban gothic gloom, romance plots and visual and verbal references to staple fictions, the film situates itself firmly and familiarly in a Gothic tradition of horror.

Generic complications render the text's contemporaneity problematic. The ending, while offering violent, even sacrificial, death for the pleasure of the audience, refuses the full unequivocal moral enjoyment of righteous ritual slaughter. An actual and well-known setting brings social and racial reality into focus, intruding on the topographical displacement usually required by the genre. Myth and reality become inextricably entangled. For Kim Newman, noting the mixture of predictability and surprise, the film has 'archetypal ingredients of the horror genre – knee-jerk shocks, stalking bogeyman, touches of dark humour – but also locates the horrors in an identifiable and credible landscape of urban decay' (Newman, 39). This combination disturbs standard expectations of horror plots and confounds critical interpretation. Colin McCabe illustrates the problem: 'while it may be plausible to read *Candyman* as a complicated utopian fantasy of multicultural reproduction, it is also possible to read it as vicarious male desire for a black man who will finally give an uppity white girl what she's been asking for' (McCabe, 24). (When offered the second interpretation the director threatened to sue.) McCabe goes on to suggest a more positive reading: he invokes 'a notion of complexity which would not be promoted as a value in itself but in terms of the force of the contradictions it is able to harness' (24). This notion of complexity, and the double, contradictory reading McCabe offers for the film, discloses an important element in its mode of representation and its deployment of horror, separating figures of horror from a more disturbing and less visible source. Indeed, in its own contradictory way, the film activates the 'incoherence' that Polan associates with popular postmodern forms, an incoherence that 'comes from the very vagueness of the logic; rational explanation becomes only one more element in a spectacular combination which one element's presence is enough to explain' (Polan, 181).

Confounding conventional oppositions, crossing boundaries, reversing associations in the manner usually ascribed to the uncanny, the film discloses something else, neither meaning nor non-meaning, but a contradictory locus where both appear at once. This is the space Gilles Deleuze identifies as 'ab-sense', a void at the centre of signifying series and systems, a point that, for Lacan, is linked to the 'vacuole' associated with the 'Thing' or the 'irreducible, traumatic, non-meaning' of *objet petit a*, the point where meaning is created and annihilated (Deleuze, 1990: 66–73; Lacan, 1977b: 250; 1988a: 280). In and beyond representation and signification, the gap enables the production of meaning, the point at which an overriding metaphor can be instituted, and refuses the authority of any single meaning, allowing interpretations to proliferate. In *Candyman*, the space of ab-sense or incoherence remains horrifyingly open, a gap in or failure of representation demanding the unsatisfactory attribution of significance and figures of horror. This is why the film is and is not about race or gender, why both issues pervade the film without finally arresting the displacements of meaning in a single figure of horror. Both racial and sexual difference, everywhere visible and embodied by Candyman and Helen,

stand in place of an unpresentable and non-consumable Thing threatening to dissolve all subjects and representations. The fate of Candyman and
Helen as iconic figures, moreover, emphasises the problematic status of
representation: the latter is canonised in a graffiti image as a transcendent,
saintly and awe-inspiring figure of beauty; the former is pictured in unspeakable anguish, mouth wide open in a silent scream. Alluding to the
painting by Edvard Munch and the mother's silent scream in Eisenstein's
*Battleship Potemkin*, the scream does more than announce the inexpressible alienation of the modern subject: it manifests an anxiety 'too stringent
for it to find an outlet in valorization', unable to utter an ab-sense so
extreme it 'cannot burst out, unchain itself and thus enter the dimension
of subjectivity'. Silent screams of this order display 'the horror-stricken
encounter with the real of enjoyment', an encounter quite different from
the horror film's representations in which anxiety and tension are released,
that is, given an object and an outlet (Zizek, 1992: 117).

What is unbearable, then, in the ab-sense disclosed by the film are not
stereotypical racist or sexist representations (for these provide outlets for
horrific expenditure) or painful social realities (which are readily identifiable), but the point of unspeakable silent screaming, the space of a Thing
that is too close to home, a gap in and inaccessible to representation, reason, sense or meaning. Race and sex, then, surround the film as much as
they are represented in it, disclosing something in-visible and traumatic to
the white, patriarchal culture in which representation takes place. In this
respect they operate in a similar manner to the film's representations of
drugs, everywhere alluded to in a culture in which cocaine and crack chart
the spectrum of social consumption and yet never, in themselves, visible.
Within and yet outside vision, drugs are another index of the consumerist
and paranoid culture in which social and symbolic boundaries have collapsed:

> Under the impacted signifier of drugs, America is fighting a war against a
> number of felt intrusions. They have to do mostly with the drift and
> contagion of a foreign substance, or what is revealed as foreign (even if it
> should be homegrown). Like any good parasite, drugs travel both inside
> and outside of the boundaries of a narcissistically defended politics. They
> double for the values with which they are at odds, thus haunting and
> reproducing the capital market, creating visionary expansions, producing a
> lexicon of body control and a private property of self – all of which awaits
> review. (Ronell, 50–1)

Objects of anxiety, drugs afford a focus for social fears and an outlet for
social antagonisms while, in their mobility and activation of consumerist
desires, they duplicate the very structures they are supposed to be outside

of. Such is the fate of *The Scream*: it becomes the title of a highly self-conscious series of movies whose villain wears a mask modelled on Munch's image, a mask that becomes a profitable item of film merchandising. Munch's image is also printed on large balloons; it featured as the logo for the 'It's a Scream' chain of bars. There is, it seems, no point or object to anchor representation and establish a perspective that restores a sense of social cohesion in the flows of desire and capital, only the horrifying void of circulation itself.

Judith Halberstam, normally a generous critical reader of horror texts, finds little to recommend in *Candyman* or the forceful contradictions it yokes together. While conceding that the film 'on some level' engages in 'social criticisms', she argues that 'the horror stabilizes in the ghastly body of the black man' and thus confirms racist attitudes regarding black sexual violence and white women victims. Where, in the nineteenth century race functioned as a mobile, conflictual surface, in *Candyman* it 'becomes a master signifier of monstrosity and when invoked, it blocks out all other possibilities of monstrous identity' (Halberstam, 5). It is true that the film offers few positive images of monstrosity and seems to confirm the worst fears of white America in the black figure who appears, with murderous intent, in the private recesses of middle-class homes. The blockage Halberstam identifies, however, may be overstated. Not only is Candyman called up by white homeowners, he is also, as Briefel and Ngai observe, presented as a tragic, suffering figure deserving pity or, at least, a little liberal guilt and sympathy. More significant, however, is the process of the displacement of figures of horror enacted in the course of the film. The horror does not stabilise on a single body, so that the victim of violence becomes its perpetrator: while the spectre of Candyman is laid to rest, Helen assumes his place and his hook, to pass on, the seriality of the movie suggests, the contagion of violence to her husband's new partner.

The film's representations of race and sex, despite and because of their stereotypical forms, unsettle supposedly legitimate objects of moral/paranoid execration. There remains something contradictory, disturbing and even unbearable in the film, a violence related to but distinct from the representation of recognisable social antagonisms, something calling for and eluding judgement and interpretation. In the tradition of academic Gothic (with its doctors, metaphysicians, scientists, psychic researchers, antiquarian scholars, professor-priests), *Candyman* situates itself at the level of the unreadable, as a challenge to critical interpretation (Rose, when living in McCabe's basement flat in London, engaged in many warm arguments with the film theorist). A sweetshop of pick 'n' mix interpretations, the film also presents a horror story of meaning's disappearance.

Apart from Candyman, an artist, the main characters in the film are academics. Three, out of four, are murdered by the end of the film. Maybe this is part of the enjoyment of the film: academics dragged down and gutted in a representational violence akin to that of their own less than surgical trade of textual dissection. The anti-academicism, however, is bound up with the critique of institutions of modernity: systems of rationalisation, explanation and normalisation have their limitations displayed; apparatuses of social cohesion and regulation like universities, hospitals, psychiatric wards, law courts and the family home itself become entwined in the unreason they would police. From the start of the film the concrete, functional forms of modern architecture and efficient systems of transportation are associated with a swarm of bees. In an early lecture scene urban legends are dismissed as 'fears of urban society'. Rationally debunked as no more than superstition, these fears are validated and rendered literal, thereby undercutting the superiority assumed by enlightened knowledge. Fears and phantasms, the film suggests, may have greater power in the patterns of everyday life, implying, furthermore, that there is no longer a single homologous framework to existence. The undecidability introduced between narrative and interpretation, in which the latter is incorporated as just another mode of narrativisation and failed explanation, occurs within a generalisation of the uncanny, an overriding spectralisation of social and intersubjective relations.

Look into a mirror and say the name five times. Candyman, bloody hook and all, will appear with horrifying violence. Invited into domestic space from the buried regions of the dark double, sexual repression and racial oppression, he will destroy families, mutilate bodies and haunt psyches. But Candyman is not simply the inverted image that gives imaginary consistency to the law-abiding subject. Smashing through the mirror, from an unknown space on its reflective surfaces, he is more than the unavowable and violent projection of a singular (unconscious) mind: a symptom of collective unease, terrorising white suburbia, white urban apartments and black ghettoes alike. The mirror of individual wholeness, the locus of social and subjective identity, fragments, opened to the dark tain that constitutes the possibility of reflection and imaginary unification. Candyman, moreover, does not exist. He says so himself: he is myth, immortal, vampirically destined 'to live in other peoples' dreams but not to be'. His murderous reappearance in the world aims to ensure the preservation of his myth. Helen must die so that the myth lives on. Phantasmatic, his effects are real, and bloody, enough. The figural becomes literal in order to preserve the world of myth and metaphor against attempts to literalise and reduce all phenomena to materialist and empirical causes. But the repeated traversal of the borders between phantasmatic figures and literal realities confounds the opposition, rendering one permeable to the other and extending a pervasive and indeterminable strangeness across all boundaries.

There is no 'terrible place' in the film, no single physical locus of haunting containing anxiety. Instead, urban estates, apartment buildings (their bathrooms especially), derelict spaces, multi-storey car parks, hospitals, all become sites of fear and insecurity. Concrete social spaces are traversed by immaterial but no less effective forms and forces. Distinctions between interiority and the external world dissolve as the film leaves open the possibility that Helen is merely delusional and Candyman the expression of her inner rage while setting that explanation against vivid images of a speaking monster whose appearances are supernatural. Seen and unseen worlds, inner disturbance and social realities are both pictured on the same flat, celluloid ribbon. In one scene, imprisoned and interviewed by a criminal psychiatrist working for her defence lawyers, Helen is confronted with video evidence of her insanity. A tape of her initial incarceration is replayed, a scene shown earlier in the film, in which strapped to a bed, she is tormented by a floating Candyman and screams for help. The tape, while resounding with her cries, shows no figure hovering menacingly over the helpless patient. Helpless again, strapped to a chair and confronted by the disbelief of the medical and legal establishment, her abjection seems complete. She turns to a mirror to prove her story by summoning Candyman. Magically he appears to gut the doctor, cut her restraints and smash through an upper-floor window, thereby providing the means of her escape. Imaginary scenarios are replaced by empirical, technical evidence and then contradicted by supernatural events. But the film leaves incompatible criminal and supernatural readings open: in leaving her the means of escape Candyman also leaves evidence for Helen's accusers: she, with insane strength could have killed the doctor and fled through the window.

The general uncanniness, with its spectral interruption of reality testing and its reversals of oppositions, operates across the film's representational surfaces. All boundaries become permeable, subjected to a strange, destabilising in-betweenness: social space, personal and psychic space, imaginary urban lines of demarcation and solid domestic walls are traversed by uncanny effects. But in *Candyman* the uncanny's strangeness is too evident, too familiar, too much part of the generic formulas popularised in the horror genre. And because the uncanny emerges, through multiple crossings, as a social as much as individual phenomenon, it cannot be restricted to a symptom of singular psychic disturbance. Lacan offers a more far-reaching understanding of the uncanny, relegating the dissolution of conventional boundaries to secondary effects: Freud's uncanny 'is linked, not, as some believed, to all sorts of irruptions from the unconscious, but rather to an imbalance that arises in the fantasy when it decomposes, crossing the limits originally assigned to it, and rejoins the image of the other subject' (Lacan, 1977c: 22). A void, a hole, horror. The encounter dissolves imaginary identity, collapses symbolic oppositions, brings the unseen void at the centre of phantasmatically organised life unbearably close. What appears is something 'unnameable', 'the ultimate real, of the essential object which isn't an object any longer, but this something faced with which all words cease and all categories fail …' (1988b: 164) At the centre of subjective and symbolic reality, the Thing is also excluded: 'fear', Lacan observes, 'is a localizable defense' against it (1992: 232). A space of projection and substitution is disclosed, a site where objects give it form: 'cultural elaborations' 'colonize the field of *das Ding* with imaginary schemes' (99). All symbolic, social and subjective existence depends on fantasy, not in the sense of an opposition to a pregiven world of objects: reality is already symbolised reality and sustained by a fantasy that forms a matrix, a locus coordinating desire and identity (Fletcher). Fantasy provides a 'screen': it occludes nameless horror and fills the gap by projecting terrifying objects in its place.

In *Candyman*'s unresolved entwining of fantasy and reality, the phantasmatic form of social and subjective spaces manifests itself in relation to racial and sexual differences. Both are conjoined in the romantic theme of the film, underlined in Candyman's deep-voiced repetition of the phrase 'I came for you'. Trite though this may be, the lost love motif runs from Universal's *The Mummy* (1932) to Coppola's *Bram Stoker's Dracula* (1992); romance demonstrates the limits of fantasy and contemporary symbolic deterioration. Denis de Rougemont's history of romance identifies passion as a 'transfiguring force' offering 'complete Desire', 'Unity' and a 'demand to embrace no less than the All' (de Rougemont, 16; 61). For all the promises of fullness, romance requires obstacles, prohibitions, suffering, death (15). But in a world that has 'lost transcendence', the world of Hollywood, the daily diet of popular romance tries to make two incompatible forms coincide. Romance, which thrives on distance, obstacles and transcendence, is, for de Rougemont, antithetical to the world of marriage with its constant contact, banal routines and all-too physical existence. This model of romance in which at least three, and not an idealised couple, are in evidence conforms to Lacan's account of the way that fantasy, a fantasy of harmony, subjective plenitude and unity in love, conceals the 'absence of the sexual relation', a relation determined, not by bodies or amorous union, but by the signifying locus of desire called the Other.

Even in the embourgeoisified and restricted economy which combines romance with the ideal of romantic union the double effects of the sexual nonrelation are evinced. Marriage binds women in a symbolic pact between men to the extent that 'the symbolic order literally subdues, transcends her'. But, Lacan contends, resistance remains: 'there's something insurmountable, let us say unacceptable, in the fact of being placed in the position of an object in the symbolic order, to which, on the one hand, she is entirely subjected no less than man.' At this point conflicts arise. An 'imaginary degradation' of man's status becomes visible. The symbolic exchange which elevates man to the extent that he is identified with the paternal signifier confers, imaginarily, the transcendent status of gods: 'men aren't gods' and thus the husband is unveiled as the 'idolatrous substitute' of universal man (Lacan, 1988b: 262). Such a symbolic deterioration is emphasised early in the film when Helen arrives at her husband's lecture: they joke about the 'dashing professor' and the 'loving wife' while he introduces some of his students. One of whom, Stacy, is clearly having an affair with him. Masculine and conjugal failure, it seems, takes some of the blame for Helen's passionate romance with Candyman, a contrast of literal and limp masculinity with that of a powerfully mythical figure. This romance, too, fails to measure up. Near the end of the movie, Helen, lost to the literal liberal world, has no option but to give in to Candyman: he sweeps her up in his arms, the camera spins 360 degrees around them and he promises her exquisite pain and immortality through death, the ultimate in *jouissance*. But he's just another degraded symbol of passionate suffering, reneging on their pact. Even as Helen seems to be seduced by the fantasy, she manages to disentangle herself from its lure, substituting her life for a black child in a way that extinguishes the power of Candyman.

If a fantasy of subjective plenitude underlies romance's passionate desire for absolute union with another, then it also informs the paranoid identification of the other, a projection of a single black killer into the deserted spaces of the Projects. The film does not simply endorse racist attitudes and stereotypes, but presents them as representations, as projections to be interrogated, and highlights the role of representation in generating fear and maintaining social tensions. Newspaper and TV reports, interviews, urban myths, lectures, dinner conversations, stories, rumours, graffiti, photographs, videos, slide projectors, are focused on throughout the film, alongside references to Gothic fiction and fairytales. One form of communication is not privileged over any other, all operating on the same plane as attempts to structure existence and provide fearful meaning in the face of uncertainty. Not only do these representational apparatuses mediate the confirmation of existing structures of reality, they replay the phantasmatic organisation of everyday life, paranoiacally reaffirming collapsing boundaries. 'I am rumour', says Candyman, feeding and feeding off the stories that generate his phantasmatic significance. This unwritten figure behind the scenes, glimpsed in graffiti or mentioned in hushed tones, occludes the in-visible cause of the social fantasies projected around and onto him. Fear and fantasy coalesce in the substitution of one figure in place of an internal and excessive social, symbolic violence, a figure whose in-visibility as myth enforces rules and boundaries.

What the film draws out of its representations of representational effects is something in excess of representation, an unwritten excess at the limit of social and symbolic meaning. The psychoanalytic term is 'Other enjoyment'. Law, composed of signifiers, needs an other over which it can establish its authority: because 'there is no Other of the Other', no metalanguage, the basis of otherness is problematic and signifiers are inadequate, reversible, exchangeable. Law is 'founded on what one imagines about the Other's *jouissance*; it is hatred of the particular way, of the Other's way of experiencing *jouissance*' (Miller, 125). Law depends on an element heterogeneous to its stated principles, reasons and values. Miller offers the example of racism: 'racist stories are always about the way in which the Other obtains a "*plus-de-jouir*": either he does not work enough, or he is useless or a little too useful …' (125). The other's imagined desire to ruin our way of life, or his/her possession of a secret, perverse or better enjoyment, is not an effect of 'immediate social reality' and the presence of others, but emerges from '*inner antagonism inherent in those communities*' (Zizek, 1993: 205, original emphasis).

The film's representations of race, representations which fail to do justice to the other, are bound up in this problematic of other enjoyment. Located in the context of failed institutions of marriage, of law, of medicine, of learning, of social planning, the film's milieu can be characterised in terms of a deterioration not only of physical urban space, nor social and subjective space, but symbolic space, the system articulating lives and meanings and communities in relation to an excessive, phantasmatic element:

> Fantasy designates precisely this unwritten framework which tells us how we are to understand the letter of the Law. And it is easy to observe how today, in our enlightened era of universal rights, racism and sexism reproduce themselves mainly at the level of the phantasmatic unwritten rules which sustain and qualify universal ideological proclamations. (Zizek, 1997: 29)

Fantasy is articulated in the gap between real and symbolic being, a bridge to intersubjective relationships and the glue of a structure that narrates or makes sense of reality. In this respect Candyman forms the double of social institutions, a fantasy figure who establishes meaning and community in the absence of any other point of symbolic credulity. 'Be my victim', he says to Helen, wanting her investment in his myth and offering her identity and significance when all other institutions have alienated her from herself. As double, of course, Candyman carries the internal violence of social institutions, the ghost of a paternal figure, an impostor called up by a delusional demand for love, meaning, order.

*Candyman*, strangely for a slasher film, often presents vicious assaults off- screen, heard but not seen, requiring imagination to fill the empty space of vision. The film refuses full moral enjoyment, curtailing visual excesses and baulking at the substitution of one figure of execration for another. Instead, it begins to suggest, in linking enjoyment and fantasy, that the problem is internal to modes of representation and perpetuated in their fear-inducing stories. In key, repeated shots, attempts are made not only to self-consciously signal textual and cinematic effects, but to emphasise their limitations as projections that depend on something that cannot be seen, on some Thing unpresentable. McCabe identifies moments 'punctuating the film where there is literally nothing in the image' (24). These begin when Helen photographs graffiti in the Projects. The camera flash obliterates the screen with its intensity, briefly whiting it out. When slides of these images are subsequently projected, the camera focuses closely on the carousel to show the darkness articulating the mechanical movement between images. Repeated throughout, the photoflashes are accompanied by moments of mental confusion and narrative disjunction. They function as disorientating puncta where sense is disturbed by something unknown, blind spots in vision and comprehension challenging representation. McCabe argues that these puncta 'provide a kind of zero-point within the film which means that all interpretations – not least the fundamental one as to whether Candyman exists – are suspended' (24). The gap that, in a visual medium, is introduced in vision shatters identifications between camera and objects, attacking visual pleasure and dislocating images from the frames that articulate them. In drawing attention to what cannot be represented, moreover, suspicion is directed towards representations themselves: the white screen breaks into phantasmatic visual fulfilment and breaks up an authoritative gaze to mark the whiteness of media presentations rather than leave them transparently neutral.

This technique is particularly significant given the film's engagement with racial and sexual differences: it turns the look away from objects of expulsion and enjoyment and highlights the means by which those objects are produced and maintained. Photoflashes are linked to a huge graffiti image of a black face, mouth gaping open. A black scream fills the screen, silently announcing something unpresentable, unspeakable. The seen scream implies a position that has yet to speak and which the film, it is clear, cannot speak in place of. All it can do is, within the web of phantasmatic and fear-inducing projections it foregrounds, disclose something other, a space, an absence within representation. It is an ab-sense never completely filled by the film's projections: it does not climax in the violent sacrificial killing of the evil object; it does not deliver the righteous execution required by a simplified moral fantasy returning its relieved audience to the literal, liberal world. Candyman still burns. But Candyman is a myth that is demythologised: the racist projection of a single black slasher goes up smoke. Lured into the bonfire that will immortalise Candyman and Helen, the latter finds the black baby he promised to release. As children light the pile, Helen breaks free of Candyman and, though fatally burned, carries the child to his mother. A gesture of self-sacrifice. The next scene overlooks her graveside: a few white people attend, her husband and the professor in the fore. The camera pans across the cemetery to show a procession of people from the Projects arriving to pay their respects. The husband looks alarmed and confused. A child throws a hook on the coffin. The next sequence returns to the apartment where the disconsolate husband sits alone in the bathroom reminiscing about his dead wife. Stacy, his student partner, is preparing dinner. She holds, provocatively for the audience, a large kitchen knife. In the bathroom, the husband starts to moan a name … 'Helen'. As he utters the name a fifth time, a burned, disfigured Helen appears, hook in hand: 'What's the matter Trevor?' She asks, 'Scared of something?' His bodily integrity is not intact for long. Stacy discovers the bloody cadaver. The last shot depicts her, knife in hand, screaming. The accursed share of a commodified bourgeois liberalism has been passed on down the line … a chain of horror and violence, integral to its de-composition and reconstitution.

In the final credit sequence, the camera returns to Candyman's derelict abode and lingers over a new graffiti image on the wall: Helen has been immortalised, pictured in white surrounded by flames. Are these flames testimony to her saintly suffering and self-sacrifice or are they the flames of a hell still burning in the hearths, and bathrooms, of white liberal reality? Ambiguity remains. Two different readings stand opposed and inter-related. The first suggests that Helen supplants the role of Candyman, a violent contagion not extinguished but spreading inexorably outwards from black estates. The repetitive, serial cycle of pleasure, violence and consumption is sustained by fantasy. Fear projected onto figures of otherness continues unabated: Trevor's fear fuels, and produces, a new escalation of violence invading the home. This model of social relations is implied at the start of the film: overhead shots of city traffic are edited with images of bees clustered together. Bees only attack when frightened. Contemporary urban life is built on fear, a pervasive paranoia articulating all relations, perpetuating antagonistic myths that occlude the excess at the heart of white liberal modernity and its self-representation.

*Candyman* shows its spectators the excesses integral to a late liberal culture whose '"exceptions" (the homeless, the ghettoized, the permanent unemployed) are the symptom of the late-capitalist universal system, the permanent reminder of how the immanent logic of capitalism works' (Zizek, 1993: 127) This system looks toward global solutions of economic development and ecological balance and overlooks the particular political contradictions that allow a system to universalise itself through exclusions. The liberal utopia, Zizek notes, imagines the harmonious inclusion of every exception. But, as in the 1980s in which global expansion was attended by diminished state responsibility, political economy produces all sorts of 'exceptions'. These larger issues are, in the film, bound up with more 'academic' concerns associated with political correctness and presented not only in terms of race and sex, but in the highlighting of smoking and unprofessional affairs. Political correctness is not exempt from horror's scrutiny. It, too, according to Zizek, involves 'fantasmatic enjoyment' in which a 'compulsive effort to uncover ever new, ever more refined forms of racial and/or sexual violence and domination' serves to maintain one position as its negative but necessary counterpart: 'all other positions can affirm their specificity, their specific mode of enjoyment, only the white-male-heterosexual position must remain empty, must sacrifice its enjoyment' (213). For Zizek, PC is not severe enough: in sacrificing 'everything that sounds racist and sexist', it fails to renounce 'the very gesture of self-sacrifice'; in evacuating the position of the white male, it maintains it 'as a universal form of subjectivity' by providing 'newer and newer answers, *in order to keep the problem alive*'. Political correctness becomes the 'protective shield' of bourgeois liberalism (214, original emphasis).

At the end of *Candyman* Helen's self-sacrifice stands out as a disarmingly illiberal gesture disturbing conventional patterns of Gothic and liberal enjoyment. She gives her life for the life of another in an ethical act recognised by a black community who cross the unmarked boundaries of fear and fantasy to signal the possibility of a quite different symbolic relationship. The horror of her death becomes the occasion, the possibility of a new, unwritten and sacred framework. The act of self-sacrifice, however, terrifies and haunts the white husband, tormenting him with something his fear refuses to countenance, a comfortable consumerist enjoyment he must lose. Instead, however, Helen is transformed into another violent phantasmatic projection threatening, and sustaining, the porous borders of property and self-identity. Between the displacements of violence from black man to white woman, from working-class estate to middle-class apartment, the film maintains a disturbing in-coherence which no single object of horror can resolve. Indeed, McCabe's two readings, separating a 'utopian fantasy of multi-cultural production' from a racist story of male desire and violence, cohere, strangely doubled, in their space of forceful contradiction, the one fuelling the other in a cycle of exclusion and retribution, each the other's unbearable inverted image, and neither ever stable enough to forestall or arrest the disarming flows of desire in which figures are projected and consumed on a cinematic conveyor belt of commodified images of horror and little *jouissance.*

# ⚔ 2 ⚔

# Tech noir

## *Doom* with a view

A HAND APPEARS, clutching an automatic pistol. Walls of grey reinforced concrete, dripping with dank slime, provide the gloomy surroundings. The flickering half-light of low ceilings, dark corridors and sliding steel doors offer little orientation as the handgun begins to negotiate the uninviting dungeon. Outside, a bleak, rocky lunar landscape is visible, as are the harsh outlines of the desolate bunker fortress that to the inmate is both labyrinth and prison. Suddenly, a shadowy movement is glimpsed through the pale glow of dials and lamps. A shot is fired. The assailant, a barely human figure in fatigues and body armour, lumbers forward out of a dark alcove, preparing to fire again. The pistol reacts, kicking slightly in the hand. It kicks again. The attacker recoils and falls, a bloody mess on the floor. More threatening figures lurch from the darkness. The pistol responds with a semi-crazed, jerky rapid fire continuing until all mutant soldiers are splattered corpses.

Welcome to *Doom*, the most advanced three-dimensional computer game in the world when it was released in 1993. And the most popular: *Doom* and *Doom II* sold 2.7 million copies, with an estimated additional 20 million copies having been circulated freely through shareware schemes (Keegan, 2). The opening sequence of the violent virtual adventure playground leaves no doubt as to its aim or content. The rules of the game are kill or be killed until there are no more monsters left and the hostile military-industrial-research complex can be escaped. There are several stages, however, for the player to negotiate, each one a maze of darkened passageways, gloomy rooms, pools of green radioactive slime, hidden tunnels, secret doors, full of murderous monsters, from fireball-throwing werewolves to radiation-breathing hybrids that have the appearance of porcine rhinoceroses. Mainly zones of terror, horror and violent sensation, bewildering labyrinths stalked by homicidal mutants, the various stages of the game also conceal secrets. There are rewards on offer: enhanced armour and an arsenal of weapons (shotgun, chain-gun, missile launcher and chainsaw) furnish the player with greater, more satisfyingly explosive or bloody firepower; repeated exposure and the discovery of secret compartments, develop an understanding of the mysterious spaces of the complex. And, of course, repetition increases the skill and speed with which monsters can be dispatched and stages can be completed. But the overwhelming and threatening contours of the virtual spaces are matched by the technological escalations of difficulty: harder levels bombard the player with more and more enemies, materialising as if from nowhere, intensifying the visual shocks and sensations of terror, requiring faster and faster reactions, and precipitating the plunge into virtual death: game over.

At the risk of playing the uncanny too cheaply (a hand employed all-too often), there is something strangely familiar about *Doom*. Its labyrinths, ghostly figures, monstrous mutants evoke primitive fears and instinctual responses; its violent shocks and graphic images quicken the blood and set the pulse racing; its repetitive structure sacrifices imaginative narrative involvement for the more immediate pleasures and terrors of desire and fear, fight and flight, a fanciful, childish game of excessive expenditures in which self-possession is lost and regained. The dissolution of self in fear and the recovery enabled through violent expulsion, of course, charts the principal dynamic of terror, most evident in contemporary culture in the screams that attend a showing of a horror movie. The development of computer games owes debts to horror cinema and incorporates some of its features and, even, some images, in game design. *Silent Hill* (1999), for example, is a horror game which involves 'tense wanderings in dark environments' that are 'interrupted with shocks, sudden appearances of blood-curdling monsters'. *Resident Evil* (itself made into a sci-fi horror film) moreover, includes scenes that are taken from George Romero's cult horror movie, *Dawn of the Dead* (Poole, 79). To close the loop, *Doom* itself became a sci-fi horror movie (dir. Andrzej Bartkwiak, 2006).

The settings, shocks, monsters and graphic violence of games provide grounds for condemnation: 'in general, the computer game, we might say, is a degenerate spectacle awash in the flood of information-images. It internalises current and archaic phantasm of pleasure, violence and control through simple narratives, crude moralising filters and forms of self-identification' (cited in MacKenzie, 257). Though the critic halts his account of 'cultural damage' and 'infantile embarrassment' and goes on to distinguish positive features of computer game-playing, terms like 'degenerate spectacle', the 'flood' of images, the 'phantasms', replay over 200 years of Gothic fiction and its criticism. Short-circuiting judgement and discrimination through excessive stimulation of emotional energies, romances were accused of hindering learning, character development and moral understanding. A base kind of love or amorous identification is evoked instead: 'but the love we mostly meet with, in such *Circulating Library* books, is devoid of *passion*; has more of *sensation*, than *sentiment*, in it. More *desire*, than *wish.* Were brutes gifted with speech and reason, they would express their *instinct*, in the very stile of modern Novelists' (cited in Ioan Williams, 277, original emphasis). Gothic fiction horrifies the discriminating critic with the spectre of a deviation from proper human qualities, with its induction of a regression to the uncivilised (animal or infantile) appetites associated with desire, sensation and instinct. The same, of course, has been remarked of computer games: a 'more primitive, kinetic' intellect is required to play; a 'visceral, animal brain' comes to the fore (Poole, 56; 63).

While game-playing has its uses in developing pattern recognition, motor coordination, reflexes and spatial imagination (Poole, 56) it is, more often, the deleterious psychological and social effects that consume concerned commentators. Like the idle indulgence in fanciful fictions that irritated so many eighteenth-century critics, game-playing wastes much time and money with no evident profitable return in either category. Noting a popular moralising media tendency to explain the dangers of video games in terms of dependency and addiction ('kiddie cocaine'), Peter Buse details the fears of players' spending excessively on their habit (Buse, 179). Such waste is, of course, immoral and antisocial: not only in its lack of concern for economic consequences, but in the way, through repeated exposure to violence, that social values and other beings are rendered inconsequential and expendable. If moral discrimination is set aside in game-playing, so, too, is reason. Indeed, the moral panic about computer games is reflected in the panic induced by them: *Doom* owes its development to Atari video games like *Battlezone* (1980) and *Missile Command* (1980), the latter a 'panic-inducing arcade game ... which initially grew out of a military simulation to see how many nuclear warheads a human radar operator could track before overload set in' (Poole, 50). Rational faculties are overwhelmed by the bombardment of images, an informational sublimity in which sense is overstimulated by sensory excitation and consciousness sacrificed to the absorbing immersion in the 'flow' of the game, 'an experience of ecstasy or bliss, losing track of time and losing the sense of self' (180). The player is magically transported into another dimension imaginarily beyond the limits and constraints of everyday temporality, economy and experience, an expenditure of sense, reason, morality and self without return.

Game-playing, however, involves more than wasteful, immoral and irrational expenditure. Besides the development of practical skills, games have a significant part to play in cultural formation (Poole, 147). This line of argument, in respect of game-playing generally, has been made by Johann Huizinga: linked to ritual, 'pure play is one of the main bases of civilisation' (Huizinga, 5). Culture, indeed, 'arises in the form of play', manifesting a 'supra-logical' characteristic of humanity that resists reduction to rational and mechanical analysis. Romanticism, too, is 'born in play': Huizinga cites Walpole's *Castle of Otranto* as its 'birth-certificate' (189). For Roger Caillois, Huizinga's argument concerning the importance of games in the development of ritual and civilisation is more 'an inquiry into the creative quality of the play principle in the domain of culture': it is 'at the same time too broad and too narrow' to account for the manner in which play '*expends*' and assumes a role in the secret and mysterious nature of institutional cultural ceremonies and the material resources of production. Games disclose an excess lying within and outside culture; they are as wasteful as they are symbolic and ritualistic:

> A characteristic of play, in fact, is that it creates no wealth or goods, thus differing from work or art. At the end of the game, all can and must start over again at the same point. Nothing has been harvested or manufactured, no masterpiece has been created, no capital has accrued. Play is an occasion of pure waste: waste of time, energy, ingenuity, skill, and often of money for the purchase of gambling equipment or eventually to pay for the establishment. (Caillois, 5–6)

Separated from the sphere of productive activity, games disclose elements crucial to cultural formation. Wasting time, resources, energy, play manifests the heterogeneous expenditures central to symbolic economies: what is lost or sacrificed in the material terms of a restricted economy may return – in ritual or ceremony – as a general symbolic value (see Bataille, 1997). With videogames, however, mechanism comes to the fore; their excess, moreover, disrupts the structures of ritual: 'play inverts ritual: if ritual (or secular narratives of progress or emancipation which ground their legitimacy in the future rather than the past) absorbs events into synchronic structures, play in all its forms articulates and even dismembers synchronic structures into events' (MacKenzie, 261). There is, then, something 'aneconomic' about play: it manifests an internal excess that disturbs the cycle of commercial or rational exchange while, at the same time, invigorating its movement in relation to another, symbolic, level, thereby disclosing a heterogeneity that can neither be contained nor expelled (see Derrida, 1992b). One can never be fully assimilated by the other. Related to ritual and to useful productive activity, play remains distinct from it: its dynamics admit something other than functional or directed development, its pleasures expending energies unregulated by the dictates of work.

Useful and useless, play activates an ambivalent energy. While Gothic narratives can be defended as dark mirrors cautioning readers against improper behaviour, identifying monstrous vices and giving form to and assuaging cultural anxieties, the dangers, for critics, remain: a loosening of social and familial bonds, the suppression of reason by enflamed passions, the breakdown of morally sanctioned reality through flights of fantasy. So, too, with computer games as technical skills are developed at the expense of social virtues and the playful, imaginative outlet for all sorts of adolescent energies and anxieties crosses the permeable line separating it from physical social expression. Games, like fictional narratives, are not, it seems, neatly contained, but spill over, with ambivalent effect, introducing a disruptive heterogeneity into the social sphere. The events of April 1999 at Columbine High School in Colorado offer an example of the way that popular media are implicated in shocking outbursts of apparently senseless violence. *Doom*, already cited in a $130 million lawsuit against videogame developers and internet companies by the relatives of victims of a school shooting in West Paducah, Kentucky, was cited again in the search for an explanation for murderous adolescent rage: Eric Harris and Dylan Klebold were 'avid Doom fans' (Keegan, 2. See also Poole, 219). Popular culture, from films like *Heathers* and *The Matrix*, to the music of Marilyn Manson and computer games, was invoked alongside discussions of racist and Nazi sympathies, mental instability and adolescent alienation, in attempts to make sense of the event. Two episodes of *Buffy the Vampire Slayer* were cancelled, an example of media 'hypersensitivity' (McConnell, 120). But, as Andrew Wernick argues, it is difficult to rationalise or explain away such an act of violence as merely media-inspired imitation. More complex economic and symbolic forces need to be invoked, two 'sacred' events in particular: 'what Harris and Klebold offered us on Hitler's birthday was a deadly counter-gift, a performative symbol as fatal strategy, a contestative transgression that staked itself in the game'. What happened leads to a 'reparative ritual' in which the shooters were defined and expelled as pathologically evil, explained away, that is, in a process of symbolic and communal restoration culminating in the ceremonial reopening of the school in August 1999. Play spills over into the community, opening up a violent counter-festive transgression which tears its structure apart and requires that it be reformed through a restorative ritual. In between, a space of excess, of senseless violence, remains to haunt the institution of community:

> a nihilism, evidently, that is mired in reactiveness and can only abstractly negate. The lack of anything to affirm is rendered positive only by becoming an active will to annihilate. At the same time, the lack of an affirmed self with which to affirm is met by identifying (to the point of personification) with the negating impulse itself. It is the hateful negation of a hateful world; destructive rage self-affirmed. Such a spirit – manifest in real and fictional moral monsters, as well as in the audio-visual surround of attack games and industrial music to which Harris and Klebold were supposedly addicted – may be the signature of the times. (Wernick)

The negativity and transgression expended in play, to no external purpose or effect, becomes, when freed from the strict bounds of game-playing, an excess which threatens social and communal limits. Play, like Gothic fiction, haunts and affirms the boundaries of cultural formations with a heterogeneity that, while necessary, often remains difficult to countenance or bear.

In Gothic texts, however, terror is more often associated with the playful expenditure of destructive energies, a consumption of excesses that, unsanctioned, have no legitimate outlet other than in fantasy or fiction. A fear remains, played upon in the texts themselves, that the boundaries between fantasy and reality are themselves insecure, preyed upon by supernatural agencies or the disturbances of superstition itself. Indeed, the first Gothic fiction with its blend of ancient and modern romance is designed precisely as a movement between worlds of inventive fancy and probable realism. The aim, Walpole asserts in his second preface to *The Castle of Otranto*, is to have his characters 'think, speak and act, as it might be supposed mere men and women would do in extraordinary positions' (Walpole, 7–8). Reality and fantasy cross in order to produce interesting situations and effects. A similar movement is undertaken in computer games. The 'first-person shooter' genre, in which a hand holding a gun functions as a perspectival illusion of involvement on the screen, offers a point of identification drawing the player into the virtual world. It is 'a clever effort to try to cross the barrier between onscreen action and the player's physical situation' (Poole, 137). For John Romero, *Doom*'s creator, this blurring is crucial. Speaking of his new game, *Daikatana*, he notes the absorption involved: 'physical reality suggests you are sitting in a chair operating a mouse and a keyboard. But with the computer screen replacing your field of vision, you believe you're actually creeping around a corner, causing your breath to shorten. Afraid an enemy is lying in wait, you feel your pulse quicken. When the monster jumps out, real adrenaline roars through your body' (Keegan, 2). Immersion in the artificial, virtual world of the screen, an immersion in a more literal and immediate visual environment than that conjured up on the page, allows very real, visceral effects to be evoked. A world of ghosts and monsters is rendered palpable in the shocks that result from visual images. Unlike the world of fiction, where superstitious credulity and imaginative identification are required to make the leap of realising, in emotional effect at least, fictions, computer games perform the work of visualisation themselves, while continuing to play with patterns of anticipation, expectation and shock that constitute the minimal Gothic plot.

Not only are Gothic structures of suspense and shock retained in computer games, their environments are designed to evoke horror and terror. The foggy world of *Silent Hill* obscures visibility and clouds the player in uncertainty and apprehension; the labyrinths, gloom and post-industrial ruins of *Doom* produce the threatening atmosphere of pursuit along with a sense of disorientation. While these environments stimulate the more basic emotions associated with terror and horror, computer games can also generate the loftier feelings pertaining to the sublime: *Tomb Raider's* 'breathtaking environments', 'awe-inspiring spaces' and 'cathedrals of fire' manifest a 'secularisation of wonder' (Poole, 236–7). More than a secularisation, the virtual space is also a digitalisation of wonder in contrast to the secularisation of a natural spirit associated with the Romantic sublime. The effects, however, remain similar: the encounter with a natural divinity found, in the eighteenth century, in the sovereign shape of rugged, mountainous landscapes, overwhelms the viewer, lost in the breathtaking enormity of the spectacle, to then regain, on an imaginative level, self-possession through identification with the magnificence and grandeur of the scene. Though terror, in Burkean aesthetics, is ultimately uplifting, the movement of loss and mastery invigorating an elevated idea of selfhood and a sense of the sacred, its energy comes from a baser, corporeal source, from the passion of self-preservation (Burke, 123). In computer games 'instinctual' emotions become central to enjoyment. They involve an 'appreciation of dynamic properties hard-wired into the species – it's essential for survival' (Poole, 63). There need not be, it seems, any recuperation of self or sense of the sacred: loss of self-consciousness may be intensely pleasurable in itself, immersion in the 'flow' of gaming engendering an experience of 'ecstasy or bliss', a joyful dissolution and expenditure of bounded selfhood (180–2).

The aesthetics of the sublime, reinvented in the context of a commercial eighteenth century, served to establish, at least imaginarily, a sense of self and agency in a rapidly changing world. In a culture dominated by the 'invisible hand' of the market the question of a civic, public spirit was raised. How, when social equilibrium was calibrated in terms of the circulation and 'mass effect of self-interested passions', can a 'disinterested public spirit' be fostered? In feudal times public service had a military outlet 'but in a peaceful mercantile state, organised on the principle of the division of labour, death in battle is an option open to a few'. The sublime thus fills the breach in a new way, vainly trying to articulate individual and socius by offering 'a private war without consequences' (Clery, 104–5):

> The sublime is a simulacrum of the external threat of violent death sufficient to arouse the strongest passions of self-preservation, while never requiring that these be surmounted in the name of public duty; it remains essentially a mind-game. Although it has the effect of catharsis and renewal, and confirmation of masculinity (here, the mental qualities that make men different from women), there is no bridge back to the sense of public spirit (such as Kant would attempt to provide, in criticism of Burke). (105)

What is delivered, in the quasi-sacred form of sublime terror, is 'a decisive alteration, an appeasement of individualist commercial values' manifesting a 'bourgeois appropriation of the political language of luxury'. The sublime indulges the bourgeois subject, allowing a glimpse of something other than commercial economy and an imaginary sense of mastery. But it remains tied to the passion of self-preservation, a mind-game in which the self is virtually lost and virtually regained in the oscillation of terror and pleasure, an expenditure of excess energies that returns to equilibrium.

As an aesthetic technique, a mode of appropriating luxurious, wasteful expenditure, an expenditure associated in bourgeois culture with the excesses of feudal aristocracy, the sublime participates in the eighteenth-century transformation of self and nature. In the natural images, architectural ruins and feudal customs that are coloured by a Gothic sublime, the past is appropriated and expelled in an attempt to separate a civilised, rational eighteenth century from its barbaric forebears: ruined abbeys and castles testify to a world that has been superseded, its wildness and extravagance tamed by the enlightened mind; natural and primitive passions of self-preservation are activated as the basis of a movement away, an elevation or progression. Remnants of the past – ruins, superstitions, passions – mark turning points in cultural historical progress and thus, in looking back, Gothic figures also provide the platform of a movement forward. Though more often associated with the return of suppressed images, ideas and energies, with hauntings, guilt and supernatural forces, Gothic texts manifest a double temporal movement in which technical advances provide the means for the future to become a site of dark projections. The hi-tech worlds of computer games are also places of destruction and decay, spectral fears and primitive energies, fictional worlds in which the future is as ruined as the past. Anxiety, and desire, leaps forward: social and corporeal disintegration lie in the future, in post-industrial devastation, in biotechnological experimentation, in alien and mutant shapes: the urban wastelands of cyberpunk (*Blade Runner's* dark and decaying Los Angeles or *Neuromancer's* 'Night City', 'a deranged experiment in social Darwinism' (Gibson, 1984: 14), depict a near-future of gloom and ruins (Sponsler). Technoscience moves beyond human control, no longer guaranteeing enlightened progress, a cause of terror and horror, harbinger of barbarism and degeneration. From *Frankenstein* onwards, it seems, scientific discovery is as much threat as promise. In *The Island of Dr Moreau* (1896) the biologist's attempt to accelerate evolution according to Darwinian principles only causes rapid regression to bestial states and unleashes a reversion to savagery and a host of horrible hybrid creatures.

Though Gothic fiction begins with the invention of a feudal, romantic and supernatural past, it maintains close and disturbing affinities with technological innovation. As Friedrich Kittler suggests, 'there is no difference between occult and technological media' (Kittler, 1990: 229). Gothic fiction, for all its trappings of the past, its ruins, feudal ranks and customs, its superstitions and ghosts, also engenders a new relationship between technology and the supernatural. Terry Castle, examining the magic lantern shows of the late eighteenth century and their phantasmagorical effects on consciousness, draws out the uncanny relation between technology and the supernatural. Technical devices disclose a 'spectralizing habit' in modernity: 'our compulsive need, since the mid-nineteenth century, to invent machines that mimic and reinforce the image-producing powers of consciousness'. The 'technological embodiment' of the habit is manifested in various new media (cinema, television, virtual reality). Photography, in the guise, becomes 'a way of possessing material objects in a strangely decorporealised yet supernaturally vivid form' (Castle, 137). Indeed, in the famous Cottingley hoax photographs of fairies, the existence of supernatural beings was held to be proven by technological means. Machines for mimicking natural and human forms and functions, too, assume an uncanny aspect. Automata, too, manifest the association between technology and spectrality: E.T.A. Hoffman's story, 'The Sandman', is a tale of psychological disorder embracing childhood fears of threatening paternal figures and the amorous allure of a feminine doll. The story, of course, is central to Freud's discussion of 'The Uncanny'. Automata participate in the development and disturbances shaping the subject in the course of the eighteenth century: 'the mechanical doll is a metaphor of, and counterpoint to, the autonomous subjectivity; the autonomous self-determination and the automaton seem to go hand in hand' (Dolar, 1994: 46). From being toys, puppets for the amusement of monarch and court earlier in the century, the significance of automata changes: the fantasy of power, machination and domination shifts from monarchical authority to enlightened knowledge and the mechanism comes to represent (in the manner if La Mettrie's Man-machine) a systematic understanding of human workings, a subjection to the inviolable principles of rational knowledge, excluding spirit and able to be utilised economically in the industrial revolution: a technological reduction is put into effect, and with it arise fears of a de-spiritualisation of humanity. Mimicking, duplicating and threatening to replace human abilities, automata manifest the doubleness that threatens individual uniqueness. Hence the horror that attended encounters with ghostly or artificial doubles, a horror linked by Zizek to emergence of Kantian or modern subjectivity: 'all of a sudden, however, in the historic moment that exactly fits the Kantian revolution, the topic of the double became associated with horror and anxiety – encountering one's double or being followed and persecuted by him is the ultimate experience of terror, something which shatters the very core of the subject's identity' (Zizek, 1999: 315). Automata, like doubles, hollow out the subject, make its workings visible and its inner private secrets subject to knowledge, power and manipulation.

The double, indeed, is a recurrent feature of the 'spectralizing habit', a figure haunting its various technological embodiments, from fiction to cinema and beyond. Cinema materialises doubles, it makes them move across a screen, a metaphor for the apparatus itself. For Kittler the double effect is that 'movies thus took the place of the fantasy of the library. All the tricks that once magically transformed words into sequential hallucinations are recalled and surpassed'(Kittler, 1990: 247). The magical, ghostly movement of cinema images is surpassed by new computer technologies. The movement of virtual images dispossesses the body of shadow and substance so that identity becomes no more than a phantasmatic electronic flickering. Moreover, the polygons composing computer graphics almost attain a spiritual life of their own: 'And now the polygons have become animated, literally, given a soul. A machine soul' (Poole, 140). Spirits and selves entwine on the spectral screens of technological media, screens on which reality is represented, simulated and supplanted, screens that serve as the site of projections of anxiety and desire, sites of repetition, in which future horrors are clothed in old figures of fear. The double movement of technological/spectral media can be identified in Roland Barthes' account of photography. As a 'living image of a dead thing', the photograph fascinates the observer with a horrified glimpse of his/her own mortality, a ghostly preservation of lost bodies intimating 'an anterior future of which death is at stake' (Barthes, 1984: 96). While being a 'fugitive testimony' of what was and what has gone, photography is also a technical invention that anticipates rapid change and hurries forward in time: it emerges, Barthes notes, in an 'age of revolutions ... explosions ... impatiences' (Barthes, 1984: 94).

## Gothic shocks

Bound up with Romanticism's movement away from styles and conventions considered overly formal, mechanical and artificial (in contrast to the insistence on natural emotion and expression), Gothic fiction fared poorly in Romantic critical judgements. William Wordsworth, in the Preface to *Lyrical Ballads*, complained of the disturbing effects of popular fictions on literary tastes: 'the invaluable works of our elder writers, I had almost said the works of Shakespeare and Milton, are driven into neglect by frantic novels, sickly and stupid German tragedies, and deluges of idle and extravagant stories in verse' (Wordsworth, 936). Samuel Taylor Coleridge also criticised the delirious and sensational effects produced by fiction, underlining the way it failed to measure up to standards of Romantic imaginative creation (Coleridge, 1975: 28). He echoes Immanuel Kant's distaste for the way in which 'romances, maudlin dramas, shallow homilies' ennervate the heart at the expense of duty and render readers incapable of respecting human values and rights (Kant, 1952: 125). Romantic criticism defines the higher literary values to which it aspires in terms of and against the debasing effects of popular fictions, thereby constructing Gothic writing as a strange double of its own. While conventional eighteenth-century judgements are reiterated in the disapproval of the lower instincts, passions and appetites that are stimulated by fiction, Romantic attacks draw out a more modern concern by associating the formulaic patterns of Gothic narratives, their 'machinery', with mechanistic conceptions of the mind. At this point, the literary status of Gothic writing is securely tied to the material and psychological implications of technological and mechanical metaphors, to suggest that a decisive, if negatively perceived aesthetic development in modern cultural production and popular consumption was taking shape.

Not all commentators hated Gothic fiction. In his *Reflections on the Novel* (1800), the Marquis de Sade, commenting favourably on the works of Lewis and Radcliffe, delivered his famous and, critically influential observation that 'twas the inevitable result of the revolutionary shocks which all of Europe has suffered' (de Sade, 109). The link between Gothic fiction and revolution was also noted by conservative critics in the 1790s: one warned that fictions, especially works by women novelists mixing politics and literature, would turn their readers 'wild with Gallic frenzy' (Matthias, 244). It is curious, however, that the fictional response to revolutionary events exacerbates, rather than assuages, the more disturbing and violent energies associated with massive social and political change. The critic sets out to describe the dangerous effects of reading Gothic (and radical philosophical) texts and warns his readers 'of the manner in which the understanding and affections are bewildered, darkened, ennervated, or degraded'. He has suffered, he notes, a similarly shocking experience:

> when I have read and thought deeply on the accumulated horrors, and on all the gradations of wickedness and misery, through which the modern systematic philosophy of Europe has conducted her illuminated votaries to the confines of political death and mental darkness, my mind for a space feels a convulsion and suffers the nature of an insurrection. (Matthias, 17–18)

The effect of reading political and philosophical works is one of shock. It seems strange, indeed, that in response to 'revolutionary shocks' writing should inflict yet more shocks. As an aesthetic effect, shock is one of the negative attributes of Gothic fiction: it registers the genre's deviation from the rules of eighteenth-century composition. A disruption of the uniformity and proportion so precious to eighteenth-century judgement, shock connotes the subjective manifestation of aesthetic deformity. As a review of Ann Radcliffe's *The Italian* underlines: 'it is a matter of great consequence, in our judgement, that in all the works of taste there should be due regard paid to the preservation of this unity of emotion, as the mind of necessity experiences a shock when perplexed with contradictory and inconsistent feelings' (Anon., 1797b: 155). Shock registers aesthetic disequilibrium; its evocation of contradictory and inconsistent emotions associates its excesses with the uplifting thrill of terror and the dark confusion of horror. It is not apparent in writings of the period, however, just why the shocks of social, economic and political transformation should be repeated in fictional texts. From the position of the moral and rational eighteenth-century aesthetic critic neither shock, nor its repetition in Gothic texts, makes any sense.

'The first shock of a great earthquake had, just at that period, rent the whole neighbourhood to its centre.' Houses crumble, streets are torn apart, a chaos of stone, bricks and scaffolding, 'Babel towers' of broken chimneys, 'carcases of ragged tenements', tangled, rusted iron, carts and general detritus, lie scattered about in 'a hundred thousand shapes and substances of incompleteness'. At the same time, 'hot springs and fiery eruptions, the usual attendants upon earthquakes, lent their contributions of confusion to the scene'. Sublime though it seems, the devastation and ruination of the cityscape, perceived as a natural apocalypse in which the fires of hell erupt in 1840s Camden Town, has little to do with nature. The cause of the catastrophic interruption of everyday life is indicated by the towering presence of the 'giant forms of cranes, and tripods straddling above nothing'. Their monstrous, mechanical shadow heralds a new engine of disastrous destruction, a new force of natural, social and experiential reordering: 'in short, the yet unfinished and unopened Railway was in progress; and, from the very core of all this dire disorder, trailed smoothly away, upon its mighty course of civilisation and improvement' (Dickens, 1982: 120–1).

The ironic juxtaposition of the calmer, more factual paragraph describing the arrival of the railway system in Camden Town offers little sense of comfort in the face of the steady march of progress and civilisation. Indeed, throughout Charles Dickens's *Dombey and Son*, first serialised between 1846 and 1848, the transformation of natural and urban life by the advances of industrialisation, demonically embodied by the railway, is marked by emotions that range from suspicion and fear to outright terror. Only the proprietors of the 'The Railway Arms' and the 'Railway Eating House', along with lodging-house keepers, show any enthusiasm for the development. From the position of the shocked and sceptical residents, these are potentially 'rash enterprises' overly imbued with commercial concerns that are redolent of what Michael Stieg describes as 'the railway-building mania' and 'Railway Panic' of the 1840s when the expansion of the system was attended by a 'fever of speculation' in shares and quick profitable returns. Cartoons of the period represent the railways in the monstrous form of 'The Great *Land* Serpent', voraciously devouring, with demonic eyes and sharp fangs, huge piles of human bodies trussed up in moneybags or, in the shape of 'The Railway Dragon', uninvited intruders terrorizing bourgeois families at their dinner tables (Stieg, 145).

The general sense of terror and fear accompanying the railway system, and all that it implied for the early Victorian encounter with the rapid mechanisation of industry, society and human life, is underlined later in *Dombey and Son* when the protagonist takes a journey by rail. Despite the procession of panoramic views of town and country, there is no pleasure in rail travel, no thrill of speed or vision, for Mr Dombey. On the contrary, the speed of movement induces sensations of monotony, foreboding and despair, distancing the traveller from a landscape that has become a wilderness and haunting him with memories of his dead son. The sense of loss and mourning is intensified by the harshly repetitive and inhuman intrusions of the machine that dominate his train of thought: 'away with a

shriek, and a roar, and a rattle ... ' Human fears are accelerated and absorbed by the might of the engine, to the extent that mortality is transferred from nature to the machinery: 'the power that forced itself upon its
iron way – its own – defiant of all paths and roads, piercing though the
heart of every obstacle, and degrading living creatures of all classes, ages,
and degrees behind it, was a type of the triumphant monster, Death'
(Dickens, 1982: 354). The mechanisation represented by the railway system, heralded by inhuman shrieks and rattles, assumes the form of a fatal
inevitability, a 'remorseless monster', an 'indomitable monster'. Life has
passed beyond natural rhythms and flows and is devoured or spat out by
the progress of a relentless, sovereign and cruel technological system.

Towards the end of the novel, the sense of inevitable destructive transformation, of natural catastrophe and human fatality, is brutally manifested. The novel's schemer, Carker, is forced by 'the crash of his project'
into a desperate flight. After a long journey by carriage, boat and train, he
arrives, tired and feverish, at a small station to await the connection that
will transport him to his place of refuge. Any rest is interrupted by the
trains that thunder through, all assuming the form of a 'fiery devil' passing
smoothly along an iron road. One of these devilish giants halts to refuel
and Carker watches in fascination 'thinking what a cruel power and might
it had. Ugh! To see the wheels slowly turning and to think of being run
down and crushed!'(872–3) Attraction lingers within the repulsive vision
of mechanical mutilation, a speculation in which the restless traveller finds
peace and respite beneath the wheels of the diabolical engine. Shortly afterwards, he succumbs to the destiny prescribed by the novel and incarnated by the machine. The modes of rapid transportation which ensured
his escape also facilitate pursuit. On glimpsing his pursuer, Carker stag-
gers and turns to run:

> He heard a shout – another – saw the face change from its vindictive passion
> to a faint sickness and terror – felt the earth tremble – knew in a moment
> that the rush was come – uttered a shriek – looked round – saw the red eyes,
> bleared and dim, in the daylight, close upon him – was beaten down, caught
> up, and whirled away upon a jagged mill, that spun him round and round,
> and struck him limb from limb, and licked his stream of life up with its
> fiery heat, and cast his mutilated fragments in the air. (875)

This is how it feels to be run over, terrified apprehension and anticipation
ceding, in a rush of instantaneous recognition, to a horrifying mechanical
consummation in a whirl of corporeal matter and industrial iron, living
energy and searing steam.

Fear, terror and anxiety were quite common responses to the railway
system and the novel experience of rail travel. Wolfgang Schivelbusch notes

that 'the breaking of a locomotive axle between Paris and Versailles in 1842 leads to the first railroad catastrophe that causes a panic in Europe' (Schivelbusch, 133). The accident, a technological failure or breakdown due to metal fatigue, resulted in the death of fifty-five passengers and serious injury to over one hundred more. It prompted concerted technical, medical and legal concern with accidents: metal fatigue and psychological trauma began to be recognised and studied in order to improve safety and deal with shock. Until the novelty of rail transport was dulled by familiarity travellers remained aware of what Schivelbusch calls an 'ever-present fear of potential disaster': one passenger, in 1829, noted the difficulty of suppressing 'the notion of instant death to all upon the least accident happening'; another, in 1845, commented upon the 'close proximity of an accident and the inability to exercise any influence on the running of the cars' (131). The terror that attends the arrival of the railway system in *Dombey and Son* is clearly linked, in Dombey's journey at least, to the strange combination of speed, comfort and ease with an irrepressible apprehension of imminent disaster. Significantly, however, rail travel was not yet established as an everyday mode of transport: it was yet to become the 'natural and safe process' that, in Schivelbusch's words, 'has become second nature' (131–2). Instead, Dickens's account resonates with Ernst Bloch's description of 'the demonic nature of the first railroads' that lies beyond any 'civilized schedule' (cited in Schivelbusch, 132). Presented as an earthquake and a diabolical incursion into everyday reality, Dickens's railway is associated with an excessive and uncontrollable natural energy and a monstrous supernatural force. Technology has not yet been assimilated nor has its reconstruction of everyday life rendered technology familiar as a 'second nature'. Schivelbusch explains the difference:

> The preindustrial catastrophes are natural events, natural accidents. They attack the objects they destroy from the outside, as storms, floods, thunderbolts, hailstones etc. After the industrial revolution, destruction by technological accident comes from the inside. The technical apparatuses destroy themselves by means of their own power (133).

Technology thereby serves as an index not only of a transformation in the meaning of the accident, shifting its significance from natural catastrophe to mechanical failure, it also transforms the experience of a natural environment from what Virilio calls a 'metabolic proximity', associated with bodily temporality and spatial movement, to a 'mechanical proximity' of the transportation revolution and its regulation of time and motion across space. 'Catastrophe,' notes Mary Ann Doane, 'is thus, through its association with industrialization and the advance of technology, ineluctably linked with the idea of Progress' so that 'technological evolution is perceived as unflinching progress toward a total state of control over nature' and 'catastrophe signals the failure of the escalating technological desire to conquer nature' (Doane, 1990: 230–1).

In Dickens, however, the devastation takes the form of an excessively natural catastrophe, so unthinkable is the scale and remorselessness of the incursion of technological progress. Nature remains on the brink of an imminent and terrifying technological conquest and the accident has yet to become a fully-fledged mechanical failure. That 'first shock of the great earthquake' reverberating through Camden Town heralds the arrival of a system which carves up the natural and built environment and replaces it with the mechanical imperatives of a commercial and industrial order, in the process transforming the realm of the aleatory and accidental from a meta-natural location to one that is 'asystematic' (237). The nineteenth century ascribes 'the cause of technological accidents to the sudden disturbance of the uncertain equilibrium of a machine': 'the modern technological accident, the sudden collapse of a highly developed machinery, is a result of the management of industry according to capitalist principles'(Schivelbusch, 134). *Dombey and Son*'s traumatic encounter with the railway system enacts a 'sacrificial crisis' articulating – linking and separating – two orders of being: the chaos, confusion and terror introduced by the railway produces a new order of mechanised existence through the catastrophe which serves 'to transcend the old violence and recreate a system of difference on another level of organization' (Attali, 34). Shock is an index of the crisis; it is the human correlate of both the technological reconstruction of lived experience and the technological accident: it marks a psycho-physiological failure akin to mechanical breakdown and signals human habituation to a mechanised order. Shock is experienced first from the outside, in the quaking earth and quaking body of a natural disaster, and then from the inside in the collision of a technological accident and the reverberation of traumatic after-effects: in the nineteenth century 'shock describes the kind of sudden and powerful event of violence that disrupts the continuity of an artificially/mechanically created motion or situation, and also the subsequent state of derangement' (Schivelbusch, 151).

A few years after Dickens described the catastrophic incursion of the railway system into the metabolic proximities of everyday life, he experienced the shock of mechanical proximity. On 9 June 1865 he was travelling from Folkestone to London when the train was derailed because routine repairs had removed part of the track near Staplehurst. Leaping the gap in the rails, the train broke up and plunged into a stream. Five carriages were crushed; ten passengers were killed and twenty injured. The last carriage teetered on the bridge. One passenger described the moment of the crash as being 'startled by a deep and heavy-sounding noise; then followed two terrible jolts or bumps, and, in an instant afterwards, from bright sunshine all became darkness, and to me chaos' (Dickens, 1985: 159). Dickens, who was in the remaining carriage and praised for his attempts to aid wounded passengers, wrote, with difficulty, of the incident four days later. The scene he describes is one of sublime devastation: 'no imagination can conceive the ruin of the carriages, or the extraordinary weights under which the people were lying, or the complications into which they were twisted up among iron and wood, and mud and water'. More significant than this description, however, are the effects of the crash on normally so productive a writer. His letter declares that he neither wants to attend the inquest nor write about the event. Though unaffected at the time, he goes on, 'in writing these scanty words of recollection I feel the shake and am obliged to stop' (151). Repetition, in writing and recollection, conjures up the crash and produces the shock after the fact: Dickens was, he notes, 'not in the least fluttered at the time'. The trauma from which Dickens suffered was a phenomenon being investigated by the medical establishment for the first time in this period: 'there are reports about railroad accidents that describe travellers as exhibiting signs of strong psychic disruption, phobias, obsessive actions, etc., without having suffered any actual injury' (Schivelbusch, 137). In 1866, John Eric Erichsen observes that 'mental shock' arises from a 'psychic blow' occasioned by fright rather than mechanical causes. Speculating on whether the trauma originates in 'the frantic terror which often seizes upon the sufferers from railway collisions' or 'some vibratory thrill transmitted through the nervous system by the peculiarity of the accident', Erichsen asserts that 'the crash and confusion, the uncertainty attendant on a railway collision, the shrieks of the sufferers, possibly the sight of the victims of the catastrophe, produce a mental impression of a far deeper and more vivid character than occasioned by the more ordinary accidents of civil life' (cited in Schivelbusch, 141). Later Max Nordau, in *Degeneration*, commented 'even the little shocks of railway travelling, not perceived by the consciousness … cost our brains wear and tear' (cited in Marcus, 177).

Noting the proximity between early accounts of technological shock and psychoanalytic theories of trauma, Schivelbusch turns to Freud for an explanation of both the habituation of travellers to new modes of transportation and the after-effects of accidents. Endorsing the hypothesis, in *Beyond the Pleasure Principle*, that organisms develop a 'protective shield' to cope with the excitations of external stimuli, Schivelbusch applies it to the experience of rail travel. As a new stimulus, the speed of travel and its effects on perception constitutes a mildly distressing and irritating experience. With habituation, however, the velocity is 'psychically assimilated', the result of a thickening of the protective shield of consciousness. Shock thus becomes 'the shattering of a stimulus shield of convention' (158). Freud's abstract model, moreover, allows Schivelbusch to theorise the relationship between culture and technology so that 'social rules and technologically produced stimuli structure the individual in a similar manner, regularizing, regulating, shaping him according to their inherent laws' (158). While technological constructs manifest the process of the external domination of nature, cultural conventions produce internal regulation according to the imperatives of civilisation and social order. This systematic alignment of bodies and technology remains invisible, until the shock of an asystematic irruption destroys any sense of equilibrium and continuity. Accidents must be explained, rationalised, normalised, returned to a set of procedures maintaining equilibrium and thereby limiting the potential for shocks. For Michel de Certeau, train travel comes to exemplify the process of homogenisation and rationalisation attendant on the movement of progress and civilisation: 'the unchanging traveller is pigeonholed, numbered, and regulated in the grid of the railway car, which is a perfect actualization of the rational utopia'. While the toilets offer an 'escape from closed system', 'only a rationalized cell travels. A bubble of panoptic and classifying power, a module of imprisonment that makes possible the production of order, a closed and autonomous insularity – that is what can traverse space and make itself independent of local roots' (de Certeau, 111). The noise, rhythm and vibration of travel quietly underline the imperative that is at work, 'the Principle responsible for all the action taken away from both travellers and nature: the machine'. The machine has become the '*primum mobile*', the 'solitary god' (113).

Shock, like accidents, becomes part of the system of modernity, the asystematic excess internal to its functioning repeatedly projected outside its field of operations. Shock contributes to technological accidents in that the many repeated impacts, stresses and vibrations of the component parts of high-powered mechanisms can lead to metal fatigue and breakdown. For travellers, the many minor jolts and vibrations of mechanical motion induce unwelcome excitation and irritation but, through repetition, enable the formation of a protective shield ensuring familiarity and habituation. For Walter Benjamin, habituation and shock of this kind form the distinctive features of urban life, the experience constitutive of the subject of modernity. Discussing the significance of the crowd in Baudelaire's writing, and the importance of shock in defining an individual's relationship to urban masses, Benjamin offers a materialist account: 'the shock experience which the passer-by has in the crowd corresponds to what the worker

"experiences" at his machine' (Benjamin, 1973: 178). The repetitive movements and jolts of the machine are replayed in the discordant and dislocating flows of everyday life. In the crowd the repetition of mechanical
shocks that overstimulate the worker, habituate the individual to a new
order of diminished experience, marking by increasing isolation, shielded
from incoming stimulation in the manner outlined by Freud, and steady
incorporation into a mechanically regulated mass: 'the replacement of the
older narration of information, of information by sensation, reflects the
atrophy of experience' (161). This, for Benjamin, is associated with the
decline of auratic experience, in which the opportunities for reflection,
imagination and uniqueness of individual experience (fuller in its sense of
personal plenitude, permanence and presence than modern 'experience')
is erased by mechanical reproduction's obliteration of distance. Experience is thus reshaped by the system of urban capitalist industrial
organisation in which 'technology has subjected the human sensorium to
a new kind of training' (176). Here shocks operate, not so much a technological breakdown, but as points of disjunction, puncta of articulation
between speeds: they signal a speeding up, a reordering of the rhythms of
the human organism according to the imperatives of system of mechanical reproduction. The worker, manipulated at the machine, rather than
manipulating it, has an equivalent 'experience' to that of the traveller as
well as the passer-by in the crowd. Noting the respective differences between the 'active-productive' and 'passive-consumptive' positions of worker
and traveller, Schivelbusch describes the latter's 'industrial experience' as
that of the consumer passively engaging in a 'change of locality' and thereby
undergoing the spatial and temporal dissociation that defines the simulta-
neity of production and consumption. Early travellers, moreover, felt that
they were transported in the manner of commodities rather than persons:
the 'esthetic freedom' of the pre-industrial subject, in the productions of
goods and travel, had been destroyed (Schivelbusch, 121–2). Shock, an
experience which signals an unexplainable disjunction between phenomena and modes of habituation, whether cultural or technological, marks a
disruptive process of subjective and corporeal reordering.

Benjamin's thesis, of course, is primarily concerned with modes of aesthetic representation and reception. In particular, his concern is addressed
to the implications of photographic and cinematic representation which
form a significant part of the restructuring of experience, involving the
decline of aura, natural distance and human imagination. Film is more
than an adjunct to the shocks of urban, industrial modernity, more than
an aesthetic reflection of the experience of crowds and machines: as a technological invention, a mode of mechanical reproduction, it itself embodies

and repeats those shocks. Writing of the reductive social and industrial mechanisms of modernity Benjamin observes:

> The camera gave the moment a posthumous shock, as it were. Haptic experiences of this kind were joined by optic ones, such as are supplied by the advertising pages of a newspaper or the traffic of a big city. Moving through this traffic involves the individual in a series of shocks and collisions. At dangerous intersections, nervous impulses flow through him, like the energy from a battery. (Benjamin, 1973: 176)

Film, a form of visual traffic akin to urban and mechanical flows, constitutes part of the process of wiring the individual into the circuits of modernity. Its shocks have two modalities: a 'shattering of tradition', involving a 'destructive, cathartic aspect' marking the experience of the dishabituating effects of technological objects and systematic requirements, signals a breakdown of an older heritage; it then cedes to the shocks that form the basic operating principles of everyday and cinematic experience. Film, Benjamin argues, does not work to occlude or assuage the shocks of everyday life. Rather, it repeats and intensifies them: 'there came a day when a new and urgent need for stimuli was met by the film. In a film, perception in the form of shocks was established as a formal principle. That which determines the rhythm of production on a conveyor belt is the basis of the rhythm of reception in the film' (177). Though strange that a need for stimuli and sensation should manifest itself in an age when shocks were increasingly incorporated into everyday life, the cinematic presentation of shocks offers a glimpse of the extent to which experience is reordered in modernity through the interventions of technology.

In 1895, at the Cafe de Paris, the Lumière brothers presented what was, so the story goes, the first moving picture. The scene of a train arriving at a station was so effective that the audience ducked in terror, apparently expecting the imminent impact of the vehicle. The crash did not happen. None the less, audiences repeatedly returned to cinematic spectacles of a similar genre. Tom Gunning, rejecting the hypothesised naivety of the first audiences at the 'primal scene' of cinema, accounts for the popularity of what he calls the 'cinema of attractions' in a way that does not assume rampant and uncivilised credulity unable to distinguish between reality and representation. Early projections, he argues, though causing shock, astonishment and terror, operated according to rules of theatrical, fairground and vaudevillian entertainment: an awareness of the illusion persists in the enjoyment of it and 'the audience's sense of shock comes less from a naive belief that they are threatened by an actual locomotive than from an unbelievable visual transformation occurring before their eyes, parallel to the greatest wonders of the magic theatre' (Gunning, 35). Fears

and screams avow wonder at technological achievement, the experience of
the display being described as a 'thrill' (37). Spectators, indeed, are very
much part of the show: a promoter introduced the films, creating expectation, curiosity and anxiety 'like a fairground barker', thereby preparing
the way for the moment of critical visual impact (36). Preparation lowers
the shock effect of moving images by arousing and fulfilling curiosity and
expectation and allowing the visual stimulus – 'a succession of shocks' – to
be encountered with thrilling pleasure. Shock is (technologically) turned
into a shocking spectacle, its event and effects aestheticised. Citing Kracauer,
Gunning notes how the thrills, satisfactions and intensities of visual spectacles depend on a lack that needs repeatedly filling: the 'modern loss of
fulfilling experience' finds its compensation in the excitements and sensation of the moving image so that 'this loss of experience creates a consumer hungry for thrills'. The cinema that itself 'exposes the hollow centre
of the cinematic illusion' thus requires more and more images to fill the
void of feeling (41–2).

Reiterating the shocks, stimulation and sensation that define modern
life, film does more than merely regulate or habituate workers and consumers to the speed and mechanical rhythms of urban, industrial systems.
It does more than harden a protective shield already hard enough to signal, for Benjamin, the atrophying of experience. Instead, it breaks through
that shield, allowing for an encounter which, though destabilising the equilibrium of the viewer, produces sensations of heightened pleasure, repeating shocks on another level in order to overcome the sense of mechanical
repetition dulling everyday experience. Freud suggests that turning a 'distressing experience' into a game, is how a child deals with shock: initially
'overpowered by experience', his repetition in the form of play, though
unpleasurable, allows him to take 'an *active* part', mastering 'the stimulus
retrospectively, by developing the anxiety whose omission is the cause of
the traumatic neurosis' (Freud, 1984: 285; 304). In an essay on detective
fiction and railway travel, Benjamin describes 'the anaesthetising of one
fear by the other is his salvation. Between the freshly separated pages of
the detective novel he seeks the leisured, almost virginal anxieties which
can help him over the archaic anxieties of the journey' (cited in Marcus,
173). In cinema, the audience, overpowered by the shocks of urban and
industrial life, are actively involved in the visual spectacle by the promoter's
introduction and their own screams: with curiosity and anxiety aroused
they can transform the unpleasurable disturbance of psychic equilibrium
into the fluctuation of pleasurable sensation. Repetition, with a difference
and on another, aesthetic plane, supersedes the repetitive jolts of experience
in the crowd or at the machine. Moreover, the film, as an aesthetic event,

compensates for the shocking overproximity of crowds and mechanical noises, jolts and collisions by inscribing a degree of distance necessary to the process of overcoming feelings of impotence and subjection to the machines of everyday automation. Thrill testifies to a certain sublimity underlying the experience in which the shock of overpowering and uncontrollable technological impact is assimilated: writing of the fear that an accident might cause a nuclear war, Frances Ferguson observes that the sublime image of utter destruction functions both 'to shield' the subject from and draw attention to a subjection to overpowering conditions: 'the sublime renewal of our consciousness of the desire for self-preservation both frees us from the sense of our being bound by the world of circumstances beyond our control and also returns us to the world of circumstances with a certain benevolence toward them' (Ferguson, 1984: 7). Shock is thus incorporated, its punctum the a-systematic interruption of aesthetic and urban industrial experience in which the protective shield of consciousness is stimulated by the screen of the cinema, a locus of projection giving form to anxieties and simultaneously a shield screening out too much stimulation through the stimulation of extra sensation. Accommodating experience to the rhythm of modern life, cinema also speeds up the process of sensation by penetrating the protective shield of consciousness. Given that repeated exposure to external stimuli also serves to harden the shield into an impenetrable shell of habituation, increased shocks are required to produce sensation and thrills. A negative dialectic of shock thus emerges at the abyssal core of modern experience: the more thrills that are presented the more shocks and sensation there have to be to avoid the process of habituation and assimilation.

Paul de Kock, in his novel *La Grande Ville* (1842) describes railways as the 'true magic lantern of nature' (cited in Schnapp, 23). In both Dickens's representations of the railway and in early cinematic techniques and subjects, technology assumes supernatural forms and produces magical effects: new technology, yet to be understood and assimilated, appears magical and evokes fearful responses. The sense of shock is initially a response to a catastrophic reordering of the rhythms and expectations of everyday life but, with repetition, becomes familiar and pleasurable. And it is the apparatuses as well as aesthetic effects that cause transformations in human sensory experience. When a journalist in 1896 viewed the Lumière brothers' short film, he described the experience as 'an excitement bordering on terror' (cited in Gunning, 44). He was drawing on the aesthetic theory of the sublime developed by Edmund Burke in the mid-eighteenth century. Accounts of early cinema have much in common with discussions of the sublime in the way that the medium sets out to produce direct emotional and sensational effects on viewers. The comparison, however, has further ramifications for a discussion of Gothic shocks: the terrifying, overwhelming image activates an instinct of self-preservation that invigorates the mind's imaginative powers.

Early cinema, as it develops from nineteenth-century traditions of vaudeville illusionism and magic theatre, takes its bearings from late eighteenth-century entertainments making spectacular, and spectral, use of projection devices like the magic lantern and the camera obscura. Phantasmagoria, as they were called, referred to the illusionist exhibitions of images projected by these devices, and were described by Lawrence Sullivan in the *Gentleman's Magazine* of 1802, as 'dark rooms, where spectres from the dead they raise' (cited in Castle, 141). Much use was made of Gothic scenes and characters to produce supernatural and sensational effects: one performance, watched by William Nicholson in Edinburgh in 1802, presented 'various terrific figures, which instead of seeming to recede and then vanish, were (by enlargement) made suddenly to advance; to the surprise and astonishment of the audience' (cited in Castle, 150). The production of effects of terror and fear were central to the phantasmagorical shows. These technical effects, ostensibly designed to puncture superstitious credulity, never lost sight of the terrors that were closer to an enlightened and revolutionary present. Describing phantasmagoria in Paris, Louis-Sébastien Mercier wrote, 'the ghosts and spectres which we so enjoyed seeing conjured up in the theatres were the reflection of the revolutionary days' (cited in Hale, 13). Indeed, one of the principal showmen in Paris during the period – a Belgian inventor named Etienne-Gaspard Robertson – closed his shows with bloody spectres of Rousseau, Voltaire and Robespierre while delivering a gloomy parting speech: 'I have shown you the most occult things natural philosophy has to offer, effects that seemed supernatural to the ages of credulity, but now see the only real horror … see what is in store for all of you, what each of you will become one day' (cited in Castle, 19). The final image was the illuminated skeleton of a young woman on a pedestal, a memento mori in new technical guise. The morbid warning played directly upon general fears and anxieties of the time, its demystification of superstition simultaneously offering a veiled criticism of political idealism and illusions.

Phantasmagoria became readily associated with the phantasms of disordered consciousness. By means of technical effects, phantasmagorical shows participated in a process which saw the internalisation of supernaturalism: ghosts moved from being effects of mere optical trickery and illusion to being things of the mind. Castle calls this process 'spectralisation': the 'absorption of ghosts into the world of thought' (142). Technical models allow ghosts to be explained as mechanical effects of internal processes. But though clever deployments of new visual technologies seemed to offer rational explanations and models of mental activity and transformed the understanding of the mind, a residue of supernaturalism and ghostliness haunted the technical devices themselves: able to present apparitions to incredulous eyes, the wondrous but disconcerting, pleasurable and threatening effects of phantasmagoria testified to the technical capacity of altering one's sense of reality, contravening the maxim that seeing was believing.

Phantasmagoria did simply present terrifying images and evoke shocking effects with greater immediacy than Gothic fictions in a spectacular technical improvement on written communication. Less reliant on narrative, they offer some insight into the techniques employed in, and effects produced by, Gothic fictions and endorse eighteenth-century critical descriptions of supernatural devices as 'machinery', an assembly of techniques designed to produce mechanical effects on the newly emerging – and less cultivated – population of readers. A review of the first Gothic novel, Horace Walpole's *The Castle of Otranto*, makes this position plain: 'those who can digest the absurdities of Gothic fiction and bear with the machinery of ghosts and goblins, may hope, at least, for considerable entertainment from the performance before us' (cited in McNutt, 163). Clara Reeve also comments on the violence of Walpole's 'machinery' and describes the effects of his extravagant fiction in terms of a mechanical metaphor: the reader's 'expectation is wound up', she writes, 'to the highest pitch' (Reeve, 4–5). Radcliffe's method of maintaining a reader's interest and heightening suspense was compared in mechanical terms: 'it has,' Coleridge noted, 'been brought to perfection along with the reader's sagacity; just as the various inventions of locks, bolts and private drawers, in order to secure, fasten, hide, have always kept pace with the ingenuity of the pickpockets and housebreaker, whose profession it is to unlock, unfasten, and lay open what you have taken so much pains to conceal' (Coleridge, 1794: 361). The analogy, making the novelist little more than an artisan and the reader little better than a thief, turns the art of fiction into the craft of home security. It also implies a mechanical process of habituation and innovation at work: the writer must continually invent new tricks and devices in order to keep the reader properly shocked and amused.

The critical focus on the gothic techniques designed to maintain mystery and suspense is developed a few years later in a review of Radcliffe's last novel:

It might for a time afford an acceptable variety to persons whose reading is confined to works of fiction, and who would, perhaps be glad to exchange dullness for extravagance; but it was probable that, as its constitution (if we may so speak) was maintained only be the passion of terror, and was excited by trick, and as it was not conversant in incidents and characters of a natural complex, it would degenerate into repetition, and would disappoint curiousity. So many cries, that 'the wolf is coming!' must at last lose their effect. (Coleridge, 1798: 166)

Coleridge's criticism of the defects of Radcliffe's machinery echoes general attacks on the formulaic, repetitive and sensational patterns of Gothic writing throughout the period. For Coleridge, however, the defects are bound up with the mechanical features of the genre and provide the basis for an important statement of literary value: in the *Biographia Literaria* he attacks 'devotees of the circulating libraries' and their indulgence in fiction as 'beggarly daydreaming' in which:

> the whole *material* and imagery of the doze is supplied *ab extra* by a sort of *mental camera obscura* manufactured at the printing office, which *pro tempore* fixes, reflects and transmits the moving fantasms of one man's delirium, so as to people the barrenness of an hundred other brains afflicted with the same trance or suspension of all common sense and all definite purpose. (1975: 28, original emphasis)

The absence of active and informed reading or a synthesising imagination is the issue here. Popular fiction enacts its own phantasmagoria in a process whereby artificial writing techniques replicate the mechanical functions of empty brains. Such a practice of reading falls below the threshold of the activity Coleridge wishes to promote as cultivated understanding: it is incapable of appreciating the unifying power of the poetic imagination. The image of a mechanised process of reading and writing – reduced to a circulation of unconscious stimuli – provides the inverted form of proper and valued literary production and appreciation.

Coleridge's criticisms of Gothic devices and their merely sensational effects on an uncultivated readership none the less offer a suggestive interpretation of their function in Radcliffe's fiction. What Coleridge does not credit is the manner in which the very mechanisms of Gothic narrative that he deplores may operate to purposeful effect in the fiction and, perhaps, also work in the service guiding readers to more varied and uplifting forms of literature. In this respect, Radcliffe's novels can be seen as popular fiction written with the design of counteracting the more distracting effects of popular fiction, precisely because of, rather than despite, the defects Coleridge criticises: to repeatedly excite a reader's expectations and curiosity to a level where gratification can only be disappointed serves to deploy techniques of suspense and illusory superstition against the reader's credulity. This strategy is noted, albeit critically, in his review of *The Mysteries of Udolpho*: 'curiosity is kept upon the stretch from page to page, and from volume to volume, and the secret, which the reader thinks himself every instant on the point of penetrating, flies like a phantom before him, and eludes his eagerness till the very moment of protracted expectation' (1794: 361). Curiosity, the wish to know, is the desire wound up by narrative techniques. The game of desire in offering and withholding the answer to mysteries, in teasing the reader with spectral secrets, does not necessarily provide satisfaction: it wears it out rather than gives it an outlet, exhausting desire and interest by stimulating it to excess: 'curiosity is raised oftener than it is gratified; or rather, it is raised so high that no adequate gratification can be given it; the interest is completely dissolved once the adventure is finished, and the reader, when he is got to the end of the work looks about in vain for the spell which had bound him strongly to it' (362). This model of reading based on the gratification of appetites and an indulgence in superstitious enchantment, a model in which as soon as texts are consumed all interest and imaginative effect is used up, may be part of Radcliffe's fictional strategy: to separate readers into a lower class caught up in sensation, thrills and passions and a more sober, rational class attentive to higher moral and aesthetic values. Playing desire against desire, even to the point of exhaustion, thus performs a practical counteraction of its elusive and illusionary appeal in which the reader is captured and strung out at the expense of satisfaction and sensational enjoyment.

The charged imbalance of pleasure and unpleasure nonetheless remains difficult to sustain. On the one hand, too readily sated, desire is expended in a speedy return to equilibrium and thus to a decline in sensation and excitement requiring further repetition of the pattern; on the other hand, extenuated too far, widening the gap between expectation and outcome, desire is worn out by its impossibility, consumed by the gap separating demand from delivery. Repeated too regularly, of course, both strategies slide into predictable and familiar patterns which elicit only boredom, another sign of the extinction of desire. Radcliffe's putative reader, captured by techniques of terror and suspense and worn out in the process, is a figure representative of the imagined audience for Gothic fiction as a whole in the 1790s. Pointing out the limitations of fictional formulas and techniques, Coleridge states that as a genre 'maintained only by the passion of terror, and excited by trick, and as it was not conversant in incidents and characters of natural complexion, it would degenerate into repetition, and would disappoint curiosity' (1798: 166–9). The evocation of wild passions and false excitements, repeated too much, disillusion the reader.

Reiterating shocks and sensational incident merely habituates the reader, exhausting rather than stimulating excitement. Fictional techniques thus enact or perform the stated moral of Radcliffe's novels in warning against – and wearing out – excessive and dangerous flights of superstitious fancy. Shocks in the stories, repeated and intensified at the level of technique, seem designed to expunge violent energies and return the reader to subjective and social equilibrium. In this way, standard criticisms of Gothic fiction are incorporated by Radcliffe into her own novels. Radcliffe's defects, the apparent failures of her narrative technique, turn out, ironically, to be marks of success. Indeed, one attack on the formulaic and repetitive features of 'terrorist novel writing' makes this strategy explicit: 'every absurdity has an end; and as I observe that almost all novels are of the terrific cast, I hope the insipid repetition of the same bugbears will at length work a cure'(Anon., 1797a: 229). Repetition contains the basis of a cure. Radcliffe's repetition of supernatural imaginings and disillusioning techniques seems to provide a cure for their own shocks. The process may even transform the revolutionary shocks of the period into aesthetic thrills possessing their own mechanical momentum.

The reader who emerges from the process, worn out perhaps, does not necessarily emerge feeling instructed; nor has she/he necessarily cast off sensational appetites. One reviewer suggests that through repetitive exposure to familiar formulas, effects and disappointments, readers will ultimately tire of the genre completely, and undergo some sort of learning experience:

> The horrible and the preternatural have usually seized on the popular taste, at the rise and decline of literature. Most powerful stimulants, they can never be required except by the torpor of an unawakened, or the languor of an exhausted, appetite. The same phenomenon, therefore, which we hail as a favourable omen in the belles lettres of Germany, impresses a degree of gloom in the compositions of our countrymen. We trust, however, that satiety will banish what good sense should have prevented; and that, wearied with fiends, incomprehensible characters, with shrieks, murders, and subterranean dungeons, the public will learn, by the multitude of the manufacturers, with how little expense of thought or imagination this species of composition is manufactured. (Anon., 1797c: 194)

What is strange about the argument is not that, through excess passion, stimulation and sensation, readers learn the higher values of thought and imagination, or, even, that repetition sates an appetite for sensation and diminishes the thrilling effects of Gothic shocks, but that weariness and boredom form the conditions for the emergence of the fiction in the first place. An originary repetition seems to be at work: an unawakened or exhausted appetite precedes the repetitive fictions whose overstimulation then enacts a second process of exhaustion.

The critic awaiting the decline of tales of terror and the return to proper aesthetic values was, it seems, indulging in rather wishful thinking. Though the formulas for Gothic fictions in the mould of Walpole, Radcliffe and Lewis were only repeated in large numbers until the end of the first decade of the nineteenth century, the writing and popularity of sensational stories carried on with new figures of terror and horror and new devices to elicit them. Indeed, shocks, cheap thrills and terrific spectacles become increasingly important in the production of popular fictions. Critical confidence that repetition would exhaust the popular readers' taste for shocks and horrors, seems, with the hindsight of over two hundred years' worth of fictional, dramatic and cinematic terrors, overly optimistic. Though a certain type of formulaic Gothic fiction declined in popularity, the critics of the time underestimated the technical capacity to invent new techniques of terror. Indeed, the hope that empty mechanical repetition would cede to a fuller and more cultivated appreciation of literature did not envisage the force of technological innovation and the developments that could produce an escalating array of shocks, sensation and thrills – in books, on stage and, later, on screens – to satisfy a ravenous popular taste that was easy to feed if difficult to control.

## Reading machines

Though particular formulas fade, the association between Gothic fictions and technical innovations persists over two centuries. As a literary term, 'machinery' predates the Gothic genre, one element of the discursive conditions that inform critical judgements. Not only is the genre repeatedly described as being mechanical in form and effect, its various manifestations in different media – fiction, drama, photography, film – suffuse those media with ghostly associations. As the industrial age developed new engines of all kinds, technological developments, powerful, life-changing, monstrous, frightening, became charged with Gothic intensity. Uncanny effects were evoked and recorded, the mark of disturbing encounters with mechanisms that mimicked or surpassed human capabilities. Such triumphs of human ingenuity and invention, like the railway described by Dickens, were simultaneously signs of the progress of reason and awful threats to older beliefs and practices. Transformed and dominated by machines, modernity was completely at home with its inventions.

Strange and unfamiliar, new machines seemed to possess supernatural or magic powers even though the rational and secular age that produced them banished superstition and spirits from its material and mechanistic world order. An excess once located in heavenly or hellish dimensions is relocated on the borders of mechanistic models of natural life: artificial, inhuman, machines take on diabolical connotations; at the same time, in Romanticism, humans find solace and spirit in a deified Nature. But reason and mechanism exert more pervasive pressure on understandings of supernatural phenomena: these are no longer otherworldly, from a different dimension, but are explained in rational terms as disorders of mental functioning, tricks of the eye or brain, irruptions of irrational energy within a mind less able to maintain itself under the control of reason.

The uncanny, as defined at the end of the nineteenth century by Freud but explored in fiction throughout the period, marks the shift of 'supernatural' phenomena from an otherworldly to an intrapsychic realm. Ghosts and monsters become effects of mental processes and disturbances, effects of hallucination, delusion or delirium, rather than 'actual' supernatural entities. The unreal moves from a location outside the mind to haunt it from within. But there is a resulting tremor which destabilises distinctions between real and unreal worlds: ghosts were real in the manner in which they appeared in the world shaped by religious beliefs, sacred manifestations of higher forces. When ghosts are perceived as products of 'internal mental processes', hallucinatory disturbance has the effect of making them seem 'more real than ever before – in that they now occupied (even preoccupied) the intimate space of the mind itself' (Castle, 165). From a conjunction of spectres and spirituality, ghosts cross over, haunt and disorder the mind from within, making reality appear as much an internal effect as it is a physical order. The uncanny describes the disturbances, uncertainties and anxieties resulting from Things which do not stay in their place, where past returns on the present, death emerges within life, fantasy and reality overlap or inanimate objects come alive. In Freud's essay, the very word 'uncanny' ('*unheimlich*') undergoes all sorts of shifts in meaning, with words often turning into their polar opposite. Unfamiliar, disquieting, the uncanny, or un-homely, comes to be linked to the familiar comforts of home. 'Un-homely', via associations with secrecy and being hidden, comes to mean both 'what is familiar and agreeable' and 'what is concealed and kept from sight' (Freud, 1955a: 224–5). Freud's resolution to the inversions of meaning is to regard the uncanny as that which 'ought to have remained secret and hidden but has come to light' (225). From this point a more developed psychoanalytic definition is introduced: it is defined as the recurrence or return of the repressed, 'in reality nothing new or alien, but something which is familiar and old-established in the mind and which has become alienated from it only through processes of repression' (241). The uncanny, furthermore, is 'easily produced when the distinction between imagination and reality is effaced' and 'occurs either when infantile complexes which have been repressed are once more revived by some impression or when primitive beliefs which have been surmounted seem once more to be confirmed' (244; 249). Relocated in the mind, the uncanny none the less continues to mark crossings between supposedly distinct realms, highlighting the insecurities, the ghostly dimensions, of mental life and the porosity of the boundaries framing human existence. Reason, curiously, in relocating ghosts as effects of irrational mental events, finds itself haunted: in disposing of ghostliness through invocations of irrationality, unreason returns upon reason as an after-effect or double effect. In Cartesian philosophy, for instance, the doubt crucial to the rationalistic method is engendered by a 'malignant demon'. Powerful and deceitful, the demon has used all his 'artifice' to trick the philosopher who, in his first meditation, must discount all external things and all sense evidence as 'nothing better than the illusions of dreams', traps set for credulity which the rational mind must penetrate in order to prove itself. In doubting all sense data, Descartes assumes he will avoid falsity (Descartes, 1981: 84). Demons, dreams, credulity, the stuff of irrationality, work doubly at the start of rationalism, snares to be guarded against even as they provide the initial condition – doubt – which is the foil that enables reasoning to proceed. The uncanny, it seems, functions as the ghost of reason. It emerges as the age of reason's 'toxic side effect' (Castle, 8). Casting ghosts from the material world and into the materiality of mind, reason remains subject to haunting: the rational human subject is defined and disturbed by unconscious processes and mechanisms. Neither the external world nor the inner recesses of mind are immune from strange machinations. Things and thoughts refuse to stay in place.

The uncanny, an effect of crossing and reversals, signals the disturbance and simultaneously marks out limits: reason, unreason, inside, outside, nature, supernature and machines become entangled. Language provides the initial locus for both uncanny crossings and definitions. Freud's long lexical introduction discussing the meaning of the word 'uncanny' is significant in this respect: definitions, orderings of oppositions and meanings are, in the etymological exercise of analysing the word, rendered uncanny, with proper meanings confounded and occluded senses brought to light. Language, an external system that, in constituting speaking beings, is internalised, is, itself, something of an automaton, a technology exterior and yet intimate to subjectivity, defining and deforming identity according to the directions of symbolic structures (Lacan, 1988b; Bataille, 1955; Stiegler). Freud, in moving from lexical concerns to discuss the psychological implications of the uncanny in Hoffman's 'The Sandman', concentrates on the return of infantile wishes and anxieties, relating them to the story's images of blinding associated with fears of castration. Freud's argument, in discounting the significance of the female automaton, Olympia, ostensibly in refutation of Ernst Jentsch's association of the uncanny with 'intellectual uncertainty', also represses the figure of woman and the machine. Although excluded from the realm of the uncanny, both women and machines, however, force psychoanalysis to encounter the spectre of castration: it is the 'lack' manifested by female genitalia that, in the castration complex, enables the oedipal shift from hating to identifying with the father. In mimicking human appearance and movement, automata threaten human self-identity; in exceeding human capacities, machines threaten man's fantasised superiority. Both materialise a (castrating) limit to man's imagined powers. Language, too, in subjecting an individual to an order that is Other to him/her, causes a kind of castration, separating biological being with its wishes and instincts, from the meanings, morals and messages shaping cultured identity.

Bound up with language and mechanisms (machines and mental processes), the uncanny is, in many ways, a technological phenomenon whose effects are accentuated by the shifts and disturbances of technical innovation. Its domain extends beyond the return of infantile beliefs alone: it circulates in the telling of stories, the reading of books, the seeing of images. Gothic fictions cannot be simply put down as merely mechanistic, formulaic and low cultural aberrations, despite the critical reiteration of mechanical metaphors to describe the effects of romances on undiscriminating readers whose minds work mechanically. The burgeoning of metaphors that entangle minds, machines and mysteries is not held in check by the variety of media which generate uncanny effects. Castle's account of the supernaturalisation of everyday life in the mediated process of rendering consciousness spectral discloses a more complex dynamic. The focus on consciousness, albeit often rendered strange by machines, places mind at the centre of her history of the uncanny. Perhaps some stranger process is at work, one that suggests that machines precede mind. For Castle, mechanical models serve reason's understanding of the mind: mechanism explains hitherto hidden internal mental processes. Here the supernatural is not only internalised and subordinated to mental mechanisms: giving mechanical form to the world of thought and explaining it in mechanistic terms also makes internal life visible through models and metaphors. Mental mysteries are brought to light by mechanical and supernatural metaphors.

The process of explaining and making visible does not arrest the generation of uncanny effects; reason does not manage to explain away ghosts: even if they are phantasmatic tricks of the brain they are perceived to be no less real. Another process, it seems, accompanies the inward momentum of rational enquiry: secular internalisations of the supernatural, transforming it into a mechanical effect, also reshape interior space through a process of externalisation, of rendering mind visible in terms of mechanical metaphors. Understood as a mechanism, a hallucinatory projection akin to that of a magic lantern, the inner workings of consciousness are brought to view, internal processes projected outwards. The uncanny, again disturbing borders of interiority and exteriority, confounding fantasy life and psychic reality testing, seeps out from the bounds of solitary minds in much the same as it entered them – by way of machines. Seeping from isolated minds, to the minds of others and by way of other media and mechanisms, the mobility of the uncanny again comes to the fore.

The supernatural enters in, mechanism is brought out. And vice versa. The process remains unstable, its movement linked only to unfixed poles of oscillation and circulating within a network of metaphors and overlapping associations. Emptied of soul or spirit, the mind is filled with ghosts or mere mechanisms. Externalised as mechanical process, mental contents can be manipulated by technical effects. Houses may be haunted, repositories of guilt and sin impersonating mental workings. Machines come to be possessed by demons monstrously simulating the powers of human thought and action. Objects and commodities, like dolls, assume supernatural agency; people behave automatically, lumbering like zombies. Images leap from their frames. Through fictional and media techniques, the uncanny spreads, located among collective and cultural spaces rather than individual interiors. Attracting associations with or projections of supernatural and uncanny phenomena, machines themselves assume the power to generate Gothic effects, spreading a sense of uncanniness still further afield. As modernity finds itself increasingly dominated by media of its own making, it, too, becomes suffused with an uncanny phantasmagorical aura.

Machines persist in Gothic fiction, media and criticism, the term 'machinery' in particular predating the appearance of the genre itself while, in respect of novels, establishing the conditions of production and reception. Machinery referred to contrivances of plot, to the introduction of magical or supernatural agents or devices into fiction, poetry or drama. In the latter, stage sets, pulleys and trap doors contrived the spectacular entrances or exits of ghosts and demons. In fiction or poetry a 'machine' described the introduction of any improbable event or 'supernatural agent' into the plot. In the eighteenth century, as the novel was beginning to distinguish itself from both ancient and modern romance, the use of supernatural devices was considered inappropriate. Henry Fielding, devoting a whole chapter of *Tom Jones* to a discussion of 'supernatural agents', questions the propriety and effectiveness of ghostly machinations in realism. He even wishes that Homer had followed Horace's rule 'to introduce supernatural agents as seldom as possible' rather than have his gods sent 'on trivial errands' (Fidding, 316). For the moderns, Fielding cautions, the rule should be strictly adhered to: 'the only supernatural agents which can in any manner be allowed to us moderns, are ghosts'. And even then, only sparingly: 'these are indeed, like arsenic, and other dangerous drugs in physic, to be used with the utmost caution' (316). Fielding is not alone in his opinion. Samuel Richardson concurred: 'I hate so much the French Marvellous and all unnatural Machinery, and have so often been disgusted with this sort of Management' (Richardson, 51–2). 'Machinery' forms one of the coordinates for the attack on romances so common in the eighteenth century. Improbable, artificial, absurd, unnatural, monstrous, romances were constructed as the antithesis of the emerging novel. As the polar opposite to the novel composed according to rules of realism and probability, romance provided the negative against which to measure value and success: where novels aimed to promote virtue, reason and duty, romances indulged in vice, passion and licentiousness. In this context, it is no surprise that one of the first reviews of *Otranto*, although relatively benignly, commented on its 'machinery of ghosts and goblins'.

Several shifts in the meaning of 'machinery' are manifested later in the eighteenth century as Romanticism begins to find neoclassical, Augustan compositions too formal and artificial. Machinery remains as a term critical of contrived conventions and formulas, but the materialism with which it is imbued allows for the reappearance of spirit, a spirit associated with Romantic Nature. Coleridge, in his criticism of Radcliffe and romances in general sets the terms for the re-evaluation. James Hogg draws a distinct line between the ineffectual and increasingly banal formulas of romance haunting and a more powerful Romantic sense of spirit. In an exchange on ghosts and fiction written in 1826, he satirises the implausibility of supernatural tales. One speaker in his dialogue comments that he 'never had any professed feeling of the super or preter-natural in a printed book'. The reason for this, he goes on, was finding out the background to a story of a ghost 'who had kept me in a cold sweat during a whole winter's midnight': it was the spirit of an enamoured and hungry tailor who wished only for a fat ham sandwich, a bottle of beer and kiss from his beloved nurse. 'After that I slept soundly', the speaker notes, having retained only 'a contempt for ghosts' (Wilson, 200–1). Familiarity with formulas has bred contempt. Real life ghosts, indeed, already seem overly familiar figures in a domestic romance. The supernatural, in the manner of Radcliffe, is explained: ghostly effects are banished to the realm of comic improbability, thoroughly tamed by domestic life and habits and divested of any trace of terror. Supernatural machinery has worn itself out through repetition.

Hogg's discussion of the banality of 'real' ghosts and fictional 'traditionary terrors' does admit another kind of haunting, one that is less concerned with spectres and more invested in discovering a sense of Spirit:

> Indeed, I canna say that I ever fan' mysel alane in the hush o'darkened nature without a beatin at my heart; for a' sort o' spiritual presence aye hovered about me – a presence o' something like and unlike my ain being – at times to be felt solemn and nae mair – at times sae awfu' that I wushed myself nearer ingle-licht – and ance or twice on my lifetime, sae terrible that I could hae prayed to sink down into the moss, sae that I micht be saved frae quaking o' that ghostly wilderness o' a world that was na for flesh and bluid. (Wilson, 201)

Sublime, numinous, awful, the intimations of 'spiritual presence' are thoroughly Romantic, a haunting in tune with a Wordsworthian appreciation of the spirit of Nature. Ghostliness of this kind, unlike the shocks and horrors of fiction, is terrible and wondrous: it tells of a more humanistic spirituality in which the individual mind is elevated and expanded. Divinity, not mechanism, lies within as much as without, the sacred is internalised at the same time Nature is spiritualised. Romantic, as opposed to romantic, ghosts are disclosed by poetic feeling and imagination, part of a communion rendering the inner realm of subjectivity more sensitive and profound. Materiality is held at bay as the spiritual dimensions of Nature are disclosed: banal ghosts, common spectres and haunting are surpassed in the approximation of religious experience which, further, valorises Romanticism's investment in individual creativity and consciousness. Its faith in the higher powers of mind and Nature encodes a spirituality that is felt to be lacking in overly rationalistic and materialistic perspectives of an increasingly secular and industrial eighteenth century.

Material, rational, repetitive, formulaic and now soulless, the machinery of Gothic fiction remains an object of criticism, held more firmly in its place by Romantic aesthetics' insistence on spirit, organicism, creativity and spontaneity. The Romantic frame informs criticism of Gothic fiction for over a century. In 1833, Thomas Babbington Macaulay's extended examination of Walpole and his work is critical of all the superficialities, indulgences and artifices on display. Walpole deals in 'charms', 'baubles',

'curiosities' (Macaulay, 144–15). All is decoration, luxury, style and surface, all without substance: the work does not appeal to reason, imagination or the heart. It is mere entertainment, an idle distraction grabbing a
reader's attention. Though the 'machinery' remains 'absurd' and 'human
actors' are never more than 'insipid', Macaulay concedes that the work is
never dull, skipping along with its excitements and spectacular occurrences
(117). Traditional distinctions between a cultivated, discriminating reader
and the masses seeking thrills, adventures, romance, are replayed. Aesthetic hierarchies divide high and low culture and insist that Gothic fictions remain very much the diet of an unimaginative and appetitive popu-
lace seeking entertainment and excitement rather than art or instruction.
The metaphor of machinery provides the mechanism for maintaining critical judgement, repeated regularly, habitually, mechanically until the middle
of the twentieth century: the mechanistic and formulaic features of the
Gothic genre are reiterated as 'unwieldy machinery' (Scarborough, 39);
'supernatural machinery' (Birkhead, 19); 'conventional machinery' (Summers, 23).

Walter Scott, at the same time as Hogg was debunking ghosts, offered
several reappraisals of romantic and supernatural fiction which consoli-
dated the use of mechanical metaphors to criticise repetitive and conventional formulas. He charted significant shifts in ways in which mechanical
terms were employed. His account of Radcliffe, though partly favourable,
echoes Coleridge and critics of the late eighteenth century. Radcliffe's narrative techniques are discussed in mechanical terms: the feelings of suspense she excites are awakened by means of 'springs which lie open, indeed, to the first touch, but which are peculiarly liable to be worn out by
repeated pressure. The public soon, like Macbeth, becomes satiated with
horrors, and indifferent to the strongest stimuli of that kind' (Scott, 1824:
566). Habituated to mechanical conventions, readers will become bored,
inured to the shocks and stimuli Gothic devices employ. Hence, Scott
notes in a subsequent essay, 'the effect of the supernatural in its more
obvious application is easily exhausted' (1881: 276). Though 'great magicians' are able to raise spectres 'amidst the shadowy and indistinct light so
favourable to the exhibition of phantasmagoria', romance writers fail to
unravel satisfactorily the complex threads of adventures they have woven
together (1824: 567). The 'supernatural machinery', though relevant to
an age of superstition is deemed less effective or pertinent in a period of
'universal incredulity' (568). For Scott, the supernatural becomes increasingly anachronistic, not only as a result of the repetitions of Gothic techniques, but in terms of cultural changes wrought by Enlightenment
progress:

> Men cannot but remark that (since the scriptural miracles have ceased,) the belief in prodigies and supernatural events has gradually declined in proportion to the advancement of human knowledge; and that since the age has become enlightened, the occurrence of tolerably attested anecdotes of the supernatural characters are so few, as to render it more probable that the witnesses have laboured under some strange and temporary delusion, rather than that the laws of nature have been altered or suspended. (1881: 272)

While, in Scott's estimation, ghosts have been exorcised and dispelled by secular rationality, their concerted persistence in the fictions and popular lore of the early nineteenth century calls for an alternative explanation: they must be things of the mind, symptoms of disordered consciousness, signs of delusion and mental breakdown. Scott again echoes Coleridge's criticism of romances, seeing them foster the spread of a delirium from writer to reader, causing a derangement of the senses through mechanical, and therefore explicable means rather than by supernatural intervention.

As ghosts move inwards, mechanically disordered consciousness becomes a standard mode of explaining spectral occurrences. Rationality, machines and troubled consciousness, however, are also implicated in the production of ghosts, providing new modes of technical trickery that both explain away and conjure up spectral events. For Scott, this ambivalence has political and cultural ramifications. Discussing the merits of Radcliffe's explained supernatural, he notes many incidents 'the mysterious obscurity of which has afterwards been explained by deception and confederacy'. Retrospectively, as with Radcliffe's technique, reason explains all superstition in terms of trickery or hallucination:

> Such have been the impostures of superstition in all ages; and such delusions were also practised by members of the Secret Tribunal, in the middle ages, and in more modern times by the Rosicrucians and Illuminati, upon whose machinations Schiller has founded the fine romance of *The Ghost-Seer*. (1824: 569)

Machinations do not occur as a result of divine or diabolical manipulation, but through the interventions of secretive and conspiratorial human hands. Reason, like Descartes' demon, has the capacity to darken, obfuscate and misdirect as much as enlighten. The techniques it employs, its machinations, can produce seemingly supernatural effects without any aid from a supernatural power. In the post-revolutionary period in which Scott writes, such capacities continue in terrifying and monstrous form. Popular accounts of the origins and causes of the Revolution in France, like those by Abbé Barruel, Robison and Edmund Burke, had, on the basis of more imagination than evidence, laid the blame for revolutionary ferment at the door of secret societies, like the Rosicrucians and the Illuminati. Like a Gothic novelist, but writing on a far larger page, these conspirators had the power to enflame passions beyond the control of reason and incite behaviour of the most monstrous kind. In a similar vein, Matthias castigated Gothic fiction for arousing 'gallic frenzy' in its readers: in this guise the 'great engine' of literature worked in a subversive rather than conservative manner. Identifying the cause of Revolution with a small group of mysterious conspirators served, if not as a rationalisation of the event, as a conservative story of its inauthentic origins as a popular revolt: having been incited to frenzy by malicious plotters, the masses had been duped, played like puppets by a deceitful few. Revolutionary enthusiasm was thereby contained: secret societies, the Iluminati, perhaps, or the Rosicrucians, isolated and demonised, were the cause of illegitimate uprising, devious reason manipulating popular irrationality.

The link between Gothic machinery and cruelly rational and conspiratorial machinations is forged in the Marquis of Grosse's novel of the 1790s, translated from the German by Peter Will under the title of *Horrid Mysteries* (1796). The translator's preface sets the context for the fiction in its discussion of secret societies and the way that 'all these associations, avowedly instituted for the improvement of mankind, either in piety, knowledge, or felicity, generally deceived the sanguine expectations of those that suffered themselves to be ensnared by the imposing veil of mysteriousness, which, at bottom, was nothing better than a cloak of their defects, and of the private, selfish views of their founders (Grosse, xv). He cites Baron de Knigge's critical comments on secret associations, made after leaving the 'Illuminators'. The Baron strenuously points out the dangers of these societies in purveying 'noxious doctrines' and misinforming their own members: the secrecy under which such societies are cloaked meant that '*unknown* Superiors frequently direct the whole institution by secret machinations' (xvii). The tangled plot of the novel sets out to demonstrate the scale of deceptions and pernicious deeds perpetrated by secret associations, charting their external, if obscure, machinations and their psychological effects. Much play is made of ghosts and machines. But, throughout the novel, the noises, lights and ghostly figures engendering superstitious and shocked reactions, are all disclosed as deceptions ultimately designed to dispel superstitious credulity.

In one sequence of events, the hero, Don Carlos, is awoken by a strange light in his chamber: 'little clouds of light floated in the air, moving to and fro; and I beheld, with horror, streams of sparkling fire dart through the apartment.' Lights, the vibration of low accents and ghastly groans intensify the horror as a 'thin vapour' rose from the floor. A figure, declaring itself to by 'thy Genius, Amanuel' approaches the bed to deliver a ghastly warning (85–6). It goes unheeded. On the day of the hero's planned elopement, the lovers are pursued by 'hissing and whistling', falling chandeliers and bright illuminations. They escape. But another ghost returns several pages later, 'a human form, encircled with a milk white light', a ghastly, disfigured and bloody appearance. This time, however, convinced this is 'no airy phantom', there is a struggle in which the 'ghost' is mortally wounded (119–20). Much later the first apparition is revealed as Don Carlos's servant and, unknown to him, his uncle. Incognito, the uncle explains that not only was he protecting his nephew from the machinations of the secret confederation, he was also its director, responsible for admitting him in the first place!

The cruel machinations, ghostly and otherwise, that have tormented the hero and excited the reader are explicitly addressed in subsequent reflections on events. Any hint of real ghostliness is discounted as occurrences are rationally explained:

> I was no stranger to the artifices wrought through natural magic; and also not ignorant what a powerful influence a heated, overflowing, and transported imagination produces on our senses. The whole now appeared to me a mere scarecrow for children. The mystic farce was continued too long, and afterwards betrayed the whole confederacy. The mysterious veil was removed from that memorable moment, and my imagination being rectified by cool reflection, the miserable artifices of the confederates rather filled me with contempt than with awe. (200)

'Natural magic', the art of smoke and mirrors, has replaced anything supernatural: mere technical artifice has enabled ghostly effects to be produced. That, of course, and the projections of unrestrained imagination. The supernatural is shown to be thoroughly mechanical in its external physical manifestations and in its subjective effects: 'heated', 'overflowing', the imagination has caused a temporary derangement of the senses. After the pause for rational reflection, the story resumes, not as an account of 'supernatural agents' and their diabolical plots, but as an unmasking of 'secret agents' and their devious schemes.

As if a definitive statement about the deceptive effects of natural magic on susceptible and overheated imaginations was not enough, the novel goes on to offer an extended comic performance of the technical trickery involved in exciting superstition into outright terror. The burlesque begins with a party game: participants are dared to enter a haunted room ('haunted' by disguised burglars) and develops into a full-blown charade designed to ridicule the credulity and cowardice of one of the companions.

A complicated and highly theatrical trick requires a chandelier to be suspended in a darkened chapel and covered with sulphur and pitch, servants breaking glass, opening and closing doors, imitating cats, blowing bellows and whistling. It also employs an 'electrical machine' emitting 'whole streams of fire' and figures 'dressed like devils', garments coated with streaks of phosphorus, their hands holding claws. Evoking as much laughter as fear, the burlesque is brought to a suitably farcical conclusion in the 'mutual terror' caused by an interruption: 'a man, clad in a white robe, armed with a large cross and carrying a lanthorn, stept forth' (217). The arrival of the local pastor and the Spirit he represents, scatters the spectres. The comedy serves to underline the story's observations on the foolishness of superstitious credulity. It also demonstrates and demystifies the mechanics and techniques for generating terror.

While reason seems to prevail in the novel's unmasking of devices of supernatural agency and magic, the reverberations of relocating spectral effects in technical devices and psychological disturbance (an overheated imagination) produce new fields for persecution and terror, along with a new understanding of affect. The pursuit of the hero is seen to be as much psychological as it is physical, in the manner that two years earlier, Godwin's Caleb Williams had found himself under the sway of imagined as much as actual persecution. The mind becomes an arena of ghostliness, haunted by internally created spectres that are difficult to dispel. In *Horrid Mysteries*, Don Carlos bemoans the impossibility of finding asylum: there is 'no place where thou are not surrounded by the myrmidons of those fiend-like Unknown'. His imagination has given the secret society demonic form. He goes on to note that their snares are everywhere: his speculation on the new forms of torment, entrapment and delusion they will impose on him indicates that the traps are planted in his mind as well: 'thou wilt catch a phantom of thy own fancy, when thinking to be near the butt of thy pursuit, and the laboursome structure of thy presumptuous wit will miserably sink down into its own pit' (105). The imagined power of the society grows in relation to the secrecy in which it is cloaked.

That mere artifices and machinations can have such devastating internal effects is part of the horror, a horror shared by commentators on the French Revolution. Though ghosts and spectres are demystified, their internalisation introduces a limit and challenge to the sway of reason: irrationality and mental disturbance show that the mind is never fully under the control of reason. Nor is the body, though it is increasingly understood in mechanistic terms. A romantic interlude towards the end of the novel contrasts a world of imagined spirits with the material realities perceived by scientific understanding: the scene presents the hero indulging his imagination by transforming the mist rising from a pond 'into spirits celebrating their nocturnal revels'. His beloved quietly approaches and touches him: 'an expected electric stroke could not have surprised me more violently' (332). Shocked back down to earth by physical presence, the hero is placed between a flight of imagination and mechanical materiality: human agency and reason is nowhere to be seen, displaced by a flight of fancy on the one hand and an involuntary force on the other. The electrical metaphor is telling, given the story's earlier emphasis on the role of an electrical machine in the generation of comic supernatural effects: there, the machine formed part of an elaborate artifice demonstrating the ease with which magical effects and superstitious terror could be technically produced. With the electrical shock being applied directly to the body, mechanism, it seems, can bypass mind entirely: there is no need for the cool reflection of reason to dispel ghosts from an overheated imagination, the injection of significant energy fulfils the task sufficiently.

## Phantasmagoria

Supernatural machinery and agency were on the wane in the 1790s. Mechanisms of the body and the mind came to the fore in the production and circulation of fictions whose conventions and topics engaged with natural and technical magic. A significant shift in the 'machinery' of fiction itself is evinced. Judith Wilt, discussing the machines of literary convention and contrivance that shape fiction in the eighteenth century, notes how 'machinery', in Walpole, 'spreads from its locus in plot to encompass character and even sentiment' (Wilt, 123). With Radcliffe another mechanical convention is added, that of setting. These formulas and their subsequent transformations, in Godwin's detective plot, Shelley's science fiction and Scott's historical romance, 'may, like machinery in factories, greatly facilitate the progress of fiction' (125). Machinery, it appears, breeds more machines. Supernatural agency is transformed into natural magic, older formulas eclipsed by the new ghosts raised by reason, science and Romanticism. In *Frankenstein*, for instance, older formulas disappear: there are no Gothic castles and evil aristocrats, nor any hint of the supernatural. Artificial creation is produced by scientific endeavour and technique, along with Romantic imagining. With its allusions to readings of the French Revolution (Victor's University, Ingolstadt, is supposedly the birthplace of the founder of the Illuminati), its references to alchemy and science, its location in modern Geneva, the novel dispenses with older Gothic trappings. It extrapolates upon the recently discovered potential of electricity, discussions of which, so the 1831 Introduction belatedly notes, informed the production of the novel in the first place. A scientific phenomenon and site of great Romantic speculation as a universal principle of life, electrical energy is infused with almost supernatural possibility. Almost: associated with the imagination, the supernatural is absorbed within a critical Romanticisation of Nature; the scientist, fantastically, unleashes natural secrets and powers that, in supplanting natural patterns, return to haunt the creator. Any magic is an effect of natural and mental processes as the ensuing drama between Frankenstein and monster elaborates: guilt, fear, fantasy and disappointment shapes the double relationship between them as, in part, a psychomachia, an internalised battle of creative and destructive components.

If the composition of the novel gives rise to a new mode, a new machine of literary production in which mental and natural processes replace feudal settings and supernatural agency, there are few descriptions in the novel of the mechanisms of scientific practice and invention. Only the 1831 Introduction, with its discussions of galvanism, foregrounds scientific technique over the imaginative possibilities played up by the story. The Introduction, moreover, discusses the frightful idea of the scientist's efforts 'to mock the stupendous mechanism of the Creator of the world'. While this comment accords with the theme of presumption attributed to the story by stage adaptations produced between the first publication and the 1831 edition of the novel, the verb also implies that derision is directed at the divinity, a Promethean deviance enacted in the human simulation of godlike and mechanistic powers. God, it seems, has been thrown out of the machine. For La Mettrie, Jacques de Vaucanson, inventor of numerous automata, seemed on the brink of achieving the impossible and creating a talking machine: it was, in the hands of a new Prometheus, a perfectly conceivable idea (La Mettrie, 69). Voltaire had already spoken of Vaucanson as a 'rival' to Prometheus (Dolar, 17).

Despite the minimal references to machines, Frankenstein and monster become rapidly associated with modernity's often disastrous technical interventions in nature. Political cartoons, concerned with the implications of the Reform Bill, employ the novel's principal characters in warnings about unleashing a democratic monster. 'The Political Frankenstein' of 1832 depicts a gowned scientist animating a paper monster, the Bill itself, with the help of bellows and chemical apparatus (Forry, 45). Frankenstein's (and, of course, the monster's) life, beyond the covers of a literary fiction, assumes an excessive and mechanical energy of its own as the metaphor spreads out of control. The novel was readily adapted for the stage in the

1820s. In burlesques and melodramas the moral and religious scandal of the story was played up with supernatural effects, pyrotechnically or mechanically-produced illusions, smoke, mirrors and trap doors inducing superstitious credulity and an unnamed but spectacular monster taking centre stage. Spectral sensations were highly successful. *Le Monstre et le magicien* (1826), a French version of *Frankenstein* starring T.P. Cooke who had played an acclaimed monster in Peake's London adaptation, *Presumption* (1823), merited the comment that 'on n'avait vu chez nous machinerie plus compliquée et plus extraordinaire' (Maurice Albert, cited in Forry, 11). The monster moves easily from stage to celluloid: the Edison Kinetogram produced its single reel *Frankenstein* in 1910. Hollywood takes up the story two decades later with James Whale's *Frankenstein* (1931) and *Bride of Frankenstein* (1935).

*Frankenstein* is not the only Gothic fiction to enjoy success on stage and screen. Early cinema abounds with Gothic tales: the Selig Polyscope presented a version of *Dr Jekyll and Dr Hyde* in 1908. German 'Schauerfilme' quickly drew on literary terrors and horrors with doubles, evil scientist and vampires in abundance: *The Student of Prague* (1914), *The Cabinet of Dr Caligari* (1919) and F.W. Murnau's versions of *Dr Jekyll and Mr Hyde* and *Dracula, Der Januskopf* (1920) and *Nosferatu* (1922). Hollywood, in the 1930s, offers its own versions of Stevenson's and Stoker's novels. Developments in photography resonate with the ghostly associations in which the dead remain alive or spectral beings realise themselves as technical effects. Magic and media intertwine. The pioneers of cinema were also regarded as magicians: George Melies was described as the 'king of fantasmagoria', a 'magician of the screen' while the Lumière brothers evoked 'the most extraordinary collective sense of the uncanny for centuries' (Gaby Wood, 178; 175). Ghostly and uncanny effects are not restricted to the mechanisms of modern media. An automaton called Euphonia, invented and exhibited by a German Professor Faber, was described as a 'wonderful toy', a 'scientific *Frankenstein* monster'; Edison's phonogram was described by *Engineering* magazine in 1878 in similar terms: 'it is impossible altogether to resist a feeling of wonderment, recalling to one's mind perhaps the feelings of Pygmalion or the hero of *Frankenstein*' (Gaby Wood, 122; 124). Automata and other inventions, seen through the lens provided by fiction, are not always so awe-inspiring. They have the capacity to evoke more disquieting emotional effects. The reporter from *Toys and Novelties* acknowledged as much in his account of a visit to the factory where Edison's talking dolls were manufactured. He recounts the feeling produced by the machine for making little dolls' hands:

I stood in front of it, fascinated by the steady stream of queer, little hands that fell ceaselessly from the iron monster – it was awful, uncanny, hypnotizing. Indeed, the whole sight was grim and monstrous. The low factory rooms were misty with steam and lit by strange, red-glowing fires; always the steel machines pulsed and clanged; and the mist sweaty giants of men went to and fro with heaps of little greenish arms and legs. (cited in Gaby Wood, 117)

The nightmarish scene combines the strangeness of little automata de-signed to mimic human functions and the alienating atmosphere of a com-mon scene of industrial production. Both become shrouded in the un-canny and monstrous veil provided by fiction. Fictional figures and ef-fects, however, have come to colour an everyday experience of industrial labour so that reality is absorbed into its hallucinatory and disturbing aura. The uncanny has extended its reach: from automata, photographs, phonographs, films and toys to industry itself, it moves beyond the con-fines of individual texts or a single subjectivity and crosses into the social sphere:

> The uncanny, in other words, had left its physical, concrete self behind; it no longer solely took the form of a single automated figure, but had become generalized, diffused throughout a new world of spectacle and magic. Into this world came another mechanized monster: the celluloid frames of the cinema, edited together by technological Frankensteins and brought to life. On film, man was made mechanical, reproduced over and over like an object in a factory, and granted movement by the cranking of a machine. (Gaby Wood, 160)

The perception of automata, moving from mere entertainments to mon-strous doubles, is shaped not only by media but by the productive pro-cesses of modern industry. Media, as Benjamin suggested, duplicate and intensify the mechanical effects of modernity, turning human into ma-chines along the way. Such a reversal is crucial to the psychological distur-bance caused by modern mechanisms and media and contributes to the pervasive sense of uncanniness and alienation in modern life.

Karl Marx suggested as much in his frequent uses of ghostly and Gothic figures. In describing the effects of capital as 'dead labour which vampire-like, lives only by sucking living labour', Marx implied that the bourgeois mode of production dehumanises workers: it is the unnatural entity a proletarian humanity must overthrow (Marx, 1976: 342). *The Commu-nist Manifesto* offers a different image of a 'spectre' haunting Europe. That spectre, generated by the system of production, composes a supernatural excess that will be the downfall of a vampiric bourgeoisie: 'modern bourgeois society with its relations of production, of exchange and of property, a society that has conjured up such gigantic means of production and exchange, is like the sorcerer, who is no longer able to control the powers of the nether world whom he has called up by his spells' (Marx and Engels, 1985: 85–6). The sorcerer's apprentice – the bourgeoisie – has, in creating mass production and a working class, prepared its means of destruction. A monster it can neither completely exploit nor fully master, will, like Frankenstein's creation, cause its demise. In opposition to a vampiric bourgeoisie, workers are simultaneously human and alive, yet are sucked dry by an undead system; as a mass of revolutionary potentiality, they are also monstrous and spectral. A page later, the workman is described as the 'appendage of the machine' (87). Mechanism, monstrosity and spectrality combine in Marx's critique of modern production.

The experience of modernity becomes increasingly uncanny when modes of cultural reproduction and consumption are taken into account. Benjamin, whose analysis of cinema ties the medium firmly to the repetitive and mechanical rhythms of factory labour, regularly employs the term 'phantasmagoria' in his discussions of modernity. The term is central to his approach:

> Our investigation proposes to show how, as a consequence of this reifying representation of civilization, the new forms of behaviour and the new economically and technologically based creations that we owe to the nineteenth century enter the universe of a phantasmagoria. These creations undergo this 'illumination' not only in a theoretical manner; by an ideological transposition, but also in the immediacy of their perceptible presence. They are manifest as phantasmagorias. Thus appear the arcades – first entry in the field of iron construction; thus appear the world exhibitions, whose link to the entertainment industry is significant. Also included in this order of phenomena is the experience of the flâneur, who abandons himself to the phantasmagorias of the marketplace. Corresponding to these phantasmagorias of the market, where people only appear as types, are the phantasmagorias of the interior; which are constituted by man's imperious need to leave the imprint of his private individual existence on the rooms he inhabits. (Benjamin, 1999: 14)

The economic basis of phantasmagorical modernity is found in the World Exhibition of 1867 where 'the phantasmagoria of capitalist culture attains its most radiant unfolding' (8). World Exhibitions 'glorify the exchange value of the commodity': pushing use value to the background, their 'phantasmagoria' distracts the spectator and turns him or her, in the same manner as the entertainment industry, 'into a commodity'. The abandonment to distraction and entertainment signals an enjoyment of alienation from others and oneself in which the individual sinks into the mass 'in an attitude that is pure reaction'. The same occurs in relation to the glitter of the commodity or the intoxicating flows of the urban mass: 'the crowd is the veil through which the familiar city beckons to the flâneur as phantasmagoria – now a landscape, now a room. Both become elements of the department store, which makes use of flânerie itself to sell its goods'. The commodities that shine from the windows of the arcades and stores are also part of the phantasmagoria and the means whereby the private domestic realm is permeated: in a world divided between work and leisure, where reality is dominated by the office, modernity's worker 'needs the domestic interior to sustain him in his illusions' (8). 'In the interior,' Benjamin continues, 'he brings together the far away and the long ago. His living room is a box in the theater of the world' (9). The illusions that mask economic realities with distractions, the theatre, the glitter of commodities also suggest that this 'phantasmagoria of the interior' relates to the inner world of the subject, signs of the false consciousness underpinning bourgeois existence (11).

Modernity's subject, intoxicated, commodified, repeatedly shocked, alienated, and living a thoroughly phantasmagorical existence, seems to be cut from a curiously Gothic cloth: she/he is not distinguished as a particularly rational and moral being, furnished with fibre and substance, but, like a heroine, somewhat superficial, hollow and pulsing with affect, a creature of phantasms. Modernity, politically, ideologically, socially and economically, defines a particular notion of the individual in the course of the eighteenth century. However, the civic and humanist being promoted by enlightenment discourse, rational, virtuous, productive and responsible, emerges alongside a counterpart whose qualities, or lack of them, are delineated in popular fictions and constructions of the readers who consume them. Critical concerns about the dangerous effects of romances emphasise passion, appetite, indulgence, licentiousness and vice. Reason and morality seem on the point of being eclipsed by a ravenous mob of readers, the new species of fiction spawning a new species of reader lured by the stimuli of sensation, luxury, romance and adventure rather than instruction and aesthetic or intellectual elevation. Such a reader, like the characters of Gothic fiction, corresponds to economic shifts. The move from use value to exchange value is inscribed in the bifurcations of Gothic character: what was internal and private in respect of the coherence and merit of individual personality finds itself measured on an external scale, inner states and qualities being defined through interrelationships and formal comparisons. Identity becomes, in Humean terms, 'an aggregate of characteristics, each of which was understood in commodity terms'

(Henderson, 227). Mackenzie's *Man of Feeling* makes explicit the implications: honour loses out to its more formal and insubstantial 'shadow', virtue, and social customs like politeness sound 'more ridiculous to the ear than the voice of a puppet' (229–30). For Henderson, 'the world of the man of feeling of the 1770s is a world of "shadowy" forms emptied of content; of hollow, powerless people who have, in essence, sacrificed their souls; a world of coins – the prototype of the gothic world' (230). Social and economic forms, empty, shadowy, hollow, are mirrored by the vapid characters and formulas of Gothic fiction, all puppets, automata, soulless mechanisms.

The machinery of fiction engenders reading machines. Indeed, the image of the Gothic reader turns out to be little more than a puppet or automaton: the reader's expectations and desires are 'wound up', as Reeve noted, by fictional techniques; he/she is subjected to a text's mechanisms of stimulation and sensation which evoke the appropriate involuntary response of shock, terror, or horror. There is no action, reason or imagination required in reading, only reaction. Coleridge's metaphor of the camera obscura combines the techniques of fiction with the mechanics of reading to present a passive, empty and delirious receptacle of fictional projections, a machine worked by textual machines. The popular text demands little reading, requiring only an unthinking, automatic addressee, a reactive puppet jerking on the strings of narrative technique. That machines beget machines is implied in Walpole's account of the aims and composition of *Otranto* in the second preface to the novel. The combination of ancient and modern romance which he promotes as his main contribution to genre, demands that the former be criticised for its lack of naturalism: 'the actions, sentiments, conversations, of the heroes and heroines of ancient days were as unnatural as the machines employed to put them in motion' (Walpole, 7). In contrast, the modern romance, or realist novel, cramps the former's imaginative range with too much naturalism. The 'reconciliation' of the two forms demands the construction of a new machine which allows naturalism and invention:

> Desirous of leaving the powers of fancy at liberty to expatiate through the boundless realms of invention, and thence of creating more interesting situations, he wished to conduct the mortal agents in his drama according to the rules of probability; in short, to make them think, speak and act, as it might be supposed mere men and women would do in extraordinary positions. (Walpole, 7–8)

The 'engine' Walpole uses is terror. His fiction is designed to transport its protagonists from a recognisable and familiar environment to one that is out of the ordinary while they remain the same. Yet the very different situations they find themselves in will require responses that, though in keeping with themselves, are also very different. Walpole assumes a consistency, privileging character over context, when he goes on to claim that even in encounters with miracles or 'the most stupendous phenomena' people 'never lose sight of their human character' (8). Humanity, Walpole assumes, is located very much within the person, independent of setting or situation. The mechanisms of his fiction, however, tend in the opposite direction. Indeed, critics frequently complained of fiction transporting readers away from real life and human paths. In taking realist characters and relocating them in romantic situations, Walpole subjects them to the new machine of his Gothic story: they become more ciphers than characters, reacting to the shocks of the plot that drives events, puppets of the supernatural agencies that appear beyond realism and probability.

Walpole's characters, for all their supposed reality and humanity, are transformed in the move from one realm to another: emptied of content and substance, they are subject only to the mechanisms of plot and form. Charged with an impossible task of remaining realistic in unreal settings, character is split, its integrity opened to the vacillations of external context. Furthermore, character, in Walpole's plan, becomes a cipher for another figure taking shape in the eighteenth century: the reader. What he expects his characters to do, to remain the same while undergoing improbable experiences, mirrors the split engendered by the reading process itself, a split bridged by the work of identification: from one situation, seated with book in hand, the reader is moved to another more fantastic setting, recognising or identifying with the similarities binding him or her to hero or heroine and feeling accordingly. To be the same and be different simultaneously, to experience oneself as someone else, or someone else as oneself, form a crucial element underlying the pleasures of fiction. Identification demands doubleness. There is something uncanny about it. Jentsch's account of the 'feeling of unease' evoked by dolls, toys and automata notes how, in the 'mechanism' and 'special effect' of fiction, strangeness and pleasure combine: it 'lies in the empathy of the reader or audience with all the emotional excitements to which the characters of the play, novel, or ballad, and so forth, are subject' (Jentsch, 12). Freud does not disagree with this part of Jentsch's analysis:

> This relation is accentuated by mental processes leaping from one of the characters to another – by what we could call telepathy –, so that the one possesses knowledge, feelings and experience in common with the other. Or it is marked by the fact that the subject identifies himself with someone else, so that he is in doubt as to which his self is, or substitutes the extraneous self for his own. In other words there is a doubling, dividing and interchanging of the self. (Freud, 1955a: 234)

All fiction appears to be underpinned by some degree of uncanniness: for fiction to work, some movement from one figure to another is required, some minimal crossing from self to other, in which both are doubled and divided. Identification, of course, discovers identity in places and figures other to the self, in mirrors and images, on screens and pages. Reading itself seems uncanny: the reader finds him/herself in situations where he/she is not, duplicated by characters that are and are not him/herself. The pleasures and strangeness of reading, it seems, are twinned.

Bound up with the mechanisms of fiction and reading, it is perhaps not surprising, Freud's efforts to exclude automata notwithstanding, that the uncanny has so often been evoked by machines, representational apparatuses in particular. Indeed, the Romantic tale, Hoffman's 'The Sandman', on which Freud's essay spends so much time, is a literary account of automatic enamoration, delirium and death. In the story, romance also falls under the sway of automatism: Nathaniel's 'love for the automaton is itself quite automatic; his fiery feelings are mechanically produced' (Dolar, 1991: 9). Olympia, a mechanical copy of the dark lady of courtly romance, is, like her literary original, 'emptied of all real substance' (Lacan, 1992: 149). The Lady is a 'terrifying', 'inhuman partner' whose function is 'nothing other than being as signifier', a figure who exposes the emptiness of the Other, locus of signifying, of the automatic circulation of pleasure and desire (214). Freud, moreover, finds it hard to offer examples of the uncanny that are not taken from the realm of literature. With romance, love assumes an automatic form; in reading, the past returns in the present, the dead come alive, cold letters animated by vital imagining. But it is a two-way process. The reverse is also the case: the reader can be animated or activated into imaginative life by the inanimate words and fictional mechanisms to respond automatically to the touch of text like a machine. The automatism associated with the uncanny does not disappear with a realignment of reality and fantasy or soothing of disturbance. While the pleasures of reading may be in part mechanical, so, too, the horrors: it depends on the identifications that are engendered and the boundaries that are disturbed. The double, indeed, straddles the narcissistic promise of immortality and the threat of death (Freud, 1955a: 235).

Historically, automata have received ambivalent responses: on the one hand merely entertaining humans, on the other threatening their livelihoods and uniqueness. Jacques de Vaucanson, inventor of the clockwork duck that simulated excretion, responded to the hostility of the silk workers threatened by his construction of an automatic loom by making another mechanism, this time operated by a donkey. The contrast between amusing duck and hateful donkey is striking: 'the first was designed for man's entertainment; the second was meant to show man that he was dispensable' (Gaby Wood, 38). The first automaton is entertaining because it does not impinge on the realm of humans except as a wonderful example of ingenuity in mimicking and mastering nature. The second directly encroaches on human activity. Automata and machinery in general begin to exert a more threatening and uncanny significance when the broader political and economic climate changes. With the rise of bourgeois industrialisation human identity is itself altered and the 'autonomous self-determination' of the subject (politically free to speak and vote, economically free to sell his/her labour) is duplicated by the automatism of mechanical performance. In this context, automata, mimicking human functions and appearance, disturbingly disclose a 'mechanical side' to men and women (Dolar, 1994: 46–7). At the same time, humans glimpse themselves in the machine, the same and yet different, as being duplicable and dispensable, replicable and replaceable. Dividing appearance from inner reality and function from value, machines begin to erase the very differences held up as definitively human: 'machines and automata have no secrets, their springs and levers are accessible to all' (53). To understand humans in rational and mechanical terms, to model living organisms on machines and tinker with their internal mechanisms, mental processes etc., subjects humans to the same discursive regime: their inner workings become accessible, made visible through mechanical metaphor at the same time that any essential difference is eclipsed. The uncertainty evoked by the uncanny, then, does not arise from the object of fascination, whether, for example, it is living or dead, but from the corresponding tremor in the subject whose identifications cause an uncertainty about its self, engendering doubt with regard to self-control and self-determination, whether human or machine. The disturbance of 'psychical harmony' reveals a 'dark knowledge' (Jenstch, 14).

Reading disturbs the boundaries between reader and character, self and other, human and machine, doubling and dividing both in the process. On the one hand reading is supposed to cultivate higher rational and imaginative powers of the mind, providing understanding, instruction, noble thoughts and sentiments. Reading raises issues of human virtue and value. But it also operates mechanically and produces machines, evoking passions, desires, instincts that bypass higher control in the stimulation of mechanistic and thoroughly corporeal responses. Hence the horror among critics of the rise of a popular readership for worthless romances: instead of (potentially) rational and dutiful subjects being fostered by instructive reading matter, critics were confronted by the spectre of a ravenous, appetitive, automatic mechanical monster. This monster, moreover, did not die or disappear, worn out by the repetitious shocks and sensations it seemed to enjoy so much. If it became habituated to or tired of certain formulaic repetitions it did not turn to higher subjects but was repeatedly reanimated by new machines of spectacular entertainment.

In the eighteenth century romances and readers were seen to be linked by excesses of passion, appetite, instinct: these excesses bypassed moral and aesthetic discrimination and appealed directly to corporeal mechanisms. Yet the evocation of feeling, outside rational and conscious control (making the hairs on the back of the neck stand up; freezing or curdling the blood), forms the principal aim of Gothic fiction: such emotional expenditure is undertaken without any higher aspiration. If the locks and springs of techniques of terror, formulaic and repetitive as they were, remain, as Scott and others emphasised, in danger of wearing out, so too, does the reader's capacity for intense emotional reactions. Repetition leads to habituation and boredom; stimulation needs to be increased to engender any affect. While new media, machines, spectacles and sensations are generated, each process reinforces the automatism of emotional production and expenditure. Here, however, the pattern of repetition, escalation and exhaustion does have significant effects, producing a parallel movement, an alteration of sameness and difference which leaves the uncanny and machines embroiled in a complex dynamic of internalisation and externalisation of mental processes and mechanisms, all of which depend on a particular and peculiarly empty kind of subjectivity.

The ease with which Gothic fiction and figures are adapted to various media, rendering them Gothic in turn, is only part of the story. While Gothic images, themes and plots provide ready-made sensational resources highly suited to melodramatic media and the shadowplay of early film, the genre offers more than exciting subject matter: its associations provide a means of reflecting on the technical and subjective effects of new media, its spectres, monsters, and undead provide figures for the processes and effects of apparatuses, encoding emotional responses to the arrival of new technologies. Printing presses create a monstrous reading public, ghosts attach themselves to phantasmagorical, photographic or cinematic projections. The uncanny wanders spectrally between readers, viewers, pages and screens, and the mechanisms of projection and the ghosts they engender occupy disturbed mental spaces as explanations of phenomena become hallucinatory and psychopathological. Romances and phantasmagoria find themselves involved in the steady incorporation of spirits and ghosts, exiled from an increasingly rational and secular world, into the mind. But the process is not only directed inwards: the internalisation of ghosts requires that mental activity itself be seen in rational and mechanical terms. The interior takes on the appearance of a machine. As technical apparatuses provide rational analogies for the workings of the mind, their effects open up an increasingly hallucinatory sphere: the delirium and phantasms of romance reading are made visible on phantasmagorical and cinematic screens. Their mechanisms serve to explain mental life and also to derange it further. Moving inwards, locating ghosts as effects of consciousness, also exteriorises mental life and renders reality ghostly: film, Castle contends, extends the imperative 'to find mechanical techniques for rendering the world itself in spectral form' (Castle, 137). Subjectivity is caught up, in the process of internalisation and externalisation, in a movement between machines and ghosts: it becomes haunted and mechanical at once, interior and externalised, and reducible to neither one nor the other. Moved inwards, ghosts disappear from the world and the mind finds itself haunted; moved outwards, the haunting spreads disturbingly across external, real spaces. As mechanism, moreover, mind is opened to an external gaze, rendered visible and transparent, machine without soul. With the intervention of newer techniques of terror and horror, the process is accelerated: emotions are stimulated and expended, an operation in which external mechanisms and internal processes combine. Emotions are drawn out, feelings ex-pressed, squeezed out by the shocks and surprises of narrative and cinematic mechanism. In repetitions and escalations of shock effects, externalisation becomes evacuation: the reader or viewer is hollowed out, emptied of content and substance, the pressure from outside drawing interiority to the surface, exhausting affect in the evocation of emotional expenditure and leaving only a puppet, automaton, doll, a mechanical subject. The uncanny unbearably presents a subject that is '*vacuum* and *plenitudo* all in one, the plenitude as the direct consequence of the emptiness' (Dolar, 1991: 20). Emptied out, the subject, of course, can be filled with new mechanisms and metaphors.

Allied, ghosts and machines eclipse human faculties. Qualities associated with depth and interiority are given mechanical counterparts and drawn to the surface for inspection and activation, switched on or off. Any essence or core is evacuated. Human faculties, rendered mechanical, can be circumvented, replaced or intensified beyond human capacities: feeling, indeed, becomes a mechanism that wears itself and its subject out in the repetitions and escalations of artificially generated shocks. Hollowed out, emptied of core, the decentring process may leave humans behind. Even ghosts might leave the mind. Cinema inscribes this trajectory. The close and longstanding relationship between film and psychoanalysis traces the proximity between mental process and the cinematic apparatus: Hugo Munsterberg described the 'magic' produced by simply reversing the film and running it backwards. In cinema, he notes, dreams are realised and 'uncanny ghosts appear from nothing and into nothing' (Munsterberg, 15). For Otto Rank, in his psychoanalytic study, *The Double*, the similarity between cinematography and the dreamwork is striking to the extent that the former has the capacity of 'visibly portraying psychological events' (Rank, 7). Gothic figures come to represent the workings of mental life and the cinema: 'in *Golem*, in *The Other*, in *The Cabinet of Dr Caligari*, in *The Student of Prague* — everywhere doppelgangers appear as metaphors for the screen and its aesthetic' (Kittler, 1990: 246–7). As media chart and render the mind visible with increasing technical efficiency, spectralisation operates in two directions: penetrating interior recesses, it also replicates and expropriates mental contents and powers so that ghosts spread outward, haunting media themselves. Kittler, commenting on developing technological capacities and their effects on aesthetic production and reception, notes the steady supplementation of human faculties by technical means to the point that hardly any human intervention, rational, imaginative, or fanciful, is required : 'once memories and dreams, the dead and the ghosts, become technically reproducible, readers and writers no longer need the powers of hallucination' (1999: 10). Imagination was bypassed in romance reading's hallucinatory 'moving phantasms'. Romantic fancy and delirium are soon made redundant, phenomena of the human interior sucked out and supplanted by cinema. Ghosts depart the mind to haunt the mechanisms of cinema: 'unconscious mechanisms which previously could only be found in human experiments, abandon us in order to populate the film studios as Doubles of dead souls' (1997: 97–100). It is not so much that humans give up the ghost, but that ghosts take their leave of humanity.

The screen, having assumed the capacity to project ghosts, looks back on a human dimension as doubly ghostly. There is, however, nowhere but the screen:

> in denouncing the ghostliness of those technologies – and of the media – one implies that there is somewhere an original form of lived existence. Whereas, if the rate of reality is falling every day, this is because the medium itself has passed into life, has become the ordinary ritual of transparency. All this digital, numeric, electronic equipment is merely incidental to the deep-seated virtualization of human beings. And if this so grips the collective imagination, that is because we are already – not in some other world, but in this life itself – in a state of socio-, photo- and videosynthesis. (Baudrillard, 1996: 27–8)

Ghosts are no longer uncanny in the sense of manifesting a return of repressed wishes, beliefs and fears from the unconscious and surmounted regions of psychic life. They become more active, rather than reactive, figures of a technological dimension from which human powers and autonomy seem increasingly alienated, videosynthesised and displaced by the machineries of post-modernity.

Franz Kafka found ghosts proliferating in every modern technological innovation. Letters, for him, took the form of 'an intercourse with ghosts, and not only with the ghost of the recipient but also with one's own ghost which develops between the lines of the letter one is writing'. Writers and readers find themselves 'denuded' by the ghosts, the content of their communications fed upon as though by some technological vampire. While some technologies may compensate for spatial and temporal distance, thereby cancelling the ghostly element feeding off natural communication, the opposing tendency of technology seems stronger: 'after the postal service it has invented the telegraph, the telephone, the radiograph. The ghosts won't starve, but we will perish' (Kafka, 229). Ghostly media increasingly displace human capacities. For Virilio, the innovations of digital imaging and telecommunications only serve to extend this 'ghostly dimension' (Virilio, 1997: 66). With virtual realities and teletechnologies, the material world, the human body and consciousness will be irreparably divided: 'we will see industrial production of a personality split, an instantaneous cloning of living man, the technological re-creation of one of our most ancient myths: the myth of the *double*, of an electromagnetic double whose presence is spectral – another way of saying a ghost or the living dead' (39). If the ghosts populate the machines rather than the borders of human consciousness then the position of humanity that was central to modernity's calls for liberty, progress and civilisation, a position shadowed by the uncanny, is significantly altered: humans, if anything, become the ghosts of ghosts.

### The small scream

The phantasmagoria of modernity's interior, in which, Benjamin notes, the living room becomes a box in the theatre of the world, is realised with the introduction of television into every western home. Banal, mundane, repetitive, the television is also a box of flows, shocks, sensations and strangeness. As in the horror film *Poltergeist* it can seem to possess a demonic energy. Entering everyday life in a more pervasive manner than cinema, television accelerates and amplifies the process of repetitive pleasures and shocks in which thrills must be continually escalated to penetrate the shields of habituation. Indeed, television brings the relation of shock and repetition closer than ever in the speed of access it seems to provide to global events. Normal programming, with its regular rhythms and staged events can be interrupted by newsflashes, the medium itself articulating the relationship of shock and repetition which, though happening elsewhere, is carried with alarming immediacy into the home: 'catastrophe coverage, "the time of the now", is represented as a moment when thinking stops, a moment of danger that might portend change, which paradoxically is both thrill and preclusion' (Mellencamp, 243). Televisual repetition constitutes a kind of punctuated equilibrium that depends on the shock of an interruption, a technological failure that it simultaneously deals with: 'TV time of regularity and repetition, continuity and "normalcy", contains the potential of interruption, the thrill of live coverage of death events' (Mellencamp, 244). TV, Mellencamp notes, is different from the models of shock proposed by Benjamin and Freud in that it 'is shock *and* therapy; it both produces and discharges anxiety'; it 'administers and cushions shocks, is both traumatic shock and Freud's "protective shield"' (246; 254). The collision and fusion of distinct poles erases the difference between shock and repetition. Shock has been steadily incorporated in the circuits of broadcasting and spectatorial pleasure: 'television contains (and pleasures us) by contradictions', the very ambivalence of the impulses of shock and repetition marking the rates of bored familiarity and excited attention on the pulses of the viewers. The small screen is distinguished by the poles that collide and collapse on its flickering surface. Its temporality 'is that of the instant – it is momentary, punctual' (232). So, too, is the medium: it operates on the principle of an 'insistent "present-ness"' and offers 'a celebration of the instantaneous' (222). Here, a new configuration of culture, shock and technology is manifested, a new order in which shocks are incorporated into the system rather than remaining instances of technological failure interrupting smooth mechanical functioning. Shock, ever more integral to operations, again signals a systemic shift, another reorganisation of (systematised modern) life according to the principles of a new system. For Virilio, 'technological speed' succeeds 'astronomical time' to the extent that 'we are living in a system of technological temporality, in which duration and material support have been supplanted as criteria by individual retinal and auditory instants' (Virilio, 1991a: 84). This system of communicational instantaneity, of virtual technologies and absolute digital speeds, replaces the orders of 'metabolic proximity' and 'mechanical proximity' with the imperatives of 'electromagnetic proximity' (1998: 186). Orders defined by the relationship of mass and energy are succeeded by a system in which information is king: the succession, in which 'reality's third dimension' appears, is marked by 'the incredible possibility of a new kind of shock: *information shock* (89, original emphasis).

The transformations attendant on the shock waves of electromagnetic information are manifold: the relationship between substance and accident, once defined by the privilege of essence over contingency, is inverted. Accidents and shocks become essential features of informational living. And they are no longer limited to the specific instances of technological failure manifested in the traffic of the transport revolution. Instead, a 'general accident' governs the globe, a 'delocalization of action and reaction (interaction) necessarily implying the *delocalization of all accidents*' (182, original emphasis). The effects of the generalised accident are widespread, socially, economically and technologically: they inscribe the pressure of an 'unprecedented temporal breakdown, in the throes of an imminent *social crash*'; demand the constant movement of substances and goods so that the pressures of global markets, prices and competition means that production must be easily relocatable and operate a '*just-in-time* inventory system' managing efficient supply and minimising stocks (184–5, original emphasis). Speed, informational speed, is of the essence; it dominates production, pressing for efficient performance, maximised profit potential, quick returns and turnarounds: corporate logistics increasingly require rapid delivery and immediate responses linked to the flows of electronic information. It makes little difference whether one is at work or at home, supposing, indeed, that those divisions continue to apply. Workers, like machines, must run at optimum efficiency: there is, notes Virilio, no longer any need 'to economize physical effort'. Instead, a 'new law' demands that a human be treated like a motor, '*a machine that needs to be constantly revved up*'; it sets out to '*promote increasing acceleration of the reflexes and stimuli of the animate being*' (1995a: 123–4, original emphasis). Like computers, employees must always be 'up to speed' or find themselves replaced by a faster model; like military aircraft, they must be engineered to the peak of efficiency, to the very edge of stability and airworthiness.

The increased pace demanded by the machine tolerates human casualties. Where factory labour once allowed the worker to adjust to, and find breaks in, the mechanical rhythm, when a computer sets the pace there is no time to pause. Instead a principle of 'hyperconductivity' means that 'a person can no longer keep up with the racing of his digital command tools'. This leads to what Virilio calls a 'new epidemic': stress (134). 'Repetitive strain injury' wears out the body while information overload and the imperatives of speed burn out the white-collar employee. In the face of technological imperatives the human body and the rational mind, as Stelarc is wont to remind us, have both become obsolete. The stresses of a machinic rhythm do not traumatise individuals in the same way that technological shocks do: demanding an escalating pace, they burn out their circuits. Or they require prosthetic enhancement, a 'CYBERNETIC programming of vital rhythms' through '*xenotransplants*' and '*technotransplants*'(126, original emphasis). Productive imperatives are mirrored by consumptive ones: the increased passivity of consumption is subjected to a 'law of stimulation' in which humans become 'hyperactivated' beings (126). This involves physical exertion, leisure time being devoted to the performance-enhancing regimes of sporting pastimes or to the 'superstimulants' that are 'the logical extension of a metropolitan sedentariness' and serve to speed up the body for pleasurable as much as work-related performance (102). For Virilio,

> Postmodern man's inertia, his passivity, demands a surplus of excitement not only through patently unnatural sports practices, but also in habitual activities in which the body's emancipation due to real-time remote-control technology eliminates the traditional need for physical strength or muscular exertion. (103)

The physical exertions of sports compensate for the redundancy of corporeal power. But mental stimulation is also demanded, a result of the technological reorganisation of human uses and skills, to compensate for the deprivations to which the senses are subjected: 'from the elimination of the physical effort of walking to the sensori-motor loss induced by the first transport, we have finally achieved states bordering on sensory deprivation' (85). Deprivation and overstimulation are linked, in a manner similar to Benjamin's experientially atrophied modernity: overload evacuates the mental system of any rational or affective capabilities. At the same time it requires more and more stimulation. Noting that theatre, video, cinema and television set out to 'arouse *natural* emotions', Virilio identifies a contrary momentum:

> But only pending the *artificial* effects of the paroxysmal acceleration of representational techniques. Tetanization, vertigo, overexcitement, a state of shock will evacuate all judgement, any system of rational evaluation, any positive, negative, or even simply deleterious selection of messages and images. (73)

Shock takes the subject beyond judgement, reason or feeling, inducing an equilibrium of permanent disequilibrium that can no longer be simply correlated with an economy of pleasure. Horror movies, sacrificing narrative coherence to the immediacy of visual and kinetic effects, participate in the process of accelerated emotional expenditure (Polan). Special effects and digital editing speed up and intensify the shocks. Media overstimulation reduces shock to a 'simple frequency signal', 'an impulse that can dispense

with any concern for plausibility': 'Proper training of the younger generation is already ensured through the success of video games exclusively based
on the virtuality of disappearance and elimination – reflex games that can
induce total loss of consciousness in photosensitive subjects similar to the
orgasmic effects of epilepsy' (Virilio, 1995a: 74). Excess of images, speed
of flow, the rapid alteration of images, repeats the intensities of an expenditure in which the subject is continually enlivened and exhausted at the
same time.

The accelerated pattern of pleasure, shock and repetition is wired into
computer games: 'we want to be shocked by novelty. We want to lose
ourselves in a space that is utterly different. We want environments that
have never been seen, never been imagined before'. This impossible demand for something totally novel, for something that exceeds imagination is counterbalanced by the observation that, at present, computer games
have not advanced much beyond the 'twin poles of attraction and repulsion' (Poole, 230–3). Repetition forms an intrinsic principle of gaming:
only by going over the same labyrinths, obstacles and hazards again and
again can the skills be acquired to reach another level, another level of
repetition with a minimal difference. Repetition is exercised to the point
of compulsion (Buse). Anxiety counteracts the dulling equilibrium of pleasure which 'increases up to a point of difficulty' (Poole, 181). Evoked by
an unknown cause, anxiety, marked by the quickening pulse, the increase
in adrenalin flow and skin conductivity forms the disturbance or disequilibrium punctuated by bursts of explosive expenditure. Too much difficulty, however, and the tension will evaporate, the player simply overwhelmed by technical demands.

In games, principles of reason and morality do not apply. Like the
Internet and Darpanet, its military forerunner, early videogames were developed as training simulations for tank crews, missile defence operators,
and pilots. *Doom* was redesigned to train US Marines in the art of 'one-
shot kills', a 'how-to manual for killing without a conscience' (Keegan, 2).
Optimum performance and rapid reactions are the key factor:

> Deaf, mute, and blind, bodies are brought up to the reaction speed of World
> War n + 1, as if housed in a gigantic simulation chamber. Computerized
> weapons systems are more demanding than autonomized ones. If the joysticks
> of Atari video games make children illiterate, President Reagan welcomed
> them for just that reason: as a training ground for future bomber pilots.
> Every culture has its zones of preparation that fuse lust and power, optically,
> acoustically, and so on. (Kittler, 1999: 140)

Being wired into computers by playing games may not serve ideological
or cultural ends but it is likely to enhance technical competence. Not

every child is destined to become a bomber pilot, no matter how hard or often she or he practices with joystick and console. The playing of games, entertaining and profitable by-products of the military-industrial complex, do not seem to have directly programmed social uses or planned outcomes. They do, however, have extensive effects on minds and bodies:

> Some accounts suggested that video games were producing new forms of consciousness in kids, hyperkinetic attunements of perception and reflex reminiscent of the preternatural sensory-motor apparatus of Anne Rice's vampires … while others depicted violence-addled teens as stupefied as the zombies shambling through George Romero's 1979 classic film of mall life, *Dawn of the Dead*. (Latham, 138)

One does not recoil from the vampire, but becomes it, playing on the screen. Bodies mutate, thumbs becoming prehensile in the operation of controls; sensory-nervous systems react at inhumanly enhanced rates. There is no time to think, the player just has to do it. Instincts are activated, energies wasted to no end other than the game itself; thought is given over to the ecstatic flow of the experience. Staring at screens oblivious to the world or others, players seem to be alien beings.

The comparison of game players to vampires stresses a perceived loss of humanity in Gothic terms. But the reference to *Dawn of the Dead* is also significant: set in a shopping mall populated by zombies, its version of culture is marked out as one utterly determined by consumption. The undead bodies, returning to the scene of so many purchases are virtually indistinguishable in habit and action from their former living selves. Divested of reason, agency or self-control and characterised as automatons whose self-possession has been hollowed out, consumers are consumed by the shiny commodities illuminated in shop windows (Modleski). Other anxieties lurk in concerns about game-players: like the zombies considered by Sontag to be the very image of 'technocratic man', their absorption in games mirrors a contemporary working life dominated by screens. The model of the individual promoted in the nineteenth century as the apex of culture and the ideal around which social cohesion established itself in ideological terms, is no longer at issue. Highly efficient operators, skilled technicians, experts in a limited field, are the preferred products of educational training (Lyotard, 1984). The adepts in video gaming are, in part, the new trainees of this commercial and performative ethos. Zombie culture. The flow in which identity and self-consciousness disappears – in games, in sport and in shopping – comes to be a determining experience of new imperatives to perform to the maximum in a mode of capitalism which does not restrain excess: 'flow involves the transcendence of meaningful units by a system whose only meaning is the fact of its global non-meaning' (Polan, 179; 183). The 'incoherence' of cultural productions actively encourages the loss of agency, reason and will: they offer 'an invitation for individuals to exceed previous boundaries, to be in excess of an analytical, literally conservative control of productivity' (178). In video games any search for an overriding meaning is pointless: the system does not operate to that end. It immerses players in 'fast-moving low-level "meanings"' (Poole, 198). There is no transcendence, no overriding logic, no self-conscious subject, just the flow of game itself.

It may be life, but not as we know it: life on the screen is something and somewhere else, vampiric, undead and quite banal. If, in line with *Dawn of the Dead*, Marx's 'gluttonous capitalist rat has been transformed into an army of consuming mall-rats' (Latham, 131) then the vampire is no longer a figure of disturbing otherness: it is very much the everyday image of consumer him or herself, sucked into the flow of shop windows and screens. Pac-Man, 'a neo-Marxist parable of late capitalism', offers a less Gothic image: 'he is the pure consumer. With his obsessively gaping maw, he clearly wants only one thing: to feel whole, at peace with himself'. Merely a disk with a slice missing to suggest a mouth, this early game figure is designed to navigate a screen maze consuming as many objects as possible while avoiding ghostly blobs that can 'kill' him: he is 'doomed forever to metaphysical emptiness' (Poole, 189). More is never enough, desire pulsing between plenitude and evacuation. Like the zombies shambling around shopping malls or transfixed before screens, Pac-Man, forever consuming, lies beyond final expenditure. Not even death arrests the flow of pixels and commodities, the flux of fullness and emptiness: absolute expenditure, a final consumption, is replaced by a succession of little losses. A life lost in the course of the game merely requires a new start. It interrupts but does not halt the game: 'getting killed is a drag because suddenly the game stops, and the only way to remain master of this intoxicating new universe is to kill' (Keegan, 3). Death has become 'multi-modal', its singularity and totality replaced by lots of little deaths. As such it manifests a transformation in the meaning of 'life': 'we are used to thinking of "life" as a single, sacred thing, the totality of our experiences. But videogames refine "life" as an expendable, iterable part of a larger campaign' (Poole, 68). Mobile, plural, replicable and expendable, this definition of life corresponds to the demands placed by late capitalism on its workforce and to the demands for instant gratification placed on the market by a fast food consumer culture: life is full, then empty, then over, then begun anew.

Death changes life. So, too, the absence of death. Parents 'should no longer ask where their children are, but what they are' (Buse, 164). Bodies and minds altered by the games they play, children are a different species.

The parental order incapable of recognising them also undergoes a transformation in structure and location: the waste-effects of gaming correspond to the flows of a global capitalism that 'encourages excessive expenditure, that desires a desire that is not sublimated or organized within the frame of an oedipalized family' (Polan, 178). No more father or mother: the familial symbolic is short-circuited. Yet family figures reappear, virtually, on screens. Computer games fill the place of the Other better than 'real' parents: 'video games give you their full attention. They don't ignore you or say they're busy; they concentrate with rock solid focus on what you "say" to them through the mechanical interface.' According to Isaac Asimov, the game functions as 'a pal, a friend' (Poole, 184). Identification with the screen, complete immersion in its superficial flows, divests subjectivity of self, structure and body to become a virtual, ghostly thing flickering and fading at speed, virtually realising Gothic doubles as everyday consuming living dead. There is little difference it seems between figures on the screen and figures twitching in front of it, puppets, zombies, mutants, vampires, automata.

## ⊰ 3 ⊱

# Dark bodies

### An-aesthetics

SHE LIES ON THE OPERATING TABLE, fully conscious. Artist, director, patient, performer, she is dressed in an Issey Miyake gown and continues talking as the first needle pushes beneath the skin, injecting local anaesthetic. Translators are ready, the signer too. Cameras are working, their operators dressed in dark gowns. Fruit bowls are arranged. Video screens flicker into life. The satellite uplink is operational. A surgeon marks the face for incision, dotting lines like a dress pattern. Longer needles slide behind the ear, under the forehead. An array of clocks on the wall tells the time in different zones. The first cut. Messages arrive by fax. They are answered. Another incision. The dotted lines from head to ear are joined up. Flaps of skin appear and begin to detach, to be peeled back revealing the gaping flesh. Readings from the canon of French psychoanalysis and feminism continue. Blood seeps from the wounds. More messages, more replies. Silicon implants are inserted. Cameras close in then pan back for the stitches …

'But this is no simulation of an operation, it is the real thing'(Lovelace, 13). Reality, however, has turned hyperreal in this conjunction of art and actuality, spectacle and surgery, performance and pain. After all, it takes place in an operating *theatre*. Orlan undergoes another of her celebrated operations, a kind of anti-cosmetic surgery in which her facial features are altered against the prevailing norms of beauty: in this case, she has two 'bumps' inserted into her forehead. The theatricality of the operation is enhanced by the design of the setting and the costumes. Vision machines relay events by a live satellite transmission to audiences in art galleries in New York, Toronto, Tokyo. The body, its flesh, its wounds, its pain, all guarantors of reality, is opened by medical and visual technologies and to mediated aesthetic gazes and communication networks. The patient does not suffer, but reads, talks, directs proceedings, engaging in a variety of telecommunications while flesh is sliced and transformed. Audiences may gape and gasp, suffering in silence and stillness, looking away from screens or loudly leaving galleries in disgust. Art cuts close to the bone. Surgery is forced into too unusual a visibility; it is made to make an exhibition of itself in disclosing what should remain an-aesthetic. Performance displaying too much and not enough becomes too real, too close to its object, its technical projections and artifices to engender a distance that is not at all safe: clinical sterility tied up with bloody abjection and ever present tele-communications. Real, unreal and overreal at the same time, the surgery-art, or performance-operation, is also a horror show.

Horror entwines spectacle and reality in an indeterminate scene of effects and affects that, further, engage and repulse audiences in the staging of often overwhelming and unbearable images. Orlan's performance art, as it draws audiences into the cosmetic surgical procedures she undergoes, stages a horror associated with the body and representations of excesses, an art that interrogates art by linking aesthetics and deformity, pleasure and pain. Emotions are not shared. The artist, though she may experience some degree of discomfort, feels no pain. That experience is saved for the audience: Orlan apologises during the show-operation performed on 21 November 1993 in New York, saying 'sorry to make you suffer, but know that I do not suffer – unlike you – when I watch these images' (Orlan, 83). Watcher and watched, eyeing the video screens monitoring her operation, the artist is, unlike the audience, anaesthetised. It is the latter who suffer. The art critic, Barbara Rose, notes the visceral effects and sensory overload of watching the operation (Rose, 125). For Parveen Adams, 'the dominant effect of the video … is horror'. The viewer is made to suffer in Orlan's staging of a 'general pain' (Adams, 142–3). Inducing effects of anxiety, shock, nausea, the spectacle is uncanny also: 'no dramatization of war or horror can surpass the knowledge that what is being observed in the operating theatre is a body that while simultaneously alive, expresses the stasis and bodily mutilation associated with traumatic death' (Clarke, 187). The uncanny crossing of borders between life and death forms part of horror's general disturbance as it tears through framed images and dissolves boundaries between art and real, image and audience.

The effects, of suspense, terror, anxiety and shock, the subsequent reactions like revulsion or the aversion of eyes, resemble those of horror cinema as it cuts up bodies and simultaneously assaults the eyes of audiences. The link is explored by Michelle Hirschhorn, comparing the effects of Orlan's art to the horror and abjection engendered by the film, *Alien*. Kristevan abjection and Lacan's object *a*, locus of symbolic dissolution,

castration and anxiety, combine to figure, in both *Alien* and Orlan's operation, as 'the image of the gaping and voracious black hole' of monstrous
female genitalia (Hirschhorn, 128). Horror makes one look away from an
unbearable image that threatens complete dissolution. The imagined integrity of the body is ripped apart and so is sense: the abject, and Orlan's
performance, slices through comfortable modes of viewing, representing a
body in pain and causing a bodily disturbance in other bodies. Also, another level of discomfort is evoked, a cognitive disturbance affecting the
capacity to interpret and analyse: 'what's difficult in my work is that it's
uncomfortable in every sense. So far as the operations are concerned, it is
physically uncomfortable for me and for those who look at the images.
But it is also uncomfortable to make sense of it' (cited in Ayers, 1999:
180). The pain, intensity and anxiety generated by Orlan's performance
does not encourage any identification with the artist, but provokes an
unbearable identification of some Thing in her, beyond her, a horror exca-
vating both image and the capacity to imagine.

Like the uncanny, the abject opens onto the real. Not the real in the
sense of the reality that is sustained in opposition to fiction of fantasy, not
empirical, material actuality, but the real in a Lacanian sense. Where reality is organised by a structure of humanised signs and symbols, and lived
accordingly, the real is put forward as a prior, unsymbolisable realm, distinguished only in the stains, disruptions, absences and disturbances punctuating everyday, humanised existence. Horror, dissolving sense, symbolic
structure, coherent frames, opens onto the real, its aesthetic effects evoking the gaps, holes and tears by which a hint of the real is broached. For
Renata Salecl, however, the ensemble of Orlan's performance, voice as well
as gaze, moves beyond the visual register highlighted in the analogy with
horror movies:

> Plastic surgery of Orlan's face is painful to watch; for viewers it is not only
> shocking to see Orlan's skin being detached from her face, but also to hear
> her monotonous voice reciting texts during her surgery. If Orlan were to be
> quiet, the observers might be able to pretend they were seeing a dead-like,
> deeply anaesthetized person being cut on the stage. In this case the shock
> for the observers would not be so very different than watching horror movies:
> when one does not want to see a scary scene in the film, one simply closes
> one's eyes. Of course, in horror movies one still hears the music and the
> screams, the voice without the picture is less frightening, since the voice
> loses power when it is not accompanied by the picture. But in the case of
> Orlan, it is the voice that is the real site of horror. If one listens to her voice
> and keeps one's eyes shut, one does not get relief, since Orlan's voice is the
> sign of deadliness and of life at the same time. (Salecl, 41–2)

Like Poe's 'The Facts in the Case of M. Valdemar', where a previously mesmerised person dies and then speaks the chilling words 'I am dead', the voice confounds life and death. In Poe's story, a characteristic of the living, speech, comes from the realm of death. In Orlan's case, the voice, its monotony and relentlessness, refuses any attempt to consign the performance to mere artifice or image. It is not a commentary added on later, but a sign of a 'live' transmission. The uncanniness which blurs life and death, ties the audience to the performance. But the life and death it announces is also undeath of the kind that Zizek associates with vampires and alien. For him, the undead, as Lacan's 'lamella' or object *a*, present the horrifying image of life outside symbolic parameters, indestructible, immortal, irrepressible (Zizek, 1999: 280–1). Indeed, the alien breeds by disfiguring its human victims, enveloping their faces with bulbous and tentacled bodies jumping from slimy egg-pods. This is not life in a nicely organised and humanised shape, but life seething, slimy, formless, horrifying, destructive and barely distinguishable from decaying, rank, worm-ridden death.

Orlan's horror, for all its investments in deformity and monstrosity, moves beyond familiar modes of Gothic representation, just as her project aims at interrogating and supplanting the norms of beauty established by the history of art. Her work, none the less, has made reference to the canon in her 'Official Portrait with Bride of Frankenstein Wig' (1990). The photograph depicts the artist as Elsa Lanchester's female monster from James Whale's second Universal film, fiercely crimped hair with its dyed lightning streaks proudly defying gravity. The striking still image arrests and holds the gaze with movie glamour, presenting a familiar figure that, while its allusions offer a reading of monstrous female sexuality, does not perform abjection or horror. Orlan's operations are of an entirely different order in respect of their relation to image, object, body and horror.

A face is cut, skin is peeled back and lifted. Suffering is produced for the spectator. Anxiety circulates throughout the scene, prevented from resting, in fear, on a single image or object. For Adams, Orlan's performance discloses, not the completeness associated with cosmetic surgery as it alters facial features to accord with an ideal of beauty, but the 'emptiness of the image'. Horror is crucial in this respect: it hollows out both object and image as the face is seen to be separate from the head. Beneath the face, nothing: it appears as mask, illusion (Adams, 145). No recognisable, formed image appears with the peeling back of the face: an empty interior is opened to a gaze. The provocation of anxiety arises with the collapse of boundaries: image and frame are rendered indistinct, viewer and fleshy emptiness, inside and outside blur. Orlan is not 'unveiled or stripped bare':

'there is no signifying interior to be discovered. Rather, the detachment of her face, a manoeuvre that reveals it as pure exteriority, is one which casts doubt on representation, which insists on its emptiness' (145). That which is most intimate, the interior core of being, is rendered visible in the un-doing of bodily and facial integrity. What appears, an intimacy exteriorised, pertains to neither body nor subjectivity: it manifests an inner/external emptiness around which images of both cohere. For Adams, this 'extimacy' is akin to the uncanny's dissolution of boundaries: it appears as a hole within subjectivity and representation.

Horror arises when boundaries are crossed and the secure relation of inside and outside is disturbed: 'there is suddenly, no inside and no out-side. There is an emptying out of the object. It is the moment, a horrifying moment of the birth of a new space which ruins habitual space' (154). Rather than filling the new space with recognisable aesthetic images, the gaping hole comes shockingly to the fore: 'an unfillable gap opens at the moment that the face is lifted' (158). The appearance of the gap is horri-fying in that it disturbs all aesthetic frames, tearing the structure of symbolised and humanised reality apart by disclosing 'a hole in the field of representation'. This hole 'does not simply ruin representation. It mends as it ruins it. It both produces a hole and what comes to the place of lack to cover it over' (151). A tear in representation and modes of perception and comprehension, the hole forms the disturbing focus for the spectator. Associated with castration and the enigma of female sexuality in psycho-analysis, the hole produces the effects of the real, its horrifying formless-ness underlying all signification, a locus of anxiety which defines all speaking beings (154). The encounter with a most basic formlessness, for Adams, delivers 'horrifying spectacle of the rawness of passion, of the *jouissance* of the body as such, the jubilation of the meat' (156). Structure, meaning, sense, fall apart in this intense encounter with the real. Nothing fits into place: the object of the gaze is 'emptied out'. This evacuation reverberates: 'the emptying out of the place of the object means that the structure of representation has collapsed' (156). The evacuation of image, object and representational structure is transmitted by holes to the spectator: 'the eyes become black holes into which the image is absorbed willingly or by force. These images plunge in and strike directly where it hurts, without passing through the habitual filters, as if the eyes no longer had an con-nection with the brain' (Orlan, 84). Bypassing the brain and its filters, the evacuating intensity of horror strikes through the dilated pupils that can barely gauge what they are seeing.

While horror comes to the fore in Orlan's performance to engender a devastation that goes beyond body and representation, the gap or space that is disclosed, Adams insists, offers a glimpse of the 'birth of a new space'. Evacuation enables a re-inscription as Adams promotes the ultimately positive programme of Orlan's aesthetic project: in challenging and deforming traditional and patriarchal norms and ideals of feminine beauty, the artist takes charge of her own image. Women, if one follows Orlan's lead, are at last in control of their self-images, free of both the constraints of nature and culture: 'being a woman is dependent on continuously being born through surgery. Birth and making are conflated in art. Orlan is only the new Orlan. She is a picture whose origin erases the difference between being born and being made' (Adams, 144). An image of an image without origin, it is only in the gap opened up by the ruination of conventional structures of representation, the voiding of traditional aesthetics and habitual perceptions, that this new birth can occur. Horror, however, arises in the stress on evacuation rather than re-creation. Its ambivalence testifies to the uncertainty underlying all the limits and boundaries supposedly securing identity: a fundamental formlessness, a structuring void, both constitutes and dissolves all imaginary articulations of identity, whether located in bodily integrity or social representations. Indeed, the aesthetic norms challenged and surpassed so forcefully in Orlan's performance do not seem so secure; the structure of representation, the Other, already seems to be crumbling, full of holes, with corresponding gashes readily visible, marks of a 'wound culture': 'the public fascination with torn and open bodies and torn and opened persons, a collective gathering around shock, trauma, and the wound' (Seltzer, 1998: 1). The only locus of shared bonds is found in their traumatic absence.

In a discussion of clitoridectomy and scarification, Salecl makes an important distinction between the body marking and mutilation of premodern societies and the current fashion for body art, piercing and tattooing. Premodern scarification serves to provide the individual with the 'answer of the big Other', providing the subject with identity and social position (Salecl, 32). The mark situates the individual as a member of a particular group, the bearer, through a rite of passage, being initiated into a community. The customs, rituals and significations that define group membership involve body markings that are charged with intensity and meaning, signs invested with affect, an emotional tie: 'the tattoo certainly has the function of being for the Other, of situating the subject in it, marking his place in the field of the group's relations, between each individual and all the others' (Lacan, 1977b: 206). The signifying function of the scar, its role in defining identity as a social and symbolic construction, changes as questions are asked of the narratives of modernity. The shared framework of bonds and meanings articulating individuals unravels: family structures, cultures, communities, become ineffective in the maintenance of social cohesion and in the furnishing of specific identity. In this context, Salecl describes body marking 'not as the answer of the big Other, but the subject's answer to the non-existence of the big Other' (32). A tattoo, a piercing, a scar, signals an attempt to identify oneself with a grouping in the absence of a prevailing structure of shared values and meanings: the transgressive gesture calls up ruined norms and in their absence tries to produce a new sense of group and identity.

Salecl's reading of body marking does not endorse a simple 'postmodern' account of identity, one that may be associated with the positive and creative aspects of Orlan's project. Its voiding of habits and norms does not signal an opportunity to remake identity in any fashion one chooses; it is not a straightforward liberation from the constraints imposed on individuals by nature or culture. Since identity, along with an imaginary sense of bodily integrity, is an effect of an inaugural inscription by symbolic structures, the absence of a shared system, while it may provide the occasion for the production of new identities, is also a cause for anger and disappointment. The ambivalence with regard to the breakdown of shared frameworks has extensive consequences for understanding the appeal of altering one's image or marking one's body. If identity, Salecl argues, was defined in respect of symbolic figures, approved role models or ego ideals with which a subject was able to identify, then the collapse of belief in social frameworks leads to a more imaginary, narcissistic investment in ideal egos through which a subject can find likeable images reflected back to him or herself: 'this narcissistic search for the perfect image results in the subject's obsession with changing his or her body with the help of excessive dieting, exercise and plastic surgery' (37). The weight of absence, the collapse of stable external and agreed structures, bears directly on the subject him or herself, manifesting an implosion in which judgement and discrimination is defined increasingly by a dual rather than triangular relationship: image and simulation comes to the fore in shaping and transforming subjective identity, a situation in which Narcissus (subject and image/other) and not Oedipus (subject and other/object/image and Other/law/culture/language) predominates (Baudrillard, 1990b).

The erosion or ruin of structures of representation which brings horror and its hollows to the fore binds subjects to the circulation of images and their underlying emptiness. For Salecl, body marking, which becomes another cultural trend, simultaneously evinces a desire to escape a system of fashion and consumption: the 'paradox' is that marks on the body present a 'realisation' of postmodern assumptions that identity is changeable and 'a reaction against them'. Cuts 'irreversibly' mark the body thus protesting 'against the ideology that makes everything changeable'. Against the play of simulacra and simulations that define contemporary hyperreality, the permanently marked body is invested as the site of a stable and anchoring real (39). Orlan's surgical performances, however, activating in horror the relation between simulation and real, exacerbate the ambivalence and the disturbing movement between them. Though staging the emptiness of the image and the technological artifices of simulation, Orlan's art does not restore the body as a guarantor of stable reality. The horror her operations provoke moves beyond body as well as image, opening it up to an excess that is both fleshly and formless. The holes and gaps are at once sites of dissolution and sites of surgical, technological and aesthetic reconstruction. Orlan's project, she notes, is not to return to the body in all its imagined integrity, but to remake it as image, unbound from cultural convention or natural law: 'in future times we'll change our bodies as easily as our hair colour', she is reported to have said (cited in Lovelace, 13–14). Her project, like that of Stelarc, brings attention to the obsolescence of the body:

> Like the Australian artist, Stelarc, I think that the body is obsolete. It is no longer adequate for the current situation. We mutate at the rate of cockroaches, but we are cockroaches whose memories are in computers, who pilot planes and drive vehicles that we have conceived, although our bodies are not designed for these speeds. We are on the threshold of a world for which we are neither mentally nor physically ready. (Orlan, 91)

Looking towards a world of new biotechnological possibilities demands the voiding of prior assumptions and frameworks, the evacuation of bodies as much as minds. Again, Orlan's and Stelarc's performances are comparable. The latter's work until recently, having an inoperative 'Third Ear' made of flesh and cartilage surgically attached to his arm, employed inorganic prostheses, supplementing the increasingly inadequate human body with technological enhancements. Technology, however, also requires the emptying out of corporeal elements in order that machines take over, and improve upon, once-human functions. Stelarc's proposal to develop a 'Stimbod' (in which he is wired up so that all his movements are operated by a computer programme) 'would,' he comments, 'be a hollow body, a host body for the projection and performance of remote agents'. Hollowed out, the body serves as 'a better "host" for packing more technology inside' (Stelarc, 1999: 121; 132). Here Stelarc's work, developed in conjunction with industry and corporate technicians, manifests its difference from that of Orlan: his project aligns itself with the goals of production in which bodies are improved in order that they function more efficiently in a workplace dominated by technological innovation and demands for innovation and optimisation. Orlan's art, involving images and cosmetic change, engages more fully with processes of consumption rather than production. Both economic poles, however, cohere around the emptying or voiding of inner spaces and traditional habits. Consumption requires an evacuation of subjective and symbolic spaces, the opening up of holes becoming sites of anxiety into which new and desirable images can be projected and consumed.

Orlan sells her body, in the process, perhaps, commenting on the abjection of the art market in the face of global commodification. In 1992, at the Sydney Biennial, her exhibition included vials of her liquefied flesh and blood drained from her body during operations. These were sold to raise money for further surgical procedures (Barbara Rose, 88). Abjection and horror can, it seems, be capitalised upon, postmodern economic imperatives having thrown off traditional values and constraints to maximise performance and productivity on a scale in which excess has no measure. For Juliet MacCannell, noting how 'rhetorical attacks, arts administration protocols, and sheer economic demands are combining to pre-empt a mental free space', economic and aesthetic practice overlap in their attempt to establish a new empire of market forces: the exhaustive conditions artists impose on themselves provide the new models of corporate practice, the worker sacrificing him or herself by being more creative, imaginative and productive, to the Other that is the corporation and its brand image. Aesthetics and business imperatives conjoin in this ardent new economic domain:

> the conditions of production of the aesthetic means of production are described by those employed in them as harsh—from Burbank to Silicon Valley, throughout the global economy. There is an undeniable demand for excess from workers, it is even written into their contracts, justified by the point that projects in these settings are creative, and thus consume the same kind of energies as the work of sublimation, enormous creative energies. Yet: situating the creative process within what is essentially a field of economic warfare (competition) is still to model it on the demand for jouissance by the Other, not on resistance to it. With this twist, we may collaboratively be producing a model for a unique new exploitation of the human soul, possibly deeper than ever before devised. (MacCannell, 58)

This is passionate labour at its most intense, eliding modern divisions between work and leisure. Jouissance, the expenditure of excessive (sexualised) energies, comes to determine corporate practices: intense energies are invested in the workplace, consuming the worker who has to give him or herself more fully to the corporate project. The intensity does not serve individual interests: jouissance is sacrificed to the Other, the company, in working harder, longer and later. Excess, then, is produced in a process of production that repeatedly demands more from workers, creativity as well as effort, imagination and emotional investment as much as time. Corporate culture has learnt from, and capitalised upon, the supposedly less alienated labour of artistic activity, to coordinate its new and relentless economic imperatives.

In this economic context, the excess generated by Orlan's performances has a double-edged significance, as does the evocation of horror. If excess has become the ordinary working principle of production and consumption in an economic movement that renders older traditions and practices redundant, then what kind of excess will exceed the conditions of contemporary capitalism? Excess of the kind exhibited by Orlan's (and Stelarc's) artistic efforts may well serve only to confirm or reinforce the excess that drives the new economy: it has, it seems, already capitalised on and incorporated aesthetic techniques and performative principles. Art no longer finds itself in the avant-garde of a revolutionary, anti-capitalist or counter-bourgeois movement but, on the contrary, plays a role in a radical economic upheaval, hence the 'creative industries'. While horror, of course, may make excess unbearable, causing a turning away in disgust, a revulsion recoiling, refusing to countenance dissolution. Orlan's project seems to engender horror in order to generate an excessive movement that turns on the body and its hollows, that opens it to the incursions of consumption and technology. Orlan draws the abject to the surface: 'in spectacular representation she offers her body as meat and pre-packages her photographic image for consumption by the art community' (Clarke, 189). At the same time, 'although seduced by the rhetoric of technology, she has turned to excess as a strategy against the benign and controlled nature of the screen, and the homogenization of body images' (202). What appears contradictory does cohere in respect of new models of consumption: emptying out older homogenised images, Orlan opens a space for the new, a space of further innovation and consumption surpassing the limitations of both body and image by engendering an empty and productive site of projection and desire.

Horror, then, works to ruin and repair, opening a hole that sees traditional images consumed, destroyed, used up; it also serves a locus of projection, capitalisation, innovation, a screen for more baseless images and their consumption. Orlan's work, so she says, 'is a struggle against the innate, the inexorable, the programmed, Nature, DNA (which is our direct rival as far as artists of representation are concerned) and God!' (Orlan, 91) In separating her creative work from anything fixed, constrained and immutable, her project accords with a range of practices, economic, technoscientific, genetic, attempting to surpass natural selection, overcome essence and rewrite code. In competition with DNA, art and the artist vie with the geneticist in the creation of new beings, beings no longer determined by convention, heritage or nature. On the horizon is a new aesthetic practice, 'transgenic art'. Taking its bearings from the 'extreme sciences' which manipulate the genome into new forms, it is one of the 'extreme arts' that 'aim at nothing less than to embark BIOLOGY on the road to a kind of "expressionism" whereby teratology will no longer be content just to study malformations, but will resolutely set off in quest of chimeric reproduction' (Virilio, 2003: 49–51). No longer anchored in nature or natural selection, the body becomes a site of monstrous recreation.

The 'meat' that comes to the fore in Orlan's operations describes the excess of the body and forms a site of both horror and consumption. For Adams, the meat is associated with the horrifying rawness of passion evoked by the performance, 'a jubilation' in excess of body and image; for Rose, it comes in the vials of flesh and blood sold off at exhibitions; for Clarke, it is the body reduced to a commodified aesthetic object. 'Meat' more generally signifies the redundancy of the body in an age that privileges image and information. In cyberpunk fiction, meat describes the prison of the flesh, a limit to the expansion of consciousness in the digital network (Gibson, 1984: 120). As meat, the body is denigrated as no more than shapeless, useless substance, the residue or leftover of technical and economic efforts to extract valuable information or energy from it as genetic or digital code. To assert that the body is obsolete, or to show that the face is detachable, is to reinforce assumptions that the body, like nature or identity, can be altered at will, that, like workers, it can be disposed of, remade, replicated or substituted. Excess is simultaneously the redundant stuff of the body, the exorbitant demands of the technological, corporate machine and the horror that articulates the two, the pulsing hole where things collapse and reform.

To see the body cut up, transformed, as nothing but a mask, an illusion of integrity, reality and coherence, is to expose a hollow, a formlessness that may be formed and re-formed by programmes or corporations. The horror, here, arises in identifying something that is both unbearable and all-too familiar. The return to the body does not, however traumatic or painful, sublimely evoke a sense of self in its delivery of an essence or reality underlying existence: on the contrary, it hollows out and carves up an existence assumed to be solid and immutable. Horror, making the body recoil in a violent shudder, inducing an intensity of feeling, does not necessarily return to a reinvigorated sense of humanity: the recoil and repulsion may just as well evoke the opposite, causing a flight from the body and the seething, formless substance imagined as the real. The very intensity of the body that shudders in horror, of the meat writhing in excess of corporeal integrity and usefulness, takes subjectivity out of itself, out of its skin, to throw it into networks of information, images and corporate commodities: it is a counter-abjection that exacerbates the abjections of all bodily stuff in a movement of the meat against and away from the meat.

'A horror story, the face is a horror story.' It is a horror story (so the mistranslation goes – but that's another story) engendered by the 'abstract machine of faciality' (Deleuze and Guattari, 1988: 168). For Deleuze and Guattari, subjectivity is constituted by a double relation exemplified by the face: the regime of signification forms the wall on which signs are projected and inscribed while affect, bound up with subjectification, is organised around black holes attracting passions and cathexes. Schizanalysis, of course, aims to move beyond the constraints of the couplet binding signification and subjectivity together: 'dismantling the face is the same as breaking through the wall of the signifier and getting out of the black hole of subjectivity' (188). Disassembling the face serves to undo the power relations that, monstrously, inhumanly, fix it in a negative and repressive regime of signification and single subjectivity. In cutting signification from affect, from the black hole of horror that holds it in place, desiring takes off in unimaginable and multiple directions: 'cutting edges of deterritorialization become operative and lines of deterritorialization positive and absolute, forming strange new becomings, new polyvocalities' (190). Perhaps 'polyvocal' should read 'polyfacial', 'superfacial', even, as the face in all its horror takes off, is taken off, and heads in new machinic and monstrous directions. Orlan takes Deleuze and Guattari's project literally. Her dismantling of the face sets out on a similar trajectory, escaping the face, body and aesthetic and signifying conventions: the black hole of horror seems to generate a field of intensities inaugurating a line of flight towards unthinkably different forms and combinations, a face taking off from itself, its own horrifying emptiness, in a space of endless simulated possibilities. But not quite. Horror remains. The flight to and of simulations continues, for the time being, however short that may be, on horror's trajectory of intense and radical ambivalence: its flight away from body, nature, even the real itself, not yet having the reserves of energy to attain escape velocity. Returning to the body, upon the body, in horror, attraction cedes to repulsion and flight begins again.

Image, it seems, is everything. It wages war on the ever-expanding meat that it leaves slumped before its screens, screens across which assorted monsters and horrors flicker and fade. Hollywood, of course, lies in the forefront of the image imperative: all excess corporeality, given that the camera's gaze is reputed to add pounds, must be cut away. 'What am I to do?' A director of a multi-million dollar movie is reported to have exclaimed to an 'overweight' famous actress, 'shoot round you?' (Heiman, 65)

When value is calibrated to dress size, huge expenditures on losing weight are demanded: diets and fitness regimes, nutritionists and personal trainers, abused medication and banned pharmaceuticals, become a major growth area. Continued employment depends on turning the body into an image, reducing it to the thinness of celluloid two-dimensionality. A 'nutritionist to the stars', Dr Tony Perrone, notes how celebrities will 'risk heart palpitations, a stroke and infertility': dieting is redefined as an 'extreme sport' (Heiman, 67; 65). 'Fat in Hollywood is a size 2. Everyone wants to be size 0', quips Joan Rivers (65). Kathy Najimy of the TV show *Veronica's Closet* emphasises the dangers: 'the glamorisation of ghastly thinness is what's truly frightening because, if it continues, I really think we are going to see a woman drop dead on one of these television shows'(65–7). Death raises the stakes in this extreme sport, the final consummation of the drive to be size 0.

In a technologised economy of digital flows all substance, all materiality, all weight must be jettisoned. Bodies must have size 0 as their goal in order to live on in a circulation of images dominated by the screens of popular consumption, the screens in relation to which unrealities are realised, lived and consumed:

> Right here and now, life-size is no longer the yardstick of the real. The real is hidden in the reduction of images on the screen. Like a woman worried about putting on weight, being overweight, reality seems to apologise for having any relief, any kind of thickness. If the *interval* becomes thin, 'infra-thin', in suddenly turning into an interface, things and objects perceived also become infra-thin and lose their weight, their bulk. (Virilio, 1997: 26)

Weightlessness is demanded by the vision machines of martial and corporate progress. The body, according to Virilio, is to be subjected to the 'de-corporation' of video screens, divested of its qualities and useful information, its functions given over to machines: eyes cede to lenses, hands to DataGloves, sexual organs to the electrodes in a datasuit (1995b). Interplanetary technologies will colonise the space of the body, evacuating its substance at a microcellular level, the hallucinatory speeds of digital processing will erase temporal and spatial distance in favour of the instant and the 'intimate perception of one's gravimetric mass will lose all concrete evidence' (1995a: 106).

Before the screens, as if to encourage those shrinking creatures on it, mass increases, levels of obesity arise, providing ballast for flight of simulations, feeding voraciously upon the emptiness of the image. A report by the Centre for Disease Control in 1998 found that the fattest people inhabit the Bible belt. New Orleans was the city with the largest occupants who 'seem like another species. They're not even the same shape; they're spherical, as if each one has been inflated by a God armed with a bicycle pump' (Coles, 17). Celluloid and cellulite duke it out. Between simulations and real, the body expands or shrinks, a battle determined by the quasi-superegoic power of the image. Norms are the first casualties when medical technology and cosmetic surgery joins forces with the inordinate imperatives of the image. Collagen injections, liposuction, nose jobs, neck tightening, tummy ticks, silicon breast enhancements … there is no limit to the work that 'needs' to be done. Inexhaustible enhancement leaves ideals of beauty behind: there is no final point where one is allowed to be satisfied or feel imaginarily complete. Contrasting London and Manhattan parties in terms of their 'freak value', a result of excessive plastic surgery, one woman underwent 'so many lifts that the skin which God had intended to give her eyelids was now so far up her forehead it was tattooed with false eyebrows. As a result, she could no longer blink – a not uncommon phenomenon' (17). The side-effect of having eyes permanently wide open is the horror of never be able to close them to the incessant influx of images.

Another woman with nearly sixty separate surgical procedures behind her looks 'otherworldly': 'her defence is that she was trying to turn herself into a human panther' (17). Beyond any desire to recover youthful beauty, cosmetic surgery charts an exorbitant trajectory elsewhere: monstrosity no longer serves as the exception guaranteeing human values but establishes only the illusion of difference and the fact of its disappearance. All frames of reference, except the image, disappear too: 'this liquidation of the Other is accompanied by an artificial synthesis of otherness – the radical cosmetic surgery of which cosmetic surgery on faces and bodies is merely the symptom' (Baudrillard, 1993b: 115). The synthesis of otherness, of course, exerts the magnetic pull of the same, an assimilation of strangeness through a 'hypostasis of the Same' that draws the subject into the gravitational flux of an unbound self-image:

> In facial traits, in sex, in illness, in death, identity is constantly 'altered'. There is nothing you can do about it: that's destiny. But it is precisely that which must be exorcized at any cost through an identification with the body, through an individual appropriation of the body, of your desire, your look, of your image: plastic surgery all over the place. If the body is no longer a place of otherness [*alterité*], a dual relationship, but it is rather a locus of identification, we then reconcile to it, we must repair to it, perfect

it, make it an ideal object. Everyone uses their body like a man uses woman in the projective mode of identification described before. The body is invested as a fetish, and is used as a fetish in a desperate attempt at identifying oneself. The body becomes the object of an autistic cult and of a quasi-incestuous manipulation. And it is the likeness [*resemblance*] of the body with its model which then becomes a source of eroticism and of 'white' [fake, virgin, neutral … ] self-seduction to the extent that this likeness virtually excludes the Other and is the best way to exclude a seduction which would emerge from somewhere else. (Baudrillard, 2002: 54–5)

Beyond an ideal of self-identification and an exorcism of destiny, however, the body is given over to an economy in which sameness and otherness are artificially recreated and exceeded. The performance artist, Orlan, has described a dinner party in America where other female guests greeted her with noticeable coolness, if not hostility. It did not take her long to discover the source of their animosity: 'they all had the same nose!' (Hirschhorn, 118) The minimal difference of Orlan's surgical facial excesses highlighted their cosmetic homogeneity.

Autoaffection, exposing the absence of otherness as it spirals inwards and evacuates all resistance, precipitates the imminent implosion of the selfsame, a final neutralisation. It thus demands a countervailing pull, a reinvention of difference that goes beyond ideals and self-identity in a deforming procession of synthesised monstrosities that, in turn, are rendered the same. And so on. Faces and bodies no longer need incessant adjustment to keep up with the pace of the image. Images are doing it for themselves. Hollywood stars who feel their employment threatened by ever thinner human actresses also have digital rivals whose size, shape and features are not limited by corporeal standards. Indeed, the 'lollipops' whose dramatic weight loss gives their appearance a deformed quality with heads too large for stick bodies, strangely resemble the cartoon and virtual characters whose features are over-accentuated to the point of being 'physically deformed by human standards' (Hamilton). Among the hugely popular 'virtual idols' of Japanese media, the attraction lies in the 'impossibility' of their appearance, their 'images free of material referent'. Kyoto Date, a pop star and television performer, as well as making CDs and videos, is a virtual idol created by Japan's top modelling agency, Horipro, and software engineers: she is an 'amalgam' of several faces, the voice of a singer and the voice of an actress and the dance style electronically mapped from the movements of another performer. Her CD sales, however, have been below expectation, a sign that her creation is flawed: 'if it is the artificiality of the image that attracts young men to virtual idols, then, perhaps the error was in Horipro's intense efforts to make Kyoto appear human'

(Hamilton). In the context of video game characters, a 'deformed aesthetic' moves images of desire beyond the human: 'unearthliness is part of
the charm' (Poole, 153). Unchecked by any weight whatsoever, untied
from corporeal identity, the image can replicate and deviate continually in
its expansive movement of form and deformity, norm and monstrosity.

The return of the real that Hal Foster identifies in twentieth-century
art raises questions about the way that horror, abjection and trauma are
put to work in culture. Andy Warhol's Pop Art, in which commodity
culture readily incorporates a supposedly higher aesthetics, also extends
processes of commodification to the most disturbing images of everyday
western modernity: his 'Death in America' series is made up of numbered
silkscreen prints of crashes repeated in blocks, like his cola bottles or images of celebrities, and tinted with a variety of colours. Mechanical and
shocking at the same time, the photographs of so many highway wrecks
and mangled bodies are both banal and horrible. Foster gives the genre a
name, 'traumatic realism', and argues that it addresses a particularly modern subject: not a 'blank subject', automated, indifferent, in the manner of
Warhol's dictum, 'I want to be a machine', but a 'shocked subject'. In the
fashion of Benjamin's definitively modern experience, shock becomes integral in the psychological armoury of contemporary subjectivity, the individual taking on 'the nature of what shocks him as a mimetic defence
against this shock' (Foster, 131). In Lacan, the distinction between *automaton* and *tuche* describes the limits of subjective existence, the former
marking out the circulations of pleasure and signification through which
individuality is constituted by the habits of language and culture; the latter '*the encounter with the real.* The real is beyond the *automaton*, the return, the coming-back, the insistence of the signs, by which we see ourselves governed by the pleasure principle' (Lacan, 1977b: 53). Repetition
and automation plot the everyday circuits of pleasure. The real registers a
shocking encounter, a limit-experience marking a beyond, a gap in excess
of the circuits of language. With traumatic realism, however, the proximity of automaton and real is increasingly evident, the latter irrupting to
evacuate and restart the rhythms of pleasure. A shocked subject, Foster
notes, is an 'oxymoron' since there is 'no subject self-present in shock'
(Foster, 131). Any sense of self is emptied out in the moment of traumatic
experience, only to be thrown back, dazed, numbed, almost automated,
to the world of familiar habits and pleasures. Shock, like horror, confronts
the subject with something incomprehensible, something registered only
as a traumatic gap in experience, something that causes a corresponding
hole in subjectivity.

Taking the form of a repetition, the literal screening of shock has a double effect as that which protects and provokes the reaction. Shock, becoming an aesthetic mechanism, assumes the form Lacan assigns to ghosts: 'fear with its ghosts is a localized defence, a protection against something that is beyond, and which is precisely something that is un-known to us' (Lacan, 1992: 323). That 'something', of course, is the Thing of horror, the gaping hollow around which signification and sense coheres and dissolves. Ghosts screen off as much as render visible the underlying, horrifying site of anxiety, putting objects of fear in place to ward off a more devastating consumption. In protecting against and producing fig-ures of traumatic disturbance, the close and ambivalent mechanism of aesthetic shock, like images of horror, implodes in its own space of evacu-ation, the emptiness it discloses and occludes repeatedly and at speed (the car, before Warhol's time, already symbolised the speeding progression of modernity) is rendered more distant and less disquieting. The distance between the gaping Thing of shock and the representations designed to evoke and screen it forms the basis of Foster's interrogation of the 'return of the real' in art. Repeated aesthetic deployments of shocking, abject, horrific or traumatic images tend, he suggests, towards the image rather than the Thing, precisely because such disturbing sites and forces cannot be rendered visible or fully exposed to culture. Instead, a 'conscientious abjection' is at work in the manipulation of images, an 'artifice of abjection' in which not the Thing but the collapse of the system of representation, the Other, is in evidence (Foster, 156). Horror, abjection, shock, absorbed by images, become less effective in breaking through the aesthetic screens that produce them: 'today, with excess heaped on excess, desensitization to the shock of images and the meaninglessness of words has shattered the world stage. PITILESS, contemporary art is no longer improper' (Virilio, 2003: 36).

None the less, Foster acknowledges the continuing appeal of horrifying images, arguing that their continued deployment in aesthetic practices derives from 'dissatisfaction with the textualist model of culture' (Foster, 166). The attraction of horror and abjection is thus an effect of an excess of artifice, signs and simulations rather than any disruption of an authen-tic reality. To seek a return of the real demands a corresponding excess, powerful enough to break through the circulations of images and disclose something fundamental, a ground against which to measure and arrest the artifices of signifying excess. But the real is impossible, formless, hor-rifying, a gap beyond the reality structured by signs. It remains a stain, a dark spot, a black hole within and beyond signifying conventions. In re-turning to the real, aesthetics only marks out the limits of representation rather than effecting escape or liberation. The gesture of return, moreover, turns upon the frames of symbolised reality, enunciating an incredulity at or disillusionment with prevailing orders of discourse. For Foster, the cultural investments in trauma and abjection stem from

> disillusionment with the celebration of desire as an open passport of a mobile subject – as if the real, dismissed by performative postmodernism, were marshalled against the imaginary world of fantasy captured by consumerism. But there are strong forces at work elsewhere as well: despair about the persistent AIDS crisis, invasive disease and death, systemic poverty and crime, the destroyed welfare state, indeed the broken social contract (as the rich opt out in revolution from the top and the poor are dropped out in immiseration from the bottom). (166)

Against the aestheticisation of horror and abjection stand more pervasive and persistent horrors of social, political and economic existence. Aesthetic horrors screen off, or divert attention from less spectacular and more horrifying realities. Horror against horror. But horror, whether commodified and simulated or not, increasingly fails, such are the effects of habituation and an-aestheticisation, to provoke much recoil. Nor does it re-establish social and symbolic limits. The collapse of credibility suffered by social and political institutions of modernity opens a horrifying hole, site of anxiety, incredulity, despair. As in Salecl's analysis of body marking, the collapse of the Other provokes extensive reverberations on individual subjectivity. Horror, individuated, internalised, becomes the response to horror, its site and screen: it is embraced, incorporated, repeated. For Foster, the role played by trauma in popular, aesthetic and public discourse is significant: it produces a subject who is 'evacuated and elevated at once' (168). Trauma, like shock and horror, empties individual, object and signifying institution, but also, sublimely, subsequently seems to return the subject to itself with a heightened awareness of him or herself. With feeling, at the limits of feeling, then, intensified, invigorated, thrilled, the subject rediscovers him or herself as a site of shocking affect. Aesthetically, economically, politically, the subject is evacuated and elevated, and evacuated again.

The polarity of simulation and real is gravitationally charged, the motions of one influencing the orbit of the other. Around the black hole of horror, however, orbits do not necessarily remain stable. Stars implode. Horror, repeated, figured, screened, lessens in effect. The more its power diminishes, the greater the need to find stronger sources of intense affect. Move up a level. The cycle restarts, horror becoming further absorbed in artifice. But art will not let go of bodily matters and related horrors, as if, despite and because of the speedy in-corporation of aesthetics in modes of commodification, a touch of excess will give it greater purchase on the resource of the real. In art and performance art bits of bodies, living and dead, fluids, faecal matter, have littered galleries and splashed across stages for years. Marc Quinn used eight pints of blood to make a frozen cast of his head. In the mock controversies, feigned indignation and sham scandal of tabloid headlines, shock and horror make for better publicity and prices. Charles Saatchi and his 'Sensation' exhibition fusing or confusing tabloid excitement and 'some sort of would-be avant-garde art' succeeds only in announcing a 'conformism of abjection', 'a habit the twentieth century has enjoyed spreading around the globe' (Virilio, 2003: 36). The 'Sensation' exhibition of British art at the Royal Academy in 1997 caused a media scandal that centred on one painting: an 11x9 ft portrait of Myra Hindley. Not only did it depict the most notorious British murderess of the post-war era, a woman imprisoned for child-killing, it was composed using the print of a child's hand. No matter how impressive and disturbing the painting itself, the indelible popular and media memory of the crime, compounded, mocked even, by the mode of composition, fuelled a predictable furore, an all-too automatic reaction on which contemporary art has learnt to thrive: the hype, of course, has superseded any idea of art itself while simulation feeds on an ever-more artificial and aestheticised real.

In 1998 another artist, Anthony Noel Kelly was prosecuted. The story did not make many headlines but it provides another instance of the aestheticisation of the real. The artist had stolen the remains of forty bodies from the Royal Academy of Surgeons in order to gather the raw material for his work. Such an injection of a little taste of death, adding fatal, real substance to art, reverses the historical relation between anatomy, art and cadavers: instead of robbing graves to provide corpses on which trainee surgeons could develop their skills and becoming a subject of ghoulish fiction, the artist stole from an anatomy department that had acquired the bodies legitimately. His art, one suspects, would have turned out too clinical, his crime too contrived to make the pages of some latter-day graverobbing romance.

When bodies are given willingly to exhibitors and no crime is committed, only a residual charge of bad taste and a vague sense of taboo may be activated. Gunther von Hagen's 'BodyWorlds' exhibition, having toured Europe with great success and, along the way, secured many eager prospective donors, reached London in 2002. Appalling many commentators and attracting large, fascinated crowds to the Atlantis Gallery in Brick Lane, the exhibition displayed human and animal bodies in various statuesque poses. The figures did not simply mimic sculptural postures, however. The bodies were stiffened and frozen into shape by a chemical procedure, developed by von Hagen, called 'plastination'. With skin stripped back to reveal tendons, muscles, vitrified flesh and organs, the show leaned heavily towards an anatomical exhibition: indeed, Von Hagen's work has been described as 'Anatomy Art' (Clarke, 34). Von Hagen's notoriety moreover increased when he announced plans to stage (and televise) a 'live' dissection. Doctor and showman, he describes his work as 'edutainment' and himself as 'chiefly a scientist who wants to enlighten people by means of aesthetic shock rather than cruelty shock' (cited in Jeffries, 3). For all the critical outrage and popular fascination, the exhibits evoke an air of the hygienic uncanny, their horror having been thoroughly sanitised and aestheticised, the seething and repulsive corruption of the flesh chemically shrinkwrapped and carefully posed: 'the abject body is made clean and proper' yet transformed (abjection now being an index of humanity) into something 'not human' (Clarke, 35). Bodies become plastic, grotesque mannequins, anatomical techniques having produced exhibits in line with the disjointed and disfigured dolls of the surrealist Hans Bellmer or his Britart heirs Jake and Dinos Chapman.

Von Hagen's work manifests a prospective trajectory, aligned with cybernetic and cyborg prognoses for the human body in which simulation leads to supercession: 'the post-human body will be a simulacrum, a representation of the wounded body which has been displaced by an artificial construct' (Clarke, 35). The uncanny arrives from the future, life and death, matter and nature subsumed by simulation. Horror becomes aesthetic and an-aesthetic at the same time. Monstrosity finds itself entangled in webs of technical artifice. Von Hagen's exhibition and overall project, in his own words, assume an uncanny tendency: 'I want to bring the life back to anatomy. I am making the dead lifeful again. This exhibition is a place where the dead and the living mix' (cited in Jeffries, 3). Life and death mix in viewing plastinated figures. The aim of 'bringing life back to anatomy', undertaken under the direction of a German scientist, automatically recalls his Gothic precursor: he is 'a modern-day Frankenstein' (3). Curiously, the easy invocation of Frankenstein does not nostalgically evoke the heady days of modern horror, but marks a return with a difference in which the figure and his monster are reinvented, retroactively posited at the origin of a post-human future. Fragmented, mutated, sutured and uncanny, Frankenstein's creation anticipates the post-human fate of the body, 'to be carved up into independent fragments' that reveal 'the machine-like function and structure of the body' (39).

The future, with its new Frankenstein and new monsters barely distinguishable, involves a double projection in the form of a throwing forwards of an old narrative and an eager anticipation of and identification with monstrosity:

to be perceived as monstrous, or consciously to construct oneself as monstrous, is to have an affinity with disorder, chaos, mutation and transformation, in an attempt to work against logic, rationality, normality, purity and science. It can often be seen as a way of both undoing and resurrecting the past and its fictions in order to create some new forms, connections, leakages and abstractions. (Clarke, 36)

To be seen as monstrous, as in so many Gothic revisions of vampirism and monstrosity, is no longer such a bad thing. The enthusiastic projection of present into future also sees the latter descend upon the former. Frankenstein 'remains a potent metaphor for the collapse of the biological and the technological':

> in the present milieu, human bodies are being carved up, fragmented and reassembled in seemingly less sinister ways through medical CAT scans, DNA splicing, genetic engineering, organ transplants, cosmetic surgery and prosthetic implants; or through media interventions in which body images are digitally manipulated. (46)

The future, plotted in the past as a Gothic story or scientific romance, collapses on the present as a common, thoroughly familiar condition. Monstrosity slips into the fabric of an everyday existence indifferent to horror. Posthumanity erases all human distinctions and differences, differences sustained precisely in the relation to monstrosity.

Monsters are neither more nor less than the norm. They are banal, unsurprising, ubiquitous, visible and overlooked at the same time. The wonders and horrors of Frankenstein's enterprise located monstrosity at the extremes of visionary experience, haunting the edges of modernity and the humanity it invented. But when monsters move from the margins to populate the stage as unremarkable extras in the crowd scenes of the future another version of Shelley's fiction has to be written. In his 'cyberpunk version', Bruce Sterling marks out the significantly altered message, context and roles of Frankenstein and monster:

> In this imaginary work, the Monster would likely be the well funded R&D team-project of some global corporation. The Monster might well wreak bloody havoc, most likely on random passers-by. But having done so, he would never have been allowed to wander to the North Pole, uttering Byronic profundities. The Monsters of cyberpunk never vanish so conveniently. They are already loose on the streets. They are next to us. Quite likely WE are them. The Monster would have been copyrighted through new genetic laws, and manufactured world-wide in many thousands. Soon the Monsters would all have lousy night jobs mopping up at fast-food restaurants ... This 'anti-humanist' conviction in cyberpunk is not some literary stunt to outrage the

> bourgeoisie; this is an objective fact about culture in the late twentieth century. Cyberpunk didn't invent this situation; it just reflects it … Jump-starting Mary Shelley's corpses is the least of our problems; something much along that line happens in intensive-care wards every day. (cited in Johnson, 101)

Monsters take their place in a corporate and consumerist world already used to technological innovation, products of corporate technoscience, genetically modified, patented creations of research and development departments. Their lives are routine and uninteresting, new versions of service sector drones existing with few prospects on the lowest ladder of the western economic hierarchy. The only threat 'they' pose to 'us', that is if any difference can be detected at all, is precisely in the indifference with which they circulate: if such a world is 'de-monstered', it is also dehumanised and 'their' tasks and existences are identical with those of their human counterparts. Such familiar daily monstrosities, notable for their dullness and absence of affect, are part of a narrowly an-aesthetic and uninspiring spectrum of opportunities and possibilities that are far from fantastic or monstrous: it ranges from floor cleaners in junk-food outlets to patients wired up on an operating tables, all varieties the same, homogenised culture of surgically, cosmetically, chemically or genetically prosthetic beings.

Simulations, aestheticising and eroding horror, fly from a real whose intensities fuel their flight. But the future does not provide the horizon into which they vanish, instead only clearing a vanishing horizon that flickers on the empty screens of the present. Monsters, once upon a time, heralded the possibility of a future outside narrative patterns and normal predictions, assuring an opening onto uncertainty and the unknown. Jacques Derrida underlines this monstrosity:

> the future is necessarily monstrous: the figure of the future, that is, that which can only be surprising, that for which we are not prepared, you see, is heralded by species of monsters. A future that would not be monstrous would not be a future; it would already be predictable, calculable, and programmable tomorrow. All experience open to the future is prepared or prepares itself to welcome the monstrous *arrivant* … (Derrida, 1992a: 386)

The programming of digital and genetic code, however, with their 'Frankenstein foods', 'designer babies' and 'Frankenstein pets' offer a predictable, homogenised and utterly non-monstrous alternative, a future that, if not monstrous, is also not a future: after all risks have been calculated, all options assessed, all genetic therapies undertaken, is a future open to otherness, surprise, change or monstrosity even possible? If the question evokes the slightest hint of anxiety, its outlet may assume the form of a desire for monstrosity, for something unknown, shocking, unpredictable, but that desire, too, is stimulated and exhausted in an endless procession of aesthetic monsters. In looking for monsters, anticipating their (posthuman) advent, their arrival is already contained by expectation and readily assimilated. The function of monsters in rendering norms visible falters into redundancy when monsters are normalised. Derrida recognises the decline of monstrosity in its heterogeneous incarnation: he proposes a barely tenable division in the category of monstrosity between an oxymoronic 'normal monstrosity' and a tautological 'monstrous monstrosity'. The former is all-too familiar to critical and aesthetic practices insisting on spurious divisions and differences. 'Monstrous monstrosities' provides a new name for monstrous forms that were once unrecognisable, disturbing, unpresentable and open to an unpredictable future. 'Monstrous monstrosities' manifest a 'formless form' in excess of anything that can be programmed, anticipated or legitimated. Nor can they be presented as monsters: 'Monsters cannot be announced. One cannot say: "Here are our monsters", without immediately turning the monsters into pets' (Derrida, 1990: 80). In readily making monsters, seeking them out in every crack and crevice of culture and subjectivity, monsters already appear too normal. One eats monsters (Frankenstein foods), loves monsters (Frankenstein pets), is monstrous and normal in every habitual technological relationship. Normal monstrosity, it seems, has become the quotidian new species that has simulated and simultaneously ousted all but the faintest idea of monstrous monstrosity.

## Horreality

Picture the operating room of an East European clinic, though its white tiles, glinting steel instruments and high wattage lamps could be anywhere. A British woman is undergoing cut-rate cosmetic surgery, with a documentary camera crew in attendance. As the surgeon works, the camera moves in over his shoulder to focus on the neat incision slicing skin from ear to chin under the jaw. The skin is lifted and excess tissue scraped from under the cheeks, the camera observing the bumps on the surface as surgical steel evacuates the fat beneath. At the same time, the woman is having liposuction on her legs. The camera pans to nozzles attached to thighs; it follows the opaque plastic tube to a metal side table. There, a transparent tank steadily fills with the gelatinous globules and bloody ooze pumped from the body of the woman anaesthetised upon the table.

With its juxtaposition of the instruments of rationality and the hyperrationality of a clinical exorcism of the flesh, the scene offers a revolting image, a striking glimpse of horror in its contemporary conjunction of surgical efficiency and fleshly slime. If, however, the focus on an increasingly common occurrence provides a symptomatic image of a horror central to contemporary culture, one is left to wonder about the role of Gothic representation once so crucial in apprehending monstrosity. The aura of surgical whiteness and cleanliness, arc lamps blazing their permanent daylight, along with the already hackneyed generic status of this scene in 'real-life' documentary reports, have nothing Gothic about them: no ghosts or demons flit in or out of visibility, no maniacal smile distorts the face of a psychotic villain, no darkness is left unpenetrated. Even the darkness of the flesh itself is pumped out for observation. Monster, heroine and scientist are elided in the obscenity and banality of the situation. Cosmetic surgery has become an everyday horror story.

Horror, so it seems, has passed beyond the capacity and comfort of anything vaguely resembling Gothic representation. Moving out of the darkness of dungeons and away from the nether regions of city, family or society, leaving gloomy forests or the shadowy realms of unconscious wishes, horror glows in the over-illuminated pulse of surgical and virtual realities. Terrors of the night are replaced by horrors of the light. Nathaniel Hawthorne's 'broad and simple daylight', which allowed no room for mystery, shadow or 'gloomy wrong', now technologically replicated, sucks horror into itself and spews out any remainder: so many lumps of useless, decomposing meat (Hawthorne, x–xi). Writing on hospital settings and anatomical effects in cinema, Pete Boss asserts that 'despite the immaculate order of the hospital, its brilliance and antiseptic surroundings, the banishing of signifiers of death and decay, it remains a sanctuary of contemporary terror'(Boss, 20). He cites Philippe Ariès' claim that assimilations or occlusions of death allow 'the old savagery to creep back under the mask of medical technology': the dying, tube-bound patient 'is becoming a popular image, more terrifying than the *transi* or skeleton of macabre rhetoric' (Ariès, 614). The meaning of death, for all its savagely sanitised returns, changes. It is absorbed into a bureaucracy furnished with a technology designed to abolish death as a sign of nature or efface it as a mark of failure, in the process wresting control and possession of dying from the patient, relatives and community, and, even, from anything resembling humanity (585–95). The 'technophobia' that Boss associates with medical and institutional horrors and which recoils from an identification of human and machine is located within a wider technobureaucratic system in which the boundaries between identity and otherness are disturbed. Cosmetic surgery, in which technology reverses the natural process of ageing in the interests of extended beauty, is also situated in this terrain.

'Horror isn't what it used to be', to misquote Louis Cyphre in Alan Parker's *Angel Heart* (1987). Nor is it *where* it used to be, having undergone a shift in temporal and geographical setting as well as object and form. Horror no longer lies in a barbaric, superstitious past, as it did for Walpole or Radcliffe at the end of the eighteenth century; it no longer concerns the return of monstrously unavowable wishes as it did for Frankenstein or James Hogg's justified sinner; it has nothing in common with the ghostly reappearance of the guilty family secrets and horrid paternal transgressions of the Victorians. Nor is it bound up with the primordial, atavistic or decadent energies embodied by Dracula. Nor does it lie in the callous sadism barely disguised by the nice veil of normality. If horror can be glimpsed anywhere, it occupies a site other than the surfaces of postmodern self-reflection: it circulates in and as the void disclosed by their obliteration of substance; in the slimy flesh scraped from just below the skin, the 'monstrous excrescence' that once was human. Imperceptible viral horrors circulate with a supplementary contamination of borders and a pervasive and free-floating anxiety. The eclipse of recognisable figures of horror is mirrored in the 'waning of affect' associated with postmodernity (Jameson, 1984: 61–2). Indeed, the disgust, loathing abhorrence and bloodcurdled revulsion proper to horror can barely be evoked by the unnatural and immoral monstrosities that once disturbed and corrupted the virtues and proprieties of modern culture with hideous spectres of mortal decay, callous violence, scientific cruelty or sexual depravity. With the waning of traditional objects of horror (for these objects, like symptoms, are always culturally specific) a shift is signalled, a transformation identifiable in the cultural formations, modes and media through which horror creeps and crawls. If horror, so long shaped in Gothic guises, has been transformed, it may also be the case that it no longer takes its bearings from Gothic fictions. Which suggests that Gothic, from its inception as a hybrid genre and its subsequent diverse mutations over two centuries, has dispersed itself so widely as to become both meaningless and redundant, a diffusion of significance and affect in the fantasies and anxieties of culture.

The first decade of the nineteenth century saw the decline of Gothic. The overproduction of titles, with recycled plots and repetitive formulas saturated the market for 'terrorist novel writing' and crossed the thin line separating sensation, excitement and desire from familiarity, convention and boredom with an excess of the same (Anon., 1797a: 227–9). In the twentieth century, the movies assume the mantle of popular Gothic. Film may be a more effective medium than fiction for the delivery of Gothic sensationalism: 'the "cinefantastic" in any case succeeds, far more efficiently and effectively and on a far greater scale than its ancestral media, in the production of sensation' (Clover, 94). Specular absorption, visual shocks and immediate realisation supplant imaginative effort in the brutal activation of a technology of terror. Movie horror, however, remains just as susceptible to overfamiliarity with conventions, since formulas structure the play of mystery and expectation producing the thrills. The exhaustion of the genre is well illustrated in Roberto Rodriquez's *From Dusk Till Dawn*. A post-heist story scripted by and co-starring Quentin Tarantino, the film suddenly turns into a Mexican vampire shocker, notable for the spectacular violence of its special effects. The second part of the film, however, makes no attempt to sustain an atmosphere conducive to horror. Instead, events unravel at the expense of the genre, enjoying the permeable boundary between horror and laughter with playful attention to cinematic devices. Having arrived at a seedy Mexican strip joint, the 'Titty Twister', a preacher's family and two desperadoes discover the place to be populated by bloodsuckers dressed as bikers. They discuss what to do:

> *Scott*: 'We got crosses all over the place. All you gotta do is put two sticks together and you got a cross.'
> *Sex-Machine*: 'He's right. Peter Cushing does that all the time.'
> *Seth*: 'I don't know about that. In order for it to have any power, I think it's got to be an offical crucifix.'

He is corrected by the preacher, played by Harvey Keitel: the symbolic power is the important factor, not the thing. The debate continues:

> *Seth*: 'So we got crosses covered, moving right along, what else?'
> *Frost*: 'Wooden stakes in the heart have been workin' pretty good so far.'
> *Sex-Machine*: 'Garlic, holy water, sunlight … I forget, does silver do anything to a vampire?'
> *Scott*: 'That's werewolves.'
> *Sex-Machine*: 'I know silver bullets are werewolves. But I'm pretty sure silver has some sort of effect on vampires.'
> *Kate*: 'Does anybody have any silver? No. Then who cares?'
>
> (Tarantino, 1996: 97)

The comedy is dominated by film references. No one, it is made plain, has read a volume, 'like a Time-Life book', on vampires (98). Their best weapon, they decide, is the preacher himself, able to bless an endless and destructive supply of holy water. But, there's 'only one problem, his faith ain't what it used to be' (99). With some determined coaching however, he gets back in the groove: 'I'm a mean, motherfuckin' servant of God' (100). They load up with crosses, stakes and holy water and blast out spraying 'Uzi squirt guns' and using water balloons as grenades.

The visual and verbal jokes draw attention, with thinly reflexive playfulness, to the surfaces, conventions and formulas of vampire fiction and film, except that *From Dusk Till Dawn* places vampires within the realistic genre, or, rather, as part of a hyperrealism determined by the media screen itself. There is no point to the movie other than its reflexive jokes on convention: the arbitrary and unexpected distribution of deaths underlines the anti-conventionality and evacuates any pretence to substance or morality. Horror film reaches its comedic apotheosis in its own formulas. 'Horrality', Brophy's suitably messy neologism for the 'horror, textuality, morality, hilarity' of 1980s movies in the genre, is succeeded by a 'texilarity' which jettisons the more sombre terms (Brophy, 3). The movie wears all the superficial pleasures of formulaic horror on its sleeve, pouring its artifices over the shiny surface of special effects, a technological realization of fantasy that absorbs all horror codes and evacuates all affect except hilarity. Ineffectual in the evocation of terror, the thin reflexive wit is empty of any significance other than its own absorbing visual spectacle. Beneath that, nothing. Hence the horror, the glimpse of the void beneath visual narrative, the recognition that there is nothing but images, a recognition which displaces the moral quest for objects of horror into a hyperrealism unable, despite the best efforts of mass murderers, to fill the gap.

A degree of sensationalism is sustained, however, despite the abandonment of the identification usually required to evoke horror: it comes purely at the level of special effects that realise, with shocking speed and technical efficiency, grotesque and repellent transformations and dissolutions of bodies. 'Like sex and blood,' one film technician notes, 'special effects have become an indispensable ingredient in making a blockbuster' (cited in Virilio, 1995a: 71). The slasher genre displays a fascination with corporeality and a 'realisation that all that lies between the visible, knowable outside of the body and its secret insides is one thin membrane, protected only by a collective taboo against its violation. It is no surprise that the rise of the slasher film is concomitant with the development of special effects that let us see with our own eyes the "opened" body' (Clover, 103). While the genre enjoys the horrifying spectacle of corporeal mutilation in which bodily identity is squashed into oozy substance (Boss, 16), *From Dusk Till Dawn* renders corporeality spectacularly insignificant as it plays with textual surfaces to disgorge the void filled by special effects. *From Dusk Till Dawn*, by eschewing all content, substance and morality, highlights the empty but effective artifice of cinematic techniques of immediate and shocking realisation. The technological process supplants rather than reinforces reality, natural emotion and subjectivity: sucked into the wake of technological realisation, human faculties are spat out: in evoking emotion to excess, artificial overstimulation brings human emotions to the surface in order to evacuate affect and supersede all sensory faculties.

Of course, the attention to surface, artifice and formula is as old as Gothic writing itself: for eighteenth-century critics, the obvious and re-cycled machinery of plots, settings and devices was sufficient cause for curt dismissal as crude and consumerist sensationalism. With its focus on surfaces, Gothic fiction retains, in the present, a limited continuity. In its demonstration of the boundaries of romance and reality, from *The Castle of Otranto* to *The Bloody Chamber*, dramatic and popular fictions remain integral to Gothic narratives. *The Mysteries of Udolpho*'s waxen image, *Frankenstein*'s textual monstrosity, *Dracula*'s mythic male romance, all draw out the superficial force of fictional evocations of horror. However, horror replicates and enhances the excess and deficiency associated by Foucault with the rise of terror literature in the eighteenth century (Foucault, 1977: 53–67). With the split between the language of objective rationality and literature, the latter's ironic expenditure multiplies the empty space of rep-resentation with doubles and figures of death while aiming, always defi-ciently, at a transparent and shocking communication of affect. Literary language is divested of density and substance and an infinite void is hol-lowed out. The void, gaping in excess of representation, remains the locus of horror.

Horror, disconcertingly without object, lies in the gaps narrative can-not fill, the empty spaces, the extimate darkness, underlying the narration where the phantasmatic form of symbolised reality is disclosed. Horror takes the formless form of a 'black hole', arousing emotions that vainly seek a referent. Following Poe, Sage notes its 'objectless' force as a reaction to an unknown but implied source, a reaction involving 'the recoil, inner and outer, of the whole organism' (Sage, xx–xxi). Effects precede cause; horror presents some Thing quite primary. Radcliffe's opposition of sub-lime terror and annihilating horror depends on the visibility of an object: with something to apprehend, the imagination can act and the subject can elevate itself. Without an object, horror delivers only bodily paralysis and mental chaos (Radcliffe, 1826: 145–52). Terror evokes sublimity, horror the uncanny. The latter has nothing to do with the return of the repressed: the overproximity of the double signals, according to Lacan, the decom-position of the fantasy underpinning the consistency of the order sustain-ing reality, desire and identity (Lacan, 1977c: 11–52). The absence of the paternal metaphor, the metaphor which is the key to all Gothic fiction, evokes ghosts, monsters and the void of dissolution. Frankenstein's mon-ster, like all phantasmagorical creatures, presents the horrifying 'void of pure self' (Zizek, 1992: 137). A fantasy of paternal creation dissolves, his world is overturned. With Dracula's monstrosity, the unpresentable horror of his unreflecting presence is transformed into a terrible object that, when defined, can be subjected to the cleansing violence of moral enjoyment. The text, in many ways, works in direct opposition to *Frankenstein*: the unseen, unknown primordial energy of the vampire is pieced together from textual fragments; his horrible being is subjected to the disciplined gaze of modern communications, science and law to the point that the obscure Thing eating away at the heart of decadent Victorian culture can be rendered visible and destroyed in the name of family values.

Unbearable horror finds an object that turns it into terror. Neither inside nor outside human linguistic bodies, horror connotes an experience of some Thing that is 'extimate', an uncanny and confounding interior exteriority (Miller, 121–31). Horror nonetheless is also made to function within systems of morality as a limit to desire, while the gap it discloses in those systems serves as a screen for the projection of fantasy and the assuaging of anxieties, for the constructions of objects of horror – monsters, vampires, demons, terminators: these figures turn horror into terror, invigorating the imaginative energy of expulsion. In *The Ethics of Psychoanalysis*, Lacan notes how the locus or void of horror, *das Ding*, also serves as a screen for the projection and production of objects of anxiety, defence mechanisms against an unbearable and horrifying *jouissance* which tears reality apart, sites for the erection of a collective imaginary which preserves cultural systems (Lacan, 1992: 99). As the screen for cultural projection and the imaginary misrecognition of cultural unity, the Thing is occluded. To define the object of horror as animal nature, or fleshly desire is to impose symbolic reality in place of the real, to establish the unimaginable Thing as the limit of human meaning by the substitution of names, reasons and explanations. The Thing is blocked out, 'fear', as Lacan observes, 'is a localizable defence' (232). Horror fiction, with its monsters, ghosts and vampires, gives retrospective form to the unknown, abyssal limit, to the horror a culture cannot avow. By elevating objects to the status of *das Ding*, substituting literary phantasms in place of the real, fiction preserves the power of the phallus and maintains the imaginary boundaries of culture. Fiction's sublimations, at the same time, allow a glimpse of the Thing, the shadow of extimate darkness, and thus maintain the relation between *jouissance* and the phallus: 'Freud was the first to articulate boldly and powerfully the idea that the only moment of *jouissance* that man knows occurs at the site where fantasms are produced, fantasms that represent for us the same barrier as far as access to *jouissance* is concerned, the barrier where everything is forgotten' (298). Fiction, as a fantasy screen, filters what cannot be represented.

The Gothic way of producing objects of horror by playing with convention and expectations becomes increasingly ineffective in the twentieth century as evil becomes banal and hyperreality outstrips fiction. Conventions are played out to the point at which they are almost instantly reversible: the nice guy is too good to be true, too nice and therefore already marked with the stain of creepiness. This, of course, is the final, playful twist in *Twin Peaks*, its shining hero succumbing to the mirror of evil's sneer. The twentieth century has, as Lyotard notes, been saturated with terror and horror:

> The nineteenth and twentieth centuries have given us as much terror as we can take. We have paid a high enough price for the nostalgia of the whole and the one, for the reconciliation of the concept and the sensible, of the transparent and the communicable experience. Under the general demand for slackening and for appeasement, we can hear the mutterings of the desire for a return of terror, for the realization of the fantasy to seize reality. (Lyotard, 1984: 81–2)

The fantasy is accelerated by technobureaucracy while the return of terror, to the morally sanctioned expulsion of objects of disgust and hatred, has not been curtailed by recent history's plentiful horrors. On the contrary, too much terror, actual or represented, only produces the habituation and boredom which demands the creation of new objects of stimulation. Such consumptive desire was identified, of course, in the late eighteenth century and applied to the gratification of appetites for sensation in Gothic fiction. In the late twentieth century, however, the objects of desire became, in consumer culture, endlessly realisable. Fantasy seizes reality, seeking ever more objects to satisfy a demand for wholeness and satisfaction: the media, in aiming to deliver the ultimate image of horror, saturate screens at vast speed, the immediacy, indifference and repetitiveness of presentation allowing no room for the imagination to work.

Unless the horror is spectacular no interest will be excited: human feeling is extinguished or anaesthetised or boredom sets in. If the reason for the wane of Gothic writing after the 1790s was the obvious and repetitive recycling of stock formulas and devices, the contemporary search for escalating sensation and new stimulation is continually threatened with a similar fading of consumptive desire. Hence the evanescence of monsters: now banal, generic stereotypes. Even serial killers, genocidal murderers, paedophiles, distinguished by their scorecards or their gruesome style, are viewed through the lenses of hype and hyperreality. Spectacular crimes produce instant celebrity status. Figures of real life horror are all the more potent because, dragging a little bit of the real with them, they have turned fantasy into shocking event. Erasing the difference between fiction and reality, these actual figures of horror, though guaranteed by real crimes, all-too quickly become absorbed by the indifference of the image. The accompanying moral responses and elegies for morality, of course, constitute the attempt to restore a credible grand narrative and an integrated subjectivity in the face of the dispersals and fragmentations of numerous little stories and plural identities. To restore humanism and its basic fantasy requires an identifiable object of horror to charge the righteous anger of justified terror. Horror, it seems, has moved out of the realms of Gothic fiction and film and into the hyperrealism of everyday occurrence. And while endless objects are presented to arouse the visual consumer, none ever seem to really fill the gap of a pervasive and unspecific anxiety. Contemporary horror films involve 'having the shit scared out of you and loving it' (Brophy, 5). To the point that no one really gives a shit. There are instances when horror film or fiction, as if to support the moralising execration of the guardians of taste, seem to cross over into reality.

In his comments on *From Dusk Till Dawn*, Clive Barker recognises the general cultural insignificance of the horror genre in contrasting the 'more realistic' part of the movie and later comedic vampire blasting:

> If we were disturbed by some of the earlier passages, it was because of they had some connection to the context of the *Six O'clock News*, but once the dance of the vampires begins the carnage becomes so excessive that the grimmest moments seem playful, driven by a mixture of gags and gore that recalls Sam Raimi's *Evil Dead* series. (cited in Tarantino, 1996: xii)

Only with an incursion of the borders of reality, with a disturbance of the reality principle, does film become offensive. Barker's comments are borne out in the reaction to another, more realistic, Tarantino movie, one viciously indicative of the proximity between desire, horror and morality: it was received as an exercise in senseless aesthetic violence, a symptom of the amoral, pathological condition of western society. Recall the scene that gave *Reservoir Dogs* its notoriety, the ear-cutting scene. Mr Blonde, after turning on the radio and dancing for a while, takes out his cut-throat razor and hacks off a helpless cop's ear for no reason at all. Some light pop music, an amusing little dance and a callous act of violence entwine humour, pleasure and torture to an unbearable degree. Positioned by the camera as the bound and gagged victim of Blonde as he leans over to sever the ear, we the spectators also participate in his psychotic enjoyment: 'Was that as good for you as it was for me?'

The moviegoers, along with earless cop and bodiless ear, are addressees of Blonde's question, complicit in the desire and horror of the act. Anticipating, imagining the event, the viewers await the moment of horror, wanting it if only to be released from the tension of its unwatchable imminence.

Drawn into the violence, we want it to be over with because it lingers too long, stimulating the imagination in excess of the event and preparing us too cruelly for an intolerable infliction of pain. But we want the violence to occur for another reason as well. To see, to endure, such a shocking spectacle of violence enables us to overcome the horror, to enjoy and expel it in a moral sense and thus transcend our utter subjection to irrational, tyrannical and ruthless force. While there may be relief at not seeing so horrible a moment, there is also disappointment. The moment of pleasure/horror (*jouissance*) is denied: at the point of incision and amputation the camera pans away to the back of the warehouse, prurience forestalled, moral desire frustrated. A sound is heard, but the gaze is blank. The blankness of the dark warehouse wall, refusing a sight of abhorrence, execration and pleasure, pre-empts censoriousness and censorship (the act of cutting is already cut) and returns the viewer to the complicity of his/her own desire, to see, overcome, reprimand and thereby enjoy. Strangely, then, it is the refusal to show the amputation of the ear that demands a look at viewing morals and pleasures.

Formally this scene bears little relation to anything Gothic. At a stretch one might consider Blonde's irrational, amoral, purposeless violence, his indifference to all rules and authority, as a contemporary incarnation of the Gothic villain. As a 'fucking psycho' and something of a romantic, he is comparable to Mickey Knox in *Natural Born Killers*. Mickey is described in Gothic terms as the culmination of all evil and inhumanity: 'you're a vampire, or the devil, or a monster, or a cyborg, or something like that. But you're not human' (Tarantino, 1995: 60). Blonde, however, is rather more banal. His 'a shooting spree in the store', which causes the trouble in the first place, positions him in terms of the consumer's shopping binge. The overly moral condemnations of Tarantino's films, resulting, perhaps, from a missed moral opportunity, echo the censorious tones of eighteenth-century criticism and manifest an antipathy to aesthetic violence couched in terms of parental, or paternal, concern. Where the reading of romances was considered a dangerous and unpoliceable act of private pleasure in the eighteenth century, threatening domestic virtues, the regulation of the private realm of home and family values finds its contemporary moral outlet in the prohibition of the video release of certain improper films. The insistence on paternal moral values, however, suggests that they are neither self-evident nor universally accepted, that, like the grand narratives of enlightened modernity, they have lost credibility. The paternal figure, once the domestic and ideological apex, no longer operates as a recognised law. Mr Blonde, indeed, acknowledges no law and no social relation, determined only by his own pleasure. Hence the importance of the organ he severs. The ear connects the subject to the voices of others and the outside world. Through the ear, in Orange's screaming at the beginning of the film, the cop's pain in the torture scene and in K-Billy's voice throughout, a human connection and compassion for others is evoked. Blonde, of course, is deaf to any appeal for mercy. Without humanity, Blonde's deafness is repeated in the severing of the ear that signals a separation from contact, protection, or law. We, like the cop, are situated in a relation akin to that of the villain and the heroine in Gothic fiction, the latter lost, abandoned or imprisoned in a hostile, vicious world, cut off from the comforts of home or the security of paternal protection.

Despite identifying rather tenuous similarities in *Reservoir Dogs* and Gothic fiction's relation to the absence of a paternal figure (and its subjective consequences), the role of the differences, especially in the versions of fiction and reality, signal the shift in the locus of horror. *Reservoir Dogs* does not oppose a fantastic world of horror to an ordered rational reality: reality is composed of violence, accidents and chance events. It is a reality – as all the filmic cross-references, intertextual allusions and the commode story scenes suggest – made up of fictions, bound together as a network of cultural, linguistic and cinematic signifiers and haunted by a hole or void in representation, an absence or gap that cannot be filled, but, like a black hole, threatens to consume all representation: beneath simulation, beyond image, there is nothing but the consumption of surfaces. Horror, or its irrational and useless manifestations, is very much a part of this hyperrealistic world; it discloses some Thing horrible at its centre, absent, unpresentable, a hole or void, like that left by the severed ear. In the scene the absence is represented by the camera looking away at the crucial moment of horror and, when we return to the poor cop, by the gaping, bloody hole that remains on the side of his head. The absence in place of an ear underlines the horror, while Blonde's playful words to the severed ear brings attention back cruelly and sickly to surfaces: jokes, of course, depend on the playful juxtaposition of images or words. The gaping hole in his self-image is of great concern to Marvin, the cop, in the discussions with Mr Orange that follow. Marvin asks 'How do I look?' and goes on to say 'I'm deformed' (Tarantino, 1994: 65–6). The great concern with one's appearance seems a little bizarre, given his predicament, but less bizarre if it is remembered that the film is set in LA, home of Hollywood and cosmetic surgery. Horror is superficial in two senses: the horror that arises when, through Marvin, we realise that it is all and only a play of surfaces without any depth or interiority, that one's intimate being is bound up with surfaces, tied to images, to the integrity and aesthetics of appearance alone; and, second, that to deform one's image is sufficient grounds, if not the only cause, of horror. Indeed, when, surgically, one can enhance one's appearance according to cultural ideals of beauty, the surface or image becomes the only measure of self. All substance discarded, one becomes one's skin, or changes it. But to discard substance is to enter a virtual world and fly unanchored into groundless multiplicity.

What distinguishes contemporary horror is its relationship to technology, the capacity to realise visually what had, before, to remain as fantasy, thereby evincing the capacity to reformat reality itself. The former depends on the imagination of readers, on their credulous investment in the restoration of a paternal symbolic order, while the latter requires only the passive consumption of the spectator, intoxicated by the realism of images generated by special effects. This is the crucial difference between modern and hyper- or post-modern forms: the technological ability to realise fantasy by way of machines rather than human imagination. It is a technical power that, emptying Gothic of affect, discloses a wider process that produces horror on a cultural scale with no reference at all to the conventional (Gothic) forms and images. Horror's production bypasses the human figure and, simultaneously, becomes the last source of human horror: it discloses the human figure as nothing but surface, a fabrication evaporating in the density of images. In more realistic than Gothic fictions, like Jonathan Demme's *The Silence of the Lambs* (1991) or Iain Banks's *The Wasp Factory*, the attention to textual surfaces, to bodily and narrative skins, discloses, beneath the text, the utter evacuation of substance and corporeal identity. *The Wasp Factory* suggests that sexual identity is fabricated, constructed, simulated for real in narratives and nowhere else: essence and substance are utterly effaced. Due to a father's hatred for a wife that left him, his daughter grows up dressed and addressed as a boy. Thus interpellated, she believes herself to be a he: genital difference is explained as the result of a nasty encounter with a dog. As evidence, a fake lost member is preserved in a jar for posterity. For the reader, the novel appears to describe a patently male infantile aggressivity and sadism, an aggressivity exacerbated by an actual as well as symbolic castration. But, in recognising the obvious signs of masculinity, readers are duped by the narrative as surely as young Frank is fooled by the fiction of his emasculation. The truth comes both too late and as something of a shock, leaving reader and Frank in the no man's land of sudden narrative denouement, subjects seduced beyond the fixities of gender as surely as in the virtual spaces of performative or digital transsexuality. Inner being is evacuated by narrative and reintroduced as the retrospective effect of fictions.

For one of the few effective figures of popular horror in recent years, humans are nothing more than objects to be consumed with a nice Chianti.

Hannibal Lecter, a psychiatrist turned psychopath, embodies a curiously contemporary horror, not only because the veneer of urbanity and intellect stretches across a cannibalistic inhumanity associated with 1980s consumer culture, but in the way that his penetrating psychiatric gaze draws everything to the surface. 'Look deep within your self', he tells FBI Agent Clarice Starling, parodying the platitudes of ego psychology. The 'your self', however, is a clue in pun form directing Starling to 'Your Self-storage'. As Judith Halberstam notes, these jokes draw attention to surfaces (Halberstam, 179–80). Inner being is rendered an effect of signifying surfaces, while the illusion of depth, of an inner private and secret self, is rendered obsolete under the superficial scrutiny of Lecter. It all comes down to puns, visual and verbal jokes, as they play with the thin screen of symbolic reality. 'I'm having a friend for dinner', he tells Clarice at the end over the phone. And a shot of the holidaying warden of the psychiatric prison leaves us in no doubt about the menu. The other villain of *The Silence of the Lambs*, too, emphasises the surfaces of sexual identity: the sensitively nicknamed 'Buffalo Bill' kills young women for their skins, turning the human into a disposable meat product whose only valuable or desirable commodity is the skin itself. The aesthetic surface, in an age in which identity is found only in surfaces, becomes all. The film's title announces the centrality of the deepest, most private and unavowable childhood fears of the young female agent. But Lecter has seen all this on the surface, inscribed on and readable in her half-concealed accent, her cheap scent and worn shoes. Without essence or a unique private depth, identity is no more than a manufactured, commodified, replicable and exchangeable skinsuit, as the next designer identity comes into fashion: any anchoring substance is scraped away and it slides precipitously across surfaces. And with the attention to surfaces comes the horror: all pleasures can be endlessly, superficially gratified by shopping or surfing, but, instantly accessible, the objects of desire are devalued and new objects must be found, a cycle that allows no escape from the vertiginous slide across surfaces. Hence, too, a pervasive want emerges at a cultural level, a want of objects so horrible that they arrest the momentum of image production with a resounding moral 'No', and allow networks of language and meaning to patch up the holes in the fabric of human reality and permit some sense of security and stability. But, sucked to the surface, the remainder guaranteeing identity and reality is discarded or, in Lecter's case, consumed as meat.

The evacuation of substance and humanity, whether through the artifice of visual technologies or the technology of the signifier, overwrites virtuality and absorbs subjects into a bodiless and weightless matrix. The 'realization of the fantasy to seize reality' reaches fruition in an age of superhumanly intelligent machines. Technology quite literally seizes and rewrites reality, stupefying visual consumers with ever more intoxicating images. What is expelled in the fantastic flight to hyperreality is the 'meat', the term employed by cyberpunk writers to denote the formless bodily excess of no use to machines. In Rudy Rucker's *Wetware*, a fiction populated by semi-organic, quasi-human yet zombified or genetically engineered entities called 'meaties' and 'meatboppers', a drug called 'Merge' is discovered that totally decomposes any body at a molecular level. Flesh dissolves, skeletons loosen and corporeal being becomes a 'flesh-puddle' (Rucker, 276). Bodily integrity can be readily reversed, to the point of the *corps morcelé*: 'a merged person is like Jell-O rolled over some bones, right. And you can … *splatter* Jell-O. Splatter a merged person into a bunch of pieces, and the drug wears off – the cells firm up – and there is this … uh … guy in a whole lot of pieces' (186–7). The drug, moreover, does not only dissolve discrete bodies, it allows for the recombination of genes and the production of monstrosities like the 'chitin', a chimerical hybrid with feathers, claws, feelers, snout, mandibles and gills (180). The body no longer constitutes a limit and basis of identity, but, reducible to a blob of cells that are as interchangeable as signifiers, it becomes no more than putty – or meat – to be manipulated and recoded by the whims of informatic and genetic engineering.

Confronted by the meat, being must shed substance and skin and leap into virtual space. Or it must remain as no more than meat, like the audience of a near-future tabloid TV show in William Gibson's *Idoru*:

which is best visualized as a vicious, lazy, profoundly ignorant, perpetually hungry organism craving the warm god-flesh of the anointed. Personally I like to imagine something the size of a baby hippo, the color of a week-old boiled potato, that lives by itself, in the dark, in a double-wide on the outskirts of Topeka. It's covered with eyes and it sweats constantly. The sweat runs into those eyes and makes them sting. It has no mouth, Laney, no genitals, and can only express the mute extremes of murderous rage and infantile desire by changing channels on a universal remote. Or by voting in presidential elections. (Gibson, 1996: 28–9)

Already recognisable, the formless, passive, oozing mass stupefied before the screen and seething with inarticulate passions outlines the fulsome identity of the future meat-bound consumer.

The image of the meat as a decomposing ooze of flesh has a recognisable place in Gothic texts. In the waxen image of the worm-ridden corpse in *Udolpho*, it is employed as an object of penitence and horrifying representation of the sinful, mortal flesh. In Arthur Machen's *The Novel of the White Powder* a chemically caused physical regression turns a young man

into 'a dark and putrid mass, seething with corruption and hideous rot-
tenness, neither liquid nor solid, but melting and changing before our
eyes, and bubbling with unctuous oily bubbles like boiling pitch. And out
of the midst of it shone two burning points like eyes, and I saw a writhing
and stirring as of limbs, and something moved and lifted what might have
been an arm' (Machen, 233). In E.F. Benson's story, 'Negotium
Perambulans', the 'Thing' of horror has the 'odour of corruption and decay', headless, hairless, 'slug-like' with 'an orifice of puckered skin which
opened and shut and slavered at the edges' (Benson, 238). Where Radcliffe's
image of decay offers a lesson in virtuous reason and morality, the 'abhuman'
figure in Machen and Benson signifies the return of an abjected in-human
state and simultaneously evokes enough repulsion and loathing for a sense
of humanity to be recovered. The ambivalence of William Hope Hodgson's
'abhuman' describes a 'not-quite-human subject' drawn towards otherness
in a movement of loss, away from human selfhood and thus towards something other (Hurley, 3–4). A site of loss, recuperation, transformation,
dissolution, the abhuman signifies the locus of the Thing in all its ambivalence. If horror marks a limit the beyond of which humanity must ab-ject,
it also opens a hole in which it is consumed. In the *Wasp Factory*, a comparable image of disintegration functions quite differently, dissolving
recognisable humanity: the glimpse inside a beatifically calm baby's skull
reveals its half-eaten brain and 'a slowly writhing nest of fat maggots'; the
horror that results precipitates psychosis (Banks, 142). As the mind, severed from the capacity to recognise itself and others collapses, the body is
reduced to matter, to dead, putrefying flesh crawling with living worms: 'a
fetid, sticky object without boundaries, which teems with life and yet is
the sign of death. It is nature at the point where its effervescence closely
joins life and death, where it is death gorging life with decomposed substance' (Bataille, 1991: 95). The effervescence of nature, moreover, occurs
at the point of excess where what is most natural and what seems hid-
eously unnatural are conjoined.

An unbearable and irresolvable identification surrounds the meat as the
juncture between body and machine. Indeed, from the late twentieth century, the meat constitutes the dominant form and meaning of humanity, a
lumpen mass of consumptive and rotting desires. At the intangible axis of
body and machine, however, a loaded choice is announced: to be meat or
machine, to enjoy the horrors of excessive corporeality or the image-satu-
rated void of virtuality. Virtualisation, with its obliteration of substance
and value and its general 'de-realization' of reality, turns humans into 'ghost-
like entities' whose subjectivities, unanchored and ungrounded, are 'finally
delivered from the pathological stain of *a*' (Zizek, 1996: 196). The last

little bit of the real underpinning reality or identity is excised. The 'meat', however, cannot be transformed or revalued as a guarantee of reality, humanity or nature. Nor does it permit a nostalgic return to the past. It signifies, and hence the horror, a negation of all those things, the last little bit of 'base matter' to be eradicated (Bataille, 1997: 160–4). Horror is not natural: it is learned, inculcated at an early age by parental vigilance: 'we will not rest until they share the same impulse that made us clean them and clothe them, until they share our horror of the life of the flesh, of the life naked, undisguised, a horror without which we would resemble the animals'. Horror thus originates in a cultural differentiation of human from animal, a process in which taboos are created in order to police the limits that preserve a definition of humanity. Horror is thus the reversal, the expulsion of the nature: 'the horror that demands from us this constant movement of rejection is not *natural*. It bespeaks rather a negation of *nature*' (1991: 63). As a negation, horror lies only in the difference between nature and culture, in neither one nor the other, the fallout between them. And when, as with virtualisation, both nature and culture are incorporated or obliterated, the gaping void of horror becomes all the more pervasive. Though a site of dissolution, such horror is not the kind of limit morality would prefer, despite contemporary condemnations of all things technological. As Bataille also notes in *Eroticism*, horror serves as an 'immediate boundary' which draws the subject into 'a state of bliss bordering on delirium'; it discloses a limit and enjoins excess: 'the limit is only there to be overreached. Fear and horror are not the real and final reaction; on the contrary, they are a temptation to overstep the bounds'. Transgression involves both horror and 'the dream of monstrous joy' (1987: 267; 144; 127).

The revulsion of horror is countermanded by a precipitous leap forward, especially when it is glimpsed in the surfaces, screens and special effects of technological realizations. It comes from the future rather than a past now possessed of a distant if consolatory aura. Gothic heritage, with its Hollywood remakes of standards like *Frankenstein, Dracula* and *Jekyll and Hyde, The Mummy, Dawn of the Dead*, with its fashions and lifestyles, nostalgically seeks the comfort of a little darkness secured and secreted in a human past. But the formulas, devices and mechanisms of Gothic fiction, perhaps, their stimulation of sensation and appetitive desire, disclose a different momentum, a machinic imperative that expectorates, technically and affectively, humanity: 'machinic desire can seem a little inhuman, as it rips up political cultures, deletes traditions, dissolves subjectivities, and hacks through security apparatuses, tracking a soulless tropism to zero control'. The replicants and terminators have landed, 'a self organizing insidious traumatism, virtually guiding the entire biological desiring-complex towards post-carbon replicator usurpation' (Land, 1993: 479). A new 'skin trade' emerges, with subjects no longer owners of their own skins but superficial migrants, 'borrowing variable and evanescent identities from intensities traversed in sensitive space. The replicants drape themselves in wolf-pelts, and cross into beserk zones of alien affect, or melt into data-suits that pulse with digitized matrix traffic streams. They do not need to be told that cyberspace is already under our skin':

> Cyberspace.
> Here it comes.
> The terminal social signal blotted out by technofuck buzz from the desiring-machines. So much positive feed-back fast-forward that speed converges with itself on the event horizon of an artificial time-extinction. Suddenly it's everywhere: a virtual envelopment by recyclones, voodoo economics, neo-nightmares, death-trips, skin-swaps, teraflops, Wintermute-wasted Turing cops, sensitive silicon, socket-head subversion, polymorphic hybridizations, descending data-storms, and cyborg catwomen stalking amongst the screens. Zaibatsus flip into sentience as the market melts into automatism, politics is cryogenized and dumped into the liquid-helium meat-store, drugs migrate onto neurosoft viruses, and immunity is grated-open against jagged reefs of feral AI explosion, Kali culture, digital dance-dependency, black shamanism epidemic, and schizolupic break-outs from the bin. (481–2)

With cyberspace comes 'cybergothic' (Land, 1998). A dream and a nightmare, utopia and distopia all at once, the future produced in the void of the present, is both horrifying and thrilling. But it is far from Gothic, made redundant along with the notions of history, modernity, ideology and national culture in which it was bound up. Horror no longer returns upon the present from a past to reveal guilty secrets, mythic energies or spectral powers: it has undergone a temporal shift, projected into and returning from a terroristic, terminating and machinic future. Hence the ambivalent excitements of the terminator: despite his red eye and black leather, he is without history: peel off the artificial skin and there is no organic substance to the sexy killing machine from the bright light of the future. Hasta la vista, baby.

## Black holes (and back again)

'In space, no one can hear you scream.' In black holes, no one can see you scream. Neither sound nor light can cross an event horizon: they have insufficient velocity to escape the gravitational pull of a collapsing star. In the black hole, all matter, all bodies, all energy are dragged by irresistible forces of gravity to an impenetrable point, a singularity, where none of the laws of physics apply and scientific knowledge reaches its limit. At this point everything in the known universe dissolves; nothing makes sense.

The idea of the black hole germinated in eighteenth-century mathematics and astronomy, among calculations charting the effects of gravitational forces on light and matter. Pierre Laplace, only in the first two editions of his *Exposition du System du Monde* (1796, 1798), proposed the existence of 'dark bodies' in the universe, dark because the enormous gravitational pull of imploding stars would prevent light escaping. Hence, these imperceptible objects would be invisible. Over a decade earlier William Michel had undertaken similar calculations establishing that a star of sufficient size would, when imploding, generate a gravitational field strong enough to counteract the speed of light. These 'black voids in space', though invisible, could be identified by their effect on other cosmic bodies, their extreme energies affecting the orbit of stars and the movement of energy (Gribbin, 24; Hawking, 81–2). Since receiving their current name from John Wheeler in 1969, black holes have exerted their powerful attraction on scientific speculation as much as astrophysical calculations. And, of course, they have attracted a great many popular imaginings.

When a star exhausts its fuel and begins to contract, its implosion draws its mass inward under an extremely strong density. The tension, or 'tug-o-war', between outward-moving energy, like heat and radiation, and the inward pull of gravity is overcome by the force of the latter (Boscough, 44). The resulting gravitational field is intensified to the extent that even light is caught within the circumference of the force of gravity, the boundary of which, the 'event horizon', marks the limit dividing inside and outside, 'a one-way membrane' where nothing – since nothing travels faster than the speed of light – can achieve the 'escape velocity' to break out (Hawking, 89). The event horizon forms 'the boundary of the region of space-time from which it is not possible to escape'. Within the black hole lies a 'singularity', a point 'of infinite density and space-time curvature'. Here, 'the laws of science and our ability to predict the future break down' (88–9). Time, space, all physical laws, constants and principles are voided. Nothing adds up or follows the rules; nothing makes sense. Black holes are 'rips in the fabric of space and time', tears in the universe that show up as limits to scientific knowledge.

The excess posed by the existence of black holes to any kind of knowledge about them also stimulates scientific endeavour and excites much speculation, speculation that borders on the realism of science fiction and fantasy. With black holes, come speculation on wormholes, white holes, and travel across space and time. For Hawking, the wormhole may allow one, supposing it is possible to bypass the singularity, to travel through a black hole and come out instantly at some imagined other side in some other part of space (89). To navigate the tremendous gravitational forces of rotating or non-rotating black holes would be to traverse a 'funnel of whirling space' and emerge elsewhere in the universe (Berry, 50). The return trip, of course, remains somewhat problematic unless, as Berry, a Fellow of the Royal Astronomical Society, proposed in 1977, black holes can be constructed to enable both departure and return. A second black hole would have to be constructed near to the point of emergence from the first. This would allow the traveller to return to the region of the space from which he or she had departed, as a 'white hole' (114–16). Such a scheme, on the boundaries of science and fiction, is outlined in Berry's book, *The Iron Sun: Crossing the Universe through Black Holes*. He elaborates extensively on the scientific problems, practical details and exorbitant costs of the project.

Black holes enable, in scientific hypotheses at least, the traversal of vast distances and even promise travel through time. The idea bolsters their popular and fantastic appeal. The term 'black hole', too, is significant, not only because, as Boscough suggests, it helps to 'have a good name for a concept' to provide 'psychological impact' and 'dramatic description'. The name also brings human elements into the speculation, with fear, anxiety and fantasy filling the gaps and inadequacies of scientific knowledge: 'it could be a good image for human fears of the universe' (Boscough, 58). At the limits of science, fear and fantasy come into play: where knowledge cannot reach, imagination boldly goes. Through fantasy and in fear, humans, fly to a wanton universe and re-emerge in a system human science identified as being almost beyond the reach of comprehension let alone physical intervention. At the same time, black holes, universal, cosmic phenomena, assume a strangely humanised shape, dark mirrors to a subjective interior and sites of promise, horror and fantasy.

The strong phantasmatic potential of black holes is not lost on Jacqueline Rose in her short reading of Hawking's *A Brief History of Time*. She focuses on his concern that the 'weak cosmic censorship hypothesis' must hold: if, as Hawking argues, singularities were not screened by an event horizon and thereby held apart from normal space-time to protect external observers from their effects, then the likelihood of time travel is curtailed. Otherwise, 'it would mean that no one's life would even be safe: someone might go into the past and kill your father or mother before you were conceived!' (Jacqueline Rose, 89) The horror of this fundamental destabilisation is also the stuff of so many science fictions, a horror oozing with great imaginative promise. The horrifying prospect of the reversibility or erasure of linear time discloses another fantasy, one readily recognisable in Freudian terms (Penley). To go back in time might not only mean the deletion of a being before it has even existed, it could also offer opportunities to kill the father and …

Rose, however, evinces little interest in pursuing obvious readings of Hawking's comment and reducing his speculations to another oedipal fantasy. Her concern lies in the question black holes pose for the relationship between science and fantasy: 'if knowledge always borders on fantasy, fantasy is always in part fantasy about (the borders of) knowledge' (174). The scientific limits darkly materialised by black holes, for Rose, are curiously akin, in subjective terms, to the unseen, almost impenetrable work of the unconscious: 'like the unconscious, a black hole is censored, the black hole wipes out the possibility of knowledge, of its own total or absolute theoretical grasp' (172). The 'extraordinary metaphorical resonance' of the black hole, a resonance which allows cosmos and subject to mirror each other, requires the figure of formlessness, and Hawking's thesis along with it, to be thought of as an investigation 'of how to think negativity and outer boundaries, the points where what we take to be the recognizable and at least partly knowable universe comes into being, goes off its own edges, collapses into itself, ceases to be …' (171). Rose's psychoanalytic coordinates for thinking negativity of this kind are Melanie Klein and Lacan: the negativity in question is not some primal, instinctual and destructive impulse erupting from a base, repressed nature, but a negative expenditure, a 'cost', that comes with language and socialisation. Negativity causes a black hole that is never covered over. It comes from a tear in the fabric of social and symbolic structure that, invisible, unknown to consciousness, still exerts a defining effect on the development of subjectivity. The black hole pulses at the vacant core of symbolised, subjective existence, an object (*a*) around which desires and signification are organised. Black holes are vacuoles, 'traumatic residues': 'around such abysmal holes … our understanding of danger, excitement, deceit and bodily being is articulated' (Broughton, 155). At the limits of scientific knowledge and at the heart of the formation of individuated beings, the black hole resonates with an emptiness and darkness as frightening as it is exciting, a locus of horror that is also a site of some possible 'positive radiation'.

The metaphorical resonance of the black hole extends to questions of modernity and culture, not only in the way that the idea has fuelled so much science fiction and fantasy but, epochally, in the breakdown or crisis associated with the postmodern condition and the tremors it perceives in the fabric of knowledge, legitimation, credulity and social cohesion. If science formed one of the grand narratives providing modernity with its bedrock and motor, a source of modern stability, progress and invention, then the black hole constitutes a significant point of limitation, a challenge to scientific principles and foundations, a site of spatial, temporal and physical instability where laws collapse and knowledge dissolves. The voiding represented by the black hole's exceeding of known physical laws offers an occasion for incredulity, for a rejection of science in favour of fantasy, religion, mysticism. Tearing the constituents of reality apart, disrupting the patterns of space and time, rendering linearity suspect if not reversible and prediction impossible, the black hole literalises a fundamental aporia in knowledge and, indeed, the universe. The rent in modernity, however, does not only force knowledge to encounter its limit and confront its disintegration, its absolute all-consuming end. As a site for fantastic scientific and fictional projection, the black hole offers opportunities for imaginative expansion, for modernity, if not to enlarge its horizons, but to be transformed into something else, something hypermodern perhaps. Black holes thus form a curiously significant absence of form, a figure of formlessness, a figure for the absence of figure that displays and screens horror, conjoining promise and threat, thrill and fear, an abyssal hyphen of post-modernity.

Black holes do not simply mark the confounding of the oppositions underlying modernity's narratives, the point where space and time collapse and fullness and emptiness conjoin. While defining the limit beyond which metanarratives like science cannot penetrate with rational explanation and calculation, the void of dissolution does not form the horrifying void around which narrative framework and symbolic boundaries are restored: formlessness is not the occasion for horrified recoil and the recuperation of a humanised and partially knowable universe. On the contrary, absence becomes an opportunity for speculation, an incitement to fantastic projection. Unlike modernity's sublime which nostalgically conceives the unpresentable as the 'missing contents' of presentation, the postmodern sublime locates the unpresentable 'in presentation itself' (Lyotard, 1984: 81). It is an 'immanent sublime' to be inscribed with an 'infinity of the transformation of "realities"' (1991: 128–9). The black hole, rather than marking a fundamental aporia conjoining and separating known from unknown, thereby anchoring both in their difference, becomes a screen to project upon and penetrate a scene of further destabilisation and deracination, a point of departure and fantastic flight. The black hole is neither the alpha nor omega of existence (Hawking compares it to the 'Big Bang') but a site of sublime possibility, a site, intimate and excluded from both cosmos and subjectivity, that operates, like a blind spot within vision, to trigger visionary projections. Hence, in confronting knowledge with its limits, black holes do not form a point of arrest: they engender a swarm of fantastic possibilities and proliferate throughout culture. Their proliferation, moreover, is not only on the cinema and televisual screens that dominate cultural production and circulation: it is in the absence, the very blankness of those screens that a potential is presented: 'why do we stand amazed before the assumed properties of the black holes of outer space? Aren't all our puncta of observation and all our quanta of action simply black holes of scientific thought? These are the black dots of a line wherein begin and end our rational representations' (Virilio, 1991a: 67). At the limit of reason and science, pulsing on screens and in everyday activities, the black holes multiply and return in form of the internal excess of culture, the constitutive absence rendered visible as the internal limit of every system of understanding.

'There is no scientific truth', commented Einstein, a comment which, for Virilio, implies that there are 'only momentary representations', a state of impermanence and evanescence in which we 'lose our grasp of any solid reference or matter':

> if forgetting is indispensable to the projectivity of imagination and the propagation of thought, the point is a point of reference of geometric projectivity only to the extent that it is a gap or lack, an absence of dimension, a black hole. As an obscurity, the point is as necessary to the revelation of physical appearances as the darkroom is to the objective appearances in photography and cinematographic photogram. (103–4)

If dark puncta constitute the possibility of imagination, thought, projection, they are also a locus of dissolution. Their pulse, their appearances as gaps that cannot be filled, becomes a space of incessant and fleeting projection, black holes inviting the rapid production of images and causing their consumption. Instead of one figure filling the gap and symbolically organising an order of meanings, identities, temporality around it, a 'swarm of images' symptomatic of psychosis manifests only the failure, the foreclosure of any paternal metaphor.

The black hole, visible only as a space of non-perception and understanding, a space of loss and mystery in which all meanings are consumed, all thought loses itself, all sense evaporates and all boundaries collapse, pulses as the void opened by the decline of the paternal figure and the incredulity towards metanarratives. Eclipsing transgression and prohibition it marks out the final limit and enjoins a plunge into limitlessness, an ultimate meaning exploding in meaninglessness, the black hole of contemporary culture. Such a powerful consuming void offers an attractive

and horrifying image of the collapse of all laws and distinctions, an ultimate expenditure, a final disappearance, without return. The image of a
cosmic consumption in which the light of enlightened modernity no longer
has the speed to overcome the dead weight of its own history or advance in
glorious progress returns to the black hole of the present, a present without escape velocity, wrapped up in the accelerating pulses of its images,
recycling the past and projecting futures yet unable to break through the
event horizon. As it oscillates back and forth the horror of an ultimate
formlessness, the void where all collapses, the horror that is a black hole
looms large.

*Event Horizon* situates itself at this point, at the same time gothicising
the black hole of science fiction. Set in the near future the film's narrative
of technological hubris looks back to a range of Gothic features and plots
to give form to a horror emanating from beyond the universe. The story is
straightforward, owing much to *Solaris* as well as to scientific speculations
on the possibility of travelling by means of black holes: a spaceship, the
'Event Horizon', powered by a revolutionary 'gravity drive', has reappeared
in the solar system after being mysteriously lost seven years earlier on its
maiden voyage. A rescue ship, the 'Lewis and Clark', is dispatched to in-
vestigate, with the inventor of the new drive, Dr Weir, on board. He explains the principles of the 'gravity drive' on the way: designed to generate
an artificial black hole, it folds space, and the ship passes through to its
now proximate destination. He has, however, no idea where the 'Event
Horizon' has been. Other mysteries surround the ship: an enigmatic last
message initially understood as 'save me' and, too late, recognised as 'save
yourselves'; visual recordings showing the crew engaged in an orgy of violence and mutilation; and numerous spectral appearances. On board the
deserted ship, described as a 'tomb', events begin to move beyond the
bounds of reason: scanners are saturated with unspecific bio-readings, the
rescuers suffer realised hallucinations in the form of vivid enactments of
past events, corpses coming alive, or horrifying visions of bleeding or burning bodies. The 'gravity drive' seems to operate under its own volition. An
incredible explanation is offered: the 'Event Horizon' is alive, animated by
a malevolent force intent on imprisoning the new arrivals. While the rescue crew vainly try to repair their own damaged ship, the scientist becomes possessed by his creation and sabotages their escape efforts. He has
discovered that the ship's drive has torn a hole in the universe and crossed
into a realm of pure chaos and evil, a dimension beyond the imagination.
'I am home', he declares.

A haunted house in space, an animated machine with diabolical powers
feeding off the lives it torments, the 'Event Horizon' is presented as a

realisation of hell. Dr Weir, of course, plays the part of the Frankensteinian scientist who, having implemented a discovery that abolishes spatial and temporal boundaries and opens the universe to human control, finds the truth of his fantasy in vivid nightmare. The machine designed to master the heavens materialises an unimaginable hell. And hell lies within as much as without. The narrative plays upon the guilt and fear of its protagonists. Weir, like Frankenstein, is haunted by dead females: his wife, a suicide who appears repeatedly with eyeless sockets, forms a manifestation of the soul he has lost in his work. The Captain of the 'Lewis and Clark', too, is pursued by memories of a previous mission on which he left a crewman to burn. The images are animated by the ship: it seems to know the most intimate of dark secrets and the most private of fears. As one crewman, pushed to suicide by the ship, observes, it activates 'the dark inside one from the other place'. The black hole within an individual corresponds to the rent in space, the other place, the other scene, of the universe. As the 'gravity drive' prepares to take everyone back to the hell beyond the black hole, the Captain sacrifices himself to save the surviving few by separating the engineering section from the rest of the ship. The survivors drift off, to be rescued seventy-two days later by another rescue ship, still in shock, still possessed by the horror they encountered. The drifting hulk, and the second rescue with its suggestion of a continuation and an unlikely sequel, manifests the problems the film has with ending: no climactic explosion destroys the evil thing which disappears into the unknown dimension from whence it came; no final expenditure declares a heroic and satisfying triumph. The possibility of any pleasurable frisson of terror is refused by the pervasive horror attendant on the last ditch escape from the pull of the void. Despite the religious tones emphasised in the scientific realisation of hell, no sacred structure erects itself in the face of ultimate dissolution. Nor is there any suggestion that the dangerously Promethean ambitions of human science can be arrested or that inner demons can be overcome. Awoken from stasis, a survivor can only scream.

Suspended in space and not free of the horror, the film closes in the shadow of the black hole, unable to see beyond the event horizon. Though it pulls away from the void there is, it seems, nowhere else to go but back again: it does not have the escape velocity to conjure up an idea of transcendence or an imaginable and inhabitable future and only pulses under the shadow of the black hole. Images of a realised hell, an orgy of mutual violence, bodies ripped apart to a soundtrack of screams, turns the jouissance of a fantasy fulfilled in crossing all barriers of time and space into an eternity of excruciating pain, human degradation and suffering: these are images of fullness and intensity so full and intense that they are unbearable. The black hole artificially created in the future returns upon the holes of the present and hollowly replays (religious and Gothic) images of the past. The collapse of all distinctions between space and time, near and far, actual and imaginary, the limitless domain of pain, subjective and corporeal dissolution represented by the hell of the film is also the realm of absolute freedom of the present in inverted form: the formless space of violent consuming mirrors the freedom to consume as a void in which subjects are anxious, uncertain, hysterrorised, subjects of flows and energies beyond knowledge and control. The sublime and unpresentable core of modernity and its aesthetics has been turned into a playful infinity of forms and presentations without end.

The future that has descended on a collapsing present, an image cast away and returning with a fading pulse, remains shrouded in old Gothic images exhausted of any strong charge. A future painted in past images and forms has worn too thin to veil the gaping hole generating objectless anxiety. Gothic fiction, which has served as modernity's black hole, serving up a range of objects and figures to solidify its various anxieties into fear and allow the pleasures of focused terror and expenditure, has become too familiar after two centuries of repetitive mutation and seems incapable of shocking anew. Inured to Gothic shocks and terrors, its protective screen become hardened and porous at the same time, contemporary culture recycles its images in the hope of finding a charge intense enough to renew the pulse of expenditure that staves off the black hole within and without. An object large enough to fill horror's black hole is wanted. But as Gothic images pervade a contemporary culture composed of rapidly oscillating and disturbing flows of anxious expenditures, a culture in which they are as much the norm as images of sex and violence, they manifest the generalisation of horror accompanying the vast economic and technological expansion into – and, phantasmatically, beyond – the black hole of post-modernity.

## ❧ 4 ❧

# Beyond the Gothic principle

### A child's game

'O-o-o-o!' 'A-a-a-a!' 'O-o-o-o!' All of Gothic fiction turns upon a simple oscillation, on a singular differentiation, a child's game: 'fort!' 'Da!' A game of loss and recovery, with the former rather than latter in the driving seat, its simplicity belies an extensive recalcitrance, its repetitions occluding some kind of excess to efforts of representation and theorisation. Away and back, disappearance and return, the exclamations and the projection and retrieval of a bobbin challenge, engender and thwart explanation: repetition defies neat models of life and self; it disrupts ordered and balanced circulations of pleasure, desire or identity; it introduces something alien into normal functions and expectations, something that, though inassimilable to sense, remains at the heart of subjectivity and culture. The death drive introduces heterogeneity, difference and something daemonic into everyday exchange.

It is Freud, of course, who speculates on the significance of the child's game. The game played by his grandson intrudes in the grandfather's hesitant, repetitive and circuitous pursuit of the hypothesis of *Beyond the Pleasure Principle*: is there a force refusing the regulation of the principle of homeostasis that seems to govern all life in the aims of lowering tension and decreasing excitation? Constancy and equilibrium are the stalwarts of pleasure which arises when unpleasurable tensions are discharged and the organism or psyche can return to balance. There is always some dynamism and interrelation, some exchange or economy, in Freud's model of pleasure. Until, of course, the ultimate stasis of life's return to an inorganic state of things. The pleasure principle asserts that the overriding mode of organic functioning takes its bearings from the diminution of tensions. But what of the 'war neuroses', the instances of 'shellshock', that, in the wake of the First World War, suggest other drives, other interpretations of

psychic functioning? (Freud, 1984: 281) Trauma, it seems, produces repetitions that defy models of pleasure, repeating distress and disturbance
rather than recovering equilibrium. So, too, the child's game as it is played
and observed while the father is away at war and the mother has left the
child to its own devices. A bobbin on a piece of string is thrown away: 'o-
o-o-o!' ('fort!') The child exclaims. It is pulled back: 'a-a-a-a!' ('Da!') While
'greater pleasure' was attached to the second part of the game, Freud is
puzzled to observe that the first part was often repeated 'as a game in itself'
(282). This does not appear to make sense in terms of the pleasure principle: while the act of retrieval imaginatively assuages the distress of loss,
distress being associated by Freud with the departure of the source of infantile satisfactions, the mother, the repetition of loss surely must heighten
anxiety and thus be driven by a something other than pleasure.

Initially baffled, Freud hesitatingly advances explanations for the phenomenon of repeated throwing away: some mode of revenge, perhaps, on
the mother who has abandoned the child, is at work, or an 'instinct for
mastery' in which the child moves, through repetition, from a 'passive
situation' in respect of the 'distressing experience' of loss to a position of
active control (285). Mimicry and repetition, Freud notes, are staples of
children's play. But mimicry does not explain repetition or extend to subsequent artistic play in which performed or represented distresses and pains
are enjoyable. These aesthetic considerations are discounted, irrelevant to
Freud in his pursuit of something beyond the pleasure principle: he is
looking for 'tendencies more primitive' and 'independent' of it (287). The
speculation proceeds. Oedipus appears, as do infantile losses and their
consequent narcissistic scars and the effects of transference and neurosis
and the sense of 'being pursued by a malignant fate or possessed by some
"daemonic" power' (292). A compulsion to repeat seems to override the
pleasure principle. Freud's speculation looks to the formation of the psyche
and proposes a 'protective shield' defending consciousness from
overstimulation caused by unbound, excitable and anxiety-provoking energies. The aim is to bind the free-floating cathexes or disturbing energies
within the psychical apparatus so that it can maintain equilibrium: repetition takes its bearings from such an aim, one lying at the evolutionary
roots of life. While life, in the form of Eros, expands outwards, death,
Thanatos, pulls it back. The 'daemonic' power that manifests itself in the
compulsion to repeat seems to disclose an instinct, a drive, 'to restore an
earlier state of things': it is life's drive to return to 'inertia', to death, through
its own 'circuitous' path (308–11).

*Beyond the Pleasure Principle*, for all its analytical detours, a labyrinth of
interpretations, for all its speculation on death and a daemonic power of

repetition, seems far from the psychoanalytical familiars of Gothic fiction and criticism. Seething sexuality, dark, unavowed wishes, cruel repression, death tinged with frissons of terror and eroticism, all of which make psychoanalysis the ready double and critical mirror of Gothic fiction, fade before a relentless, almost mechanical procession of metapsychological speculation. *Beyond the Pleasure Principle* does not parade the dark psychic secrets so beloved by the successors of scandalised Victorian modernity happy to embrace the venal vicissitudes of libidinal nature and, among a ripe range of repressions, find promises of phantasmatic possibilities, sexual subversions, or liberations of self. Contrary to the illusions and myths about psychoanalysis, its modernity is not reassuringly human. The energies it discloses are technological effects, products of mental mechanisms, apparatuses and processes, as much as primitive, even animalistic returns. While it may emerge in the late nineteenth century among discussions of degeneration and regression and seem eager, in its preoccupations with repression, to apprehend the beast within, it is pressed forward by the metaphors and mechanisms of technological modernity (Kittler, 1999; Doane 1996). Mystic writing pads, photoplates, telescopes, telegraphy and typewriters, though not cinema, are among its tools. Such is the mechanism moving *Beyond the Pleasure Principle* as it looks back to an earlier state of things while being pressed forward by another power. Pulled back, pushing forward, its dual momentum stems from the expansions of Eros and the retractions of Thanatos. The return to inertia, to death, is a restoration to come: death rides with life until its return to ultimate homeostasis arrives from the future, in its own time. Away and back, life casts itself out on its own fatal string, its repetitions ending in a place other than where they began.

In the dark mirror Gothic holds up to psychoanalysis repetition reduces the image to sameness, an inertial reflection occluding difference. Its dark surface of desire is readily seen as depth: human, mysterious, deep in its labyrinthine unfolding of truths, passions, secret centres, narcissistic returns, possessed by me, mummy and her plenitudes. But the surface and its repetitive flickering remain unseen, a difference among the self-centred circulations of sameness-difference. For all its explorations of a fatal, elusive drive in life from its evolutionary beginnings to war-torn modernity, *Beyond the Pleasure Principle* repeatedly returns to repetition itself, repetition that is almost mechanistic in its determinism, compulsiveness and daemonic insistence. Freud's text, only indirectly assimilable to 'human' concerns, whether base or elevated, does not dispense with the more familiar propositions of psychoanalysis, but, in foregrounding a drive that is central and alien to life in general, places them in a less recognisable or dominant position. The death drive discloses something alien, in-human and uncanny at the same time, something strange and familiar that confounds the safe distinctions between life and death:

> The death drive is precisely the ultimate Freudian name for the dimension traditional metaphysics designated as that of *immortality* – for a drive, a 'thrust', which persists beyond the (biological) cycle of generation and corruption, beyond the 'way of all flesh'. In other words, in the death drive, the concept 'dead' functions in exactly the same way as '*heimlich*' in the Freudian '*unheimlich*', as coinciding with its negation: the 'death drive' designates the dimension of what horror fiction calls 'undead', a strange, immortal, indestructible life that persists beyond death. This is the 'infinity' compatible with the Lacanian theoretical edifice: not the 'spurious (bad) infinity' of endlessly striving to achieve the final Goal or Ideal that forever eludes our grasp, but an even *worse* infinity of *jouissance* which persists for ever, since we can never get rid of it. (Zizek, 1999b: 294)

The persistence of life beyond death, that is, as a negation or undeath, remains horrifying because it is a force that is as much internal to the organism as it is external. Like the death that courses through and directs life on its own path, as Freud claims, the drive pulses with energies and intensities that continually upset the equilibrium of any system.

Oedipus, with its maternal desires and castration anxieties, and the uncanny, with is doublings, narcissisms and return of the repressed, lurk in the shadows of *Beyond the Pleasure Principle*. One variation of the game, Freud notes, involves the casting away of the bobbin with the accompanying exclamation, not of 'fort', but of 'Go to the fwont!' The child, it seems, does not miss the father, away at war: 'on the contrary he made it quite clear that he had no desire to be disturbed in his sole possession of his mother' (Freud, 1984: 285). At the same time, of course, the game may also attempt to compensate for maternal dispossession. Published in 1920, *Beyond the Pleasure Principle* follows directly the essay on the uncanny, in 1919, where the 'compulsion to repeat' is mentioned in association with a Nietzschean eternal recurrence of the same. The daemonic, like belief in the omnipotence of thoughts, is associated with the return of pre-oedipal wishes and beliefs that ought to have been surmounted: the primary narcissism of a mind that has yet to dissociate itself from the satisfactions and gratifications attached to maternal presence finds curious consolation in the mirrors and doubles of uncanny phenomena. But a secondary narcissism transforms the significance of uncanny doubles: they become signs of separation and death, returns of oedipal fears, reinforcing the main argument that the uncanny is less to do with the intellectual uncertainty of distinguishing between humans and automata and more an effect of castration anxieties. In the fort-da game, loss is privileged over recovery, repetition, perhaps, an effect of the 'narcissistic scar' left by maternal separation (291). Repetition involves a kind of self-(re)making, the activity of projection differentiating the child from the mother, from objects in the world and thereby identifying itself in imaginary and symbolic registers: 'baby o-o-o-o!', exclaims the child making himself disappear in another variation of the game played in front of a mirror (284 n.). In the process of making himself through doubling, the child makes a double of himself. Overcoming loss and, through repetition, actively reshaping his relations to himself, as image, and the world, the child moves from dependence to identity, almost forsaking the real in the process. Repetition, however, suggests that the traumatic effects of loss are never fully surmounted.

Where Oedipus places the dialectic of psychic development in the severing and redirection of maternal attachments and the uncanny emerges in the return of wishes and anxieties that ought to have remained hidden in the process of 'surmounting' infantile beliefs, the repetition linked to the death drive leaves open the reverberating effects of psychic conflict: it moves beyond psychic stages, opening onto evolutionary and cultural development as a whole, rendering individual human dramas as mere side-effects of a larger process. In his speculations on the game Freud identifies a 'great cultural achievement' on the part of the child: throwing away is associated with 'instinctual renunciation', 'that is,' Freud qualifies, 'the renunciation of instinctual satisfaction' that the child 'had made in allowing his mother to go away without protesting' (285). Culture is opposed to, a movement away from, the realm of nature and instinct. Freud's account of individual acculturation invokes modern models of progress, socialisation, development, and is predicated upon a difference from (maternal) nature, on renouncing, overcoming, rejecting natural impulses. The shift from nature to culture, from animal to human, however, never remains unilinear or irrevocable in direction or momentum: nature, supposedly surmounted, returns in many, often sublimated, ways. The movement away is impeded, held up, redirected and set off-course by a countervailing pull. Away goes nature and instinct as culture is embraced. But back comes its loss in the shape of repetitions, frustrations, aggressions, destructions. A dual momentum, of Eros and Thanatos in combination and opposition, turns repetition into oscillation.

Culture as a whole is shaped by the double movement of Eros and Thanatos. In *Civilization and Its Discontents*, Freud returns to the thesis of *Beyond the Pleasure Principle* to explain the entire dynamic of social and cultural development, dissolution and change:

I may now add that civilization is a process in the service of Eros, whose purpose is to combine single human individuals, and after that families, then races, peoples and nations, into one great unity, the unity of mankind. Why this has to happen, we do not know; the work of Eros is precisely this. These collections of men are to be libidinally bound to one another. Necessity alone, the advantages of work in common, will not hold them together. But man's natural aggressive instinct, the hostility of each against all and of all against each, opposes this programme of civilization. This aggressive instinct is the derivative and the main representative of the death instinct which we have found alongside of Eros and which shares world-dominion with it. And now, I think, the meaning of the evolution of civilization is no longer obscure to us. It must present the struggle between Eros and Death, between the instinct of life and the instinct of destruction, as it works itself out in the human species. This struggle is what all life essentially consists of, and the evolution of civilization may therefore be simply described as the struggle for life of the human species. And it is this battle of the giants that our nurse-maids try to appease with their lullaby about heaven. (1955b: 313–14)

Binding, combining, expanding, unifying, civilization's 'programme' is undertaken in relation to forces of unbinding, decomposition and destruction. One does not move without the other; one does not win out over the other: the restless, relentless dynamic, a 'battle of giants', is not resolved when a paradise of unity and harmony is reached (the closest approximation that is allowed is the homeostatic inertia of dead matter).

The appeasements of religion are little more than infantile fantasies papering over a battle that is human and inhuman at the same time: while it 'works itself out in the human species', its agency remains alien to humanity. It might be explained, tempered and rendered relatively reassuring in nursery terms as a 'lullaby', but such ineffectual appeasements put about by nurse-maids only heighten the utterly incomprehensible nature of the battle. The lullabies of religion are not far from those of science. The giant metaphor invoked by Freud remains close to the myths propagated in the nursery: beyond the grasp of psychoanalytical speculation and empirical knowledge, the 'giants' that are Eros and Thanatos battle it out for reasons that remain unknown. Even to Freud. Why does Eros combine or unify, thereby promoting the growth of culture and civilization? Why does Thanatos destroy? 'We do not know', says Freud. That is, so it seems, just what they do.

An absence appears at the heart of speculation and observation. 'We do not know' why Eros, or death, does what it does. The gap in knowledge does not, however, halt speculation and projection: on the one hand lullabies occlude struggle with a singular heaven; on the other the battle between two mythological gods rages on. Without discovering a cause, the death drive, so Freud notes in *The Ego and the Id,* remains 'elusive', 'mute' (1955c: 383; 387). The only evidence, if, indeed, evidence it is, comes from the compulsion to repeat: instead of giants, a mysterious daemonic power appears in the gap of causality. Speculation proceeds. It folds back. It moves on. Only a gap remains. And repetition. If culture and civilization are split between Eros and death, so, too, is nature itself: repetition opens gaps between and within them. The dual momentum, away and back, is not a movement from nature to culture and back again, not a war fought between two opposed and fixed antagonists, but a struggle of drives whose un-bindings constantly shift. Freud does not resolve the duality within a single dialectical movement but proposes a dynamic and perhaps interminable struggle of shifting, fluid forces. Drives, rather than instincts, are reducible to neither nature nor culture. The effects of the movement between nature and culture, the renunciation and return of one on the other, suggest that drives are not tied to a single pole but manifest a gap in oppositional structures. The very idea of a death instinct is a 'biological oxymoron' (Boothby, 75). It cannot relate to nature alone. Inimical to nature, drives are inaccessible to the cultured subject. The death drive is not the aim of life, in the sense of a conscious goal to be attained, but a force within: humans are not driven 'toward' death 'by' it (Ragland, 88). Distinct from animal and nature, drives remain outside and integral to subjectivity:

> Animals have bodies, too, but not such exotic pleasures, such perverse tastes. Their instincts, like our drives, are at kind of non-conscious knowledge of what they must do. The difference is that instinct, which suits animals for survival, are determined by nature, while drives, which are determined neither by nature nor culture, often jeopardise survival. Yet it would be a mistake to confuse drive with will or whim, since drive does not appear to be at the disposal of the conscious subject; on the contrary, it exerts an unrelenting, internal pressure which mere will is unable to oppose and the body is unable to escape. (Copjec, 2000: 36)

A strange double subtraction, neither natural nor cultural, drive appears (and disappears) in the gap of separation and connection, a gap that itself gives rise to repetition, to the circulations of representation and symbolisation operating according to the pleasure principle:

> Drives are material, but they are not solely biological since they both connect and differentiate the biological and symbolic within the dialectic of the signifying body invested in a practice. Neither inside nor outside, drives are neither the ideational interior of the subject of understanding, nor the exterior

> oratory of the Hegelian force. Drives are, instead, the repeated scission of
> matter that generates signifiance, the place where the always absent subject
> is produced. (Kristeva, 1984: 167)

Signification never fills the gap, the absence determining subjectivity; it
only temporarily arrests the destabilising momentum by freezing the disruptions of death under the dead letters of language. Death is split in this
respect, a 'constant destabilizing of language for which death itself may
well be the ultimate signifier (since there can only ever be a signifier for
death)', it is 'also figured (it is above all figured) in this internal hollowing
out of language which only ever rests on so "lawless and uncertain" a base'
(Jacqueline Rose, 128).

The movement from nature and instinct, a movement associated by
Freud with the renunciation of maternal satisfaction, leaves a gap that is
not filled by culture and language. Death remains, a signifier without a
signified, a signifier with too many inadequate significations, an absence
in signification, a split, rupture, hollow, a void that calls for and refuses
repeated attempts by representation to fill it. Repetition, then, like death,
works ambivalently, even vainly: its attempts to close the gap are driven by
a momentum that keeps it open. The death drive 'enacts the absence of
mastery'; it 'writes itself into life in two directions – towards an anterior
position of inanimate unity and towards division and supplementation'
(Bronfen, 31). It is a 'mother drive' (Goux, 1990a: 237). But the mother
to which it returns is no more than another manifestation of absence, a
repetition of death, a paradise postponed: the death drive 'defines the place
of the unconscious representatives as both one's native land of exile and
lost paradise to be regained' (Leclaire, 43). Pressed forward by life, one
cannot return home, though this promise itself presses on Eros. Hence
death is bound up with the double that divides narcissistic plenitude from
the strangeness of phantasmatic, uncanny returns: 'the double, simultaneously denying and affirming immortality, is a metaphor of the uncanniness of the death drive' (Bronfen, 114). One cannot return home to mother:
she is long gone. That particular wish only returns in the form of fantasy
tinged with uncanniness: dark, enclosed spaces are simultaneously threatening and promising, places of both fear and desire. Intrauterine fantasies
are uncanny because they mark a crossing of borders between life and
death, like those disturbed in premature burial: the wish for maternal
plenitude, for primary narcissism's blissful immortality, confronts a suppressed cognisance of the work of death, division and absence in the constitution of subjectivity. Unable to return, one can only be pressed forward in repetition, with only the groundless comforts of fantasy to screen
the absence.

The death drive remains elusive, ghostly, revenant, daemonic. Evinced in the compulsion to repeat, anchored nowhere in nature or culture, death repeats. What it repeats, however, remains in question. Its repetitions only return to absence and fantasy which is 'never anything more than the screen that conceals something quite primary, something determinant in the function of repetition' (Lacan, 1977b: 60). Fantasy takes the form of another nurse-maid's lullaby as it screens the unspeakable real. An 'encounter with the real' ('tuche'), death announces that something, something unknown and unpresentable, lies 'beyond the *automaton*, the return, the coming-back, the insistence of the signs, by which we see ourselves governed by the pleasure principle' (53). The death drive: repetition is the return of some unsymbolisable excess within the signifying circulations of pleasure. If death has no signified, if it cannot be represented, if it marks only a gap in what can be signified, then no thing, no object can be identified in the compulsion to repeat. This suggests that the death drive itself has no substance, no materiality other than the compulsion to repeat. Its object seems neither organic nor inorganic, but an 'anorganic state of life' (Bronfen, 19). Grounded in neither biology nor cultural representations, 'the being of the drive, he [Freud] claims, *is* the compulsion to repeat' (Copjec, 1994: 46). For Neil Hertz, in an examination of the uncanny and the compulsion to repeat, strangeness, like the death drive, is associated with the activity of repetition rather than the repetition of something: 'it is the emergence of compulsion that they fear, as much as the reappearance of a particular fear or desire.' Repetition compulsion itself becomes a site of fear, drawing attention to work of representation, figures and the absence that grounds them: 'repetition becomes "visible" when it is colored by something being repeated, which itself functions like vivid or heightened language, lending a kind of rhetorical consistency to what is otherwise quite literally unspeakable' (Hertz, 102). Death drives the institutions, repetitions, displacements and destructions of metaphors, figures, images. It discloses only the point of excess which cannot, despite repetition, be represented. The 'daemonic' power intimated in the compulsion to repeat is no more than revenance itself, the very excess that constitutes and motivates signifying circulation. Everything comes back to repetition as it moves around a fundamental absence, forwards and back. For all the scaffolding of speculation, theorisation, explanation and representation that radiates throughout the meshwork of psychoanalysis from the hypothesis of a drive beyond the pleasure principle, it all comes down and back to a game, its double, repetitive, ambivalent movement instituting itself nowhere, giving form to nothing: 'o-o-o-o', 'a-a-a-a', 'o-o-o-o' ...

## Go-o-o-othic

'O-o-o-o', nature, instinct, infantile superstitions are rejected. 'A-a-a-a', dark desires and emotions return with a vengeance on culture. 'O-o-o-o', again nature is discharged. An ambivalent momentum, looking backwards, pressing forwards, drives Gothic productions from the start, fictions of feudal barbarism, religious superstition, aristocratic tyranny and natural wildness emerging in an age of civic humanism, bourgeois morality and enlightened rationality. Gothic romances, like the ruins, old and new, littering fictional and actual landscapes, serve as bobbins on strings, cast away and pulled back in the differentiation between modern culture and its dark precursor. If the throwing away of feudal beliefs, customs and trappings testifies to the moral and rational superiority of eighteenth-century modernity, the move towards progress in science, industry, society and politics opens a gap in the imagined continuity with a natural past, a gap which allows the return of suppressed figures and energies. Loss and return underlies the dynamic of fictional production and consumption: in the outlay and recouping of the costs of printing and distributing books in a period in which commerce was assuming a leading role; in stories' accounts of multiple losses of reason, morality, sense, family, honour; in readers' lack of discrimination and virtue, tensions in social and familial life are evinced. Duty, law and restraint all seem to disappear in the reading of modern romances: pleasure comes to the fore in the enjoyment of wild, fantastic adventures and tumultuous distresses. The repetitive, mechanical formulas of romance all seem to have one end: to increase excitement, terror, to overstimulate the senses.

The separation between an enlightened and rational age and a dark, superstitious feudal past often introduces the metaphor of the child: where the knowledge and attitudes of the former are associated with wisdom and maturity, the primitivism and ignorance of the latter belongs to a less developed stage. The metaphor articulates the continuity of a natural shared heritage with a model based on distinct stages of development and admits a hierarchy in which the superiority of one over the other is incontestable. Joseph Addison, writing on taste and the imagination in the early eighteenth century, sets out terms for the critical judgement of numerous aesthetic productions. He has 'endeavoured', he notes, 'to banish the Gothic taste which has taken possession among us' (Addison, 174). But he goes on to consider those productions which induce horror as well as those which allow the discernment of beauty. He discusses types of writing, in which the writer 'loses sight of nature', that appeal to imagination with depictions of fairies, witches, magicians, demons and spirits. Citing Dryden,

Addison finds this 'fairy way of writing' odd: it requires immersion in 'legends and fable, antiquated romances, and the traditions of nurses and old women, that he may fall in with our natural prejudices, and humour those notions which we have imbibed in our infancy' (199–200). While Addison's tone displays an assurance in the superiority of his judgement, it is neither disgusted nor appalled by these works but maintains a position of curious liberal detachment.

Addison goes on to consider the way a 'pleasing kind of horror' might 'amuse' the imagination with 'strangeness and novelty'; he distinguishes himself from 'men of cold fancies, and philosophical dispositions' who might object to the improbability of such works. Addison, however, admits a degree of pleasure in these works of imagination: 'they bring up into our memory the stories we have heard in our childhood, and favour those secret terrors and apprehensions to which the mind of man is naturally subject'. These memories, terrors, apprehensions are neither, the dispassionate and unruffled commentary suggests, uncanny nor disturbing to the mature and rational mind. They remain firmly in their place, bound up in the natural stage of childhood, a stage that has been comfortably negotiated. Addison maintains a secure, benevolent and knowing paternal position. His confidence extends to the comparison he makes between evocations of childhood memory and the pleasures of surveying the 'habits and behaviours of foreign countries': works of imagination, of 'new creation' and 'another species', will similarly delight and surprise (200). The comparison extends, as it pushes aside concerns about falsity and delusions, to a consideration of other times and the feudal origins of works of poetic imagination. Emerging in 'darkness and superstition', their function is both amusement and the terrifying reminder of duty:

> Our forefathers looked upon Nature with more reverence and horror, before the world was enlightened by learning and philosophy, and loved to astonish themselves with the apprehensions of witchcraft, prodigies, charms and enchantments. There was not a village in England that had not a ghost in it, the churchyards were all haunted, every large common had a circle of fairies belonging to it, and there was scarce a shepherd to be met who had not seen a spirit. (201)

Addison looks back to a bygone age, his maturity and detachment underlining its distance from the enlightened eighteenth century that he represents. 'Gothic' works remain the products of a particular time, a period that has well and truly gone, has been thoroughly surpassed by learning and philosophy. The context in which stories of witchcraft and enchantments occur is dominated, Addison's images emphasise, by nature, religion, rural life and agriculture, all far removed from a world of urbane civility, social sophistication and scientific enquiry. Far removed, Addison's forefathers, with their superstitions and natural simplicity, appear primitive, child-like in their innocence and credulity. The 'charming' picture presented by Addison is pleasing in the manner of the childhood memories evoked by poetic imaginings. Indeed, the works that continue to have effects comparable to the return of childhood memories and apprehensions originate in the same period: the material, pleasing though it is, comes from a primitive stage and remains suited to superstitious and uncultivated minds.

The equation of childhood and pre-Enlightenment culture establishes the difference privileging Addison's rational and learned present. It distinguishes a past that has been overcome by a process of individual and social cultivation. But that past remains, none the less, in the very metaphor employed by Addison: children still have to be educated in the present; reason and cultivation are, by definition, not natural processes. Addison, however, exudes the confidence appropriate to his knowing paternal position: he is not alarmed at the possibility of childhood memories, fears and apprehensions reappearing with damaging or threatening effects. The cultivation of taste and reason, in placing childhood and primitive cultures on the same, lower level, has risen to a superior and unassailable stage of development. The child is not, not yet at least, father of the man. Addison's confident assumptions and secure distance from the feudal past and its childlike beliefs are outlined in an earlier aesthetic discussion: beauty, in works of art as much as human forms, serves to encourage the multiplication of the species. Ugly or ill-formed creations do not reproduce:

> for 'tis very remarkable that wherever Nature is crossed in the production of a monster (the result of any unnatural mixture) the breed is incapable of propagating its likeness, and of founding a new order of creatures; so that unless all animals were allured by the beauty of their own species, generation would be at an end, and the earth unpeopled. (182)

Aesthetic judgement is supported by natural philosophy: the same argument made self-evident by nature holds for works of imagination. Monsters of the imagination, like monsters of nature, cannot breed (tell that to Frankenstein).

Addison's critical framework establishes an influential model for aesthetic judgement in the eighteenth century, setting the many of the terms, but not the tone, for subsequent accounts of art, romances, beauty, imagination and sublimity. His prognosis, implying a straightforward development in which beauty rather than monstrosity flourishes, is less secure. In speaking of 'species' and 'monsters', in assuming a knowing, paternal authority in his discussions of aesthetics, Addison offers a critical vocabulary and position that is readily adopted in the course of the century. Writing in 1712, however, before Horace Walpole delivered his 'new species' of fiction, a hybrid of ancient and modern romance, and before the appearance of vast quantities of romances and novels in circulating libraries, booksellers' windows and on drawing-room shelves, Addison was in no position to predict how works he associated with childhood memories and earlier cultures, would dominate an expanding market for fiction. 'Monsters' and 'new species' proliferate with remarkable fecundity: the terms are used repeatedly in critical denunciations of fictions that are improbable, unnatural, and immoral. Paternal authority, the values and duties attendant on familial, and even social, structures are threatened by unrealistic and licentious tales of adventure, mystery and love (Ioan Williams). Children, young readers and women, less firm in their understanding and morals, are cited as particular objects of concern as childhood memories, secret apprehension and primitive beliefs reappear in fictions with alarmingly regularity and disarming effects in the course of the eighteenth century. The return of and to settings, customs and beliefs that are both imaginary and belong to a non-rational age are imagined by critics to herald the loss of familial, social and moral order, reason, virtue, taste and good sense disappearing in a tide of disobedient romanticism, sentimental and amorous indulgences, unchecked pleasures, fancies and excitements. The popularity and proliferation of romances and novels was described as an overwhelming 'flood', an apocalyptic 'deluge'. The imagined disappearance of social values, critically at least, provoked strident conservative calls for their recovery.

In presenting the increase of fictional texts as flood and deluge threatening to overwhelm proper behaviour, values and judgement, critics were drawing on imagery associated with biblical apocalypse and the sublime. As a branch of aesthetics reaching back to Longinus, the sublime was a perfectly proper topic of aesthetic enquiry. Its examination of pleasure, terror, horror and wonder in responses to natural phenomena and imaginative productions was also suited to studies of 'Gothic' and 'romantic' texts. In the encounter with the wildness of natural grandeur, the viewer feels overwhelmed: unlike beauty, in Edmund Burke's discussion, which rests harmoniously before the eye, rugged and immense scenery cannot be taken in at a glance. The sublime initially describes a loss: the senses are overcome, the mind is threatened by the vast scale of things. Self is gone, lost in the immensity of nature. At this point, the experience of loss is turned round: the imagined threat to comprehension, self and integrity evokes instincts of 'self-preservation', Burke argues, so that terror awakens and renews a sense of self that imaginatively overcomes dissolution, to

participate in the scene, intimate its wholeness and experience the elevation of awe and wonder. From loss to recovery, the energy and elevation
turns distress into excitement: for all its terrors and horror, the sublime is
pleasing and delightful. Ann Radcliffe's careful posthumously published
re-examination of the sublime distinguishes between the effects of terror
and horror to emphasise the activity of the subject: where terror expands,
elevates and 'awakens the faculties to a high degree of life', horror paraly-
ses, confounds and 'nearly annihilates them'. The difference turns on an
object or rather, the absence of an object: in the play of light and dark, the
frisson of pleasure and fear at work in sublime terror, there is 'something
for the imagination to exaggerate'; 'obscurity, or indistinctness, is only a
negative which leaves the imagination to act upon the few hints that truth
reveals to it'. In the chaos and confusion of horror, 'the mind can find
nothing to be magnificent, nothing to nourish its fears and doubts, or to
act upon in any way' (Radcliffe, 1826: 49–50). Horror leaves one in a
state of shock, overcome by experience; terror allows for imaginative action and the assumption of a degree of control, a movement from loss to
recuperation, an awakening of the faculties and a thrilling regeneration of
a sense of self through emotional expenditure.

There is a double movement in the sublime in which the subject is,
imaginatively and emotionally, cast away and returned to its self. Sense,
reason, self are overcome and then through emotional energy (the instinct
of self-preservation is one of the strongest passions, says Burke) recovered.
The doubleness is further developed in Immanuel Kant's analysis of the
experience:

> The mind feels itself *set in motion* in the representation of the sublime in
> nature; whereas in the aesthetic judgement upon what is beautiful therein it
> is in *restful* contemplation. This movement, especially in its inception, may
> be compared with a vibration, i.e. with a rapidly alternating repulsion and
> attraction produced by one and the same Object. The point of excess for
> the imagination (toward which it is driven in the apprehension of the
> intuition) is like an abyss in which it fears to lose itself; yet again for the
> rational idea of the supersensible it is not excessive, but conformable to law,
> and directed and drawing out such an effort on the part of the imagination:
> and so in turn as much a source of attraction as it was repellent to mere
> sensibility. But the judgement itself all the while steadfastly preserves its
> aesthetic character, because it represents, without being grounded on any
> definite concept of the Object, merely the subjective play of the mental
> powers (the imagination and reason) as harmonious by virtue of their very
> contrast. For just as in the estimate of the beautiful imagination and
> *understanding* by their concert generate subjective finality of the mental

faculties, so imagination and *reason* do so here by their conflict – that is to say they induce a feeling of our possessing a pure and self-sufficient reason, or a faculty for the estimation of magnitude, whose pre-eminence can only be made intuitively evident by the inadequacy of that faculty which in the presentation of magnitudes (of objects of sense) is the itself unbounded. (Kant, 107)

Kant stresses the role of reason and understanding in stabilising the experience, at pains to distinguish the significance of mental powers in the process: an experience without a definite idea of the object and in which the perceptual faculties are at sea requires the imagination to supplement reason with a 'feeling' that returns rationality to itself. For Kant, the experience distinguishes mind and nature and, precisely at the point that the former seems overwhelmed by the latter, it recovers with a greater and more elevated sense of itself: 'sublimity, therefore, does not reside in any of the things of nature, but only in our own mind, in so far as we may become conscious of our superiority over nature within, and thus also over nature without us (as exerting influence upon us)' (114). Nature, then, within and without the mind, is overcome: mere things and objects are subordinated to the power of ideas generated by the self-conscious subject: indeed, it is the very intimation and imagination of loss (of sense, reason, self) that generates such consciousness.

The sublime, it seems, operates according to a dialectical model in which loss on one level leads to recovery on a higher plane: on the one hand, mind, self, sense are negated by the overwhelming experience of ungraspable natural magnitude but, in confrontation with loss and excess and in the conflict of imagination and reason, mental superiority is recovered. Perceptual and emotional faculties, awash in natural immensity, are conserved and supplemented by the superior powers of mind. Reason defines itself in the surmounting of nature. The philosophical resolution, however, depends on baser and less well-formed energies. Kant's account also draws attention to the dynamism of the process: it is a 'movement', a 'vibration', a 'rapidly alternating repulsion and attraction' in which 'excess' turns into an 'abyss'. Though the hollowing out of experience serves as the condition for the productive conflictual institution of imagination and reason, the move from nature to mind, the very agitation which sets it in motion emanates from an obscure 'Object' that is at once here and not here, there and not there, too much and too little: its excess implies too great a presence for the mind to cope with, too much object, while, as 'abyss', there is too little, a gaping void where an object should have been. In Kant's reading, the excessive and abyssal nature of the object cedes to the indefiniteness of some 'concept' of the object and so gives way to a focus on mind's superiority over natural things. But excess and abyss remain at the core of the experience, the emptiness, the voiding of objects marking the site of the dynamism, the rapid alternation of attraction and repulsion. Is it such an alternation that itself opens the abyssal space in (the relation of) mind (and) or nature, its rapidity the very excess that hollows out a void? What drives this alternation? What causes this fluctuating, excessive and abyssal rhythm? Nature? Mind? Like the object, the cause remains obscure: is a 'daemonic' power, perhaps, imperceptibly at work? To look to mystery, however, returns to a Kantian path, mind imagining reasons where, maybe, there are none. All that is left is the alternation itself, a double movement, with or without resolution, appearing and disappearing, away and back, repulsing and attracting, lost and recovered.

The sublime, a double movement, is itself split between a dialectical and dynamic mode. In the former the resolution may only be temporary, a short-lived check to the rhythm of rapid alternation. The play of loss and recuperation, repulsion and attraction runs through criticism of romances and novels, and articulates the rhythms of the tales themselves. The game, perhaps, orchestrates the appeal and rejection of Gothic forms in the eighteenth century, crucial, excessive and abyssal to its self definition: its play instantiates the sublime rhythms of cultural differentiation. Reinvented in the context of a commercial eighteenth century, the aesthetics of the sublime served to establish, at least imaginarily, a sense of self and agency in a rapidly changing world. It remained an individual, private experience and, moreover, one that was both virtual and which served as a 'solution to the defects of a commercial society' (Clery, 104). The sublime fills the breach in a new way, vainly trying to articulate individual and socius by offering 'a simulacrum of the external threat of violent death sufficient to arouse the strongest passions of self-preservation'. A 'mind-game' having 'the effect of catharsis and renewal', it manifests 'a decisive alteration' (105). Self is virtually lost and virtually regained in the oscillation of terror and pleasure, an expenditure of excess energies that returns to equilibrium. In the movement of loss and recovery structuring Gothic fiction, sublimity exceeds individual or familial concerns. In association with fictions produced in the eighteenth century and depicting a feudal past, its deployment of loss involves two cultures. Replaying eighteenth-century anxieties in feudal costumes and settings seems to mourn an absence and regain a lost continuity. Alternating between loss and recovery, even as it distinguishes and interrelates a Gothic past from an enlightened present, the sublime hollows out a space for projection and fantasy in which the past is rendered both proximate and distanced. The provenance of Horace Walpole's own country house, bought by aristocrat

from a toyshop owner, turns it into 'a "theme park" treatment of aristocratic ascendancy', feudalism no more than 'the plaything of a whimsical
hobbyist' (Clery, 76). A 'plaything', little more than a child's toy, a creation of dream and fantasy, the house is as much a fiction as the novel it
inspired. Like the ruins bought and sold with country estates, or, even,
freshly built, along with bankrupt aristocrat's estates, the shift in material
power is shadowed by all sorts of more immaterial meanings and associations, simulations and recreations of the past adapted to a bourgeois context. As commercial power comes to dominate social organisation, the
remnants of feudalism are decoratively reconstructed in an idle aesthetic
fashion. Lost, they are recovered in another form, subject to a different
arrangement of economic practices, given a new meaning as the
phantasmatic antithesis, the heritage history, of the present.

Sublimity, in the terrifying spaces of natural wildness and mountainous
grandeur, repeatedly occasions heady flights of sensibility in eighteenth-
century fictions. Dark forests, gloomy castles, dungeons, caverns, labyrinths, form the horrifying counterpoint to the geography of imagined
terror and awe. In the paralysing spaces of the latter, a more internalised
vista unfolds. Phantasmatic as much as actual realms, dark enclosures entwine fear (premature burial) and desire (maternal presence), activating
uncanny returns of infantile wishes along with the spectre of death in life.
Externally, in the negotiations of beauty and sublimity, and internally, in
the dynamic of terror and horror, the subject of Gothic writing, the heroine, say, or the reader who, through identification, participates in her flights
and frights, is constituted through a movement of loss and recovery. Gothic
narratives, indeed, are based on and punctuated throughout by a series of
losses. The loss of property, protection, family, name and social status
precipitates heroines into an unkind world, while imagined losses of life,
reputation or virtue threaten both body and identity. These losses impeach paternal power and symbolic authority, dividing bad, Catholic, aristocratic and cruel fathers from good, responsible, rational, moral ones in a
fluctuation from one to the other that only eventually casts out evil excesses. Fiction presents numerous actual losses: mothers are often dead,
fathers dishonoured or absent; excesses of superstitious imagining overwhelm rational good sense, while too much terror frequently causes heroines to lose consciousness entirely. The wild social and natural landscapes
of the fictions, moreover, present worlds that have abandoned principles
of morality and propriety, places outside the rule of law, that is, without
proper paternal regulation. The cautionary element of Gothic fiction, its
deployment of monstrosity, depends on loss and recovery: demonstrating
what happens when one strays from the bounds of proper protection, it

announces the importance of, and at the end restores, sanctioned values and behaviour.

With the exception of villains whose vices are too extreme to be rehabilitated, and must be expelled, punished by death or law, the losses suffered in the course of fictions are (extended) preludes to the moment of recovery: in coming to her senses, morally and rationally, the heroine also comes into property, money and matrimony. A symbolic, familial and moral economy is re-established in a movement backwards and forwards: what was lost in the Gothic journey through wildness, vice and superstition, an absence of good order defining the world of the genre, is recovered at the end, in the case of Walpole's, Reeve's, or Radcliffe's fiction, as a divinely sanctioned order. Disequilibrium, the threats, fears, shocks, pursuits, wild fantasies, vices and crimes, that consume most of the narrative interest, is succeeded by a return to equilibrium, a return, ironically, to an order that barely existed in the fiction except in nostalgic reminiscence. The return, however, occurs on another level: like the sublime which, in Kant's more than Burke's account, charts the movement from overwhelmed senses to subjective recuperation at the level of ideas and reason, a move from disordered superstition to the good forms of rationalised imagination, the heroine masters herself and her faculties, identifies her place in a providential morally defined order of things. From an indulgence in excesses of fancy and sensibility, she regains an acceptable symbolic position. The movement, as in the sublime, also enables a satisfying expenditure of excess energies: too much sensation, passion, curiosity, desire and fancy consumes them, discharging the surplus in a cathartic release. There is also a movement from passivity to activity, in the manner described by Freud. The heroine is initially the victim of actual and imagined threats, subjected to cruel circumstances and possessed by terrible speculations. Through repetition, however, she begins to assume the necessary levels of self-control that define her as a proper rational eighteenth-century subject. Strangely, and unconvincingly for many critics, the heroine undergoes a learning process: 'all excess is vicious', the soon-to-be dead father of Emily in *Udolpho* declares. His daughter, through loss and excess feeling, must learn to appreciate the truth of this statement: her fancies, superstitions, vices must be exposed to the point that they can be replaced by reason and firm moral sense.

The losses pictured repeatedly in violent terrifying threats thus seem to serve as a prelude to recovery: the shocks intimating imminent ruin and destruction invigorate a sublime recuperation of bourgeois economic and familial order. But that order remains threatened by the mass of romance readers, by revolutionary mobs and the diabolical machinations of mysterious conspirators. The threat is repeated: losses of sanity, domestic security, bodily integrity are imagined in new figures and places from one's own psyche to the dark labyrinths of urban existence. In imperial fantasies of the nineteenth century, culture as a whole is threatened by dark powers from the East, while a similar darkness occupies culture and its civilised bodies: deviance, degeneration, disease haunt the sacred spaces of home and society. As readers become familiar with culture's familiars, the machinery of fiction churns out yet more objects of fear and ever greater threats to self and civilisation to shock them with a sublime sense of loss. In fiction the past is recalled and expelled. In the natural images, architectural ruins and feudal customs that are coloured by a Gothic sublime, appropriation and expulsion attempt to separate a civilised, rational eighteenth century from its barbaric forbears: ruined abbeys and castles testify to a world that has been superseded, its wildness and extravagance tamed by the civilised mind; natural and primitive passions of self-preservation are activated as the basis of a movement away, an elevation or progression. Remnants of the past – ruins, superstitions, passions – mark turning points in cultural historical progress and thus, in looking back, Gothic figures also provide the platform of a movement forward. *Dracula*, for all the return of primitive and supernatural energies embodied by its eponymous villain, is also suffused with signs of modernity: railways, telegrams, typewriters, phonographs, set present and past in dynamic interchange. Gothic texts manifest a double movement: looking back, they hasten forward, cast by a momentum of shock that eschews the resolutions of sublimity. Machinery, shock, the vacillations of pleasure and recoil, throw Gothic images forward. Factories, cities, science – all sites of progress – are simultaneously rendered desolate and disturbing. The temporal ambivalence of the momentum, forwards and back, allows the future to serve as a site of dark projections. Anxiety leaps forwards as well as back: social and corporeal disintegration lurks in industrial devastation, in genetic experimentation, in alien and mutant form, as threatens from the past, in decaying castles, in demonic or bestial shapes. Science and technology, markers of knowledge and progress, are both realisations of human power and achievement and harbingers of barbarism and degeneration. From *Frankenstein* onwards, it seems, scientific discovery is as much threat as promise, a doubleness that defines the momentum of Gothic modernity.

The lines from past to future and from future to past also evacuate the present: an empty site of anxious projections. At this point, the double movement of technological/spectral media rush back and forwards: like the child's bobbin, an exterior and technical object in the constitution of individual subjectivity, the machinery of Gothic fiction discloses a daemonic movement pressing within and at the edges of mechanisms which organise historical narrative and explanation. The movement backwards and forwards, pulsing over a space of inexplicability, charts what may be described as a 'history of the future' and follows the dynamic pattern that Foucault termed 'the history of the present'. In the second volume of the history of sexuality, *The Use of Pleasure*, he outlines the process:

> I am neither a Hellenist nor a Latinist. But it seemed to me that if I gave enough care, patience and modesty, and attention to the task, it would be possible to gain sufficient familiarity with the ancient Greek and Roman texts; that is, a familiarity that would allow me – in keeping with a practice that is doubtless fundamental to Western philosophy – to examine the both the difference that keeps us at a remove from a way of thinking in which we recognize the origin of our own, and the proximity that remains in spite of that distance which we never cease to explore. (Foucault, 1987: 7)

The play of difference and proximity, the movement shaping history, sees past return upon present while maintaining a distance, a gap for the movement to occur. The movement also describes the relationship between Gothic texts and the past they fabricate: a bourgeois eighteenth century returns to the remnants of barbaric feudalism to distance its enlightened present from the uncivilised dark ages while, at the same time, in its fictional constructions of that period, it recognises a comfortable image of itself in the very differentiation it enacts. The retrospection casts out the past and returns it in negated form. But the movement is prospective: in the sublime fear of losing itself in the immensity of a ruined and barbaric past, as ruinous as the devastating impressions of (super)natural Power, the self-image of the present is pressed forwards in an anticipatory, imaginary recovery of self on another plane, that is, a recovery with a difference. But as the movement speeds up, in repetitious shocks and pleasures, recuperation vanishes quickly in the face of the rapid alternating rhythms.

Backwards and forwards, hollowing out and filling up, the movement does not necessarily return to the same place: it is not a movement between fixed poles, a movement that leaves either past or present intact, but a rhythm in which history and writing are mobile:

> The modern time of writing which is set against the Gothic past eventually comes round to being the past of succeeding generations of readers and writers; and so by the 1930s we find F.M. Mayor and Isak Dinesen both setting their stories in the early nineteenth century, now become 'Gothic' itself, its customs cruelly repressive in twentieth-century eyes. (Baldick, xv)

The Gothic past, cast back and moved forwards, is relocated in the process. Repression is projected backwards, the game of casting away the very difference that secures the illusion of a present that is free and liberal: the later nineteenth century, in Coppola's *Bram Stoker's Dracula*, returns to the scene of Stoker's fiction to present the *fin de siècle* in gloomy and degenerative tones. The novel's 'modern' present is rendered Gothic itself, an effect of alternating polarisation, repulsion and attraction constituting a sense of proximity and distance in nothing more than repetitive disappearances and reappearances. Repetition's mobility, introducing a momentum of difference within the return of the same, comes to the fore with a double aspect: the casting away and coming back does not only hollow a space for the institution and maintenance of cultural frameworks, but depends on an activity of unfixing and destabilisation, destructive as well as creative. In repetition and under the appearance of the same that returns, there presses the daemonic difference of the death drive, a drive that may be no more than repetition's destructive and destabilising movement.

## Dark precursor

Loss and recovery, repetition and the shock of overwhelming stimulation underlie the attempt to identify what lurks 'beyond the pleasure principle'. The child's game holds a prominent position in Freud's speculations on the economic, dynamic and topographical factors organising mental functioning, more prominent perhaps than is credited by the writer: a 'daemonic' power associated with the 'compulsion to repeat' affects his own writing, even as, at times, it seems that all mental phenomena come under the regime of the pleasure principle. In various interpretations of the fort-da game, pleasure seems to hold sway, diminishing tension, compensating for loss, even, as an 'instinct for mastery', consolidating psychic experience. But repetition begins to disclose a movement beyond pleasure, in which pleasure does not dominate: 'we are therefore left in doubt as to whether the impulse to work over in the mind some overpowering experience so as to make oneself master of it can find expression as a primary event, and independently of the pleasure principle'. Freud, however, vacillates, unwilling to let go of the string, to offer the counter speculation that the child may 'only have been able to repeat this unpleasant experience in play because this repetition carried along it a yield of pleasure of another sort but none the less a direct one' (Freud, 1984: 286). The game's challenge to the economic dominance of the pleasure principle remains inconclusive. Freud's argument departs from the topic of the repetitive game, though returning to it on occasions throughout the essay, to examine a range of other examples and more confidently assert the existence of 'a compulsion to repeat which over-rides the pleasure principle' (293). His willingness to speculate extends to the 'protective shield' and the flows of cathexis and anticathexis that bind neural energies, two forms of which appear, 'a freely flowing cathexis that presses on towards discharge and a quiescent cathexis' (303). Here the role of repetition is evinced as the mastering or binding of excitations, an operation that, while not opposing itself to the pleasure principle, works independently of it.

On the basis of these speculations Freud is led to propose an enduring tension, a double movement, in which polarised instincts or drives (between life and death, preservation and destruction) operate in a dynamic, oscillating manner, drawing the organism backwards and forwards. Repetition compulsion manifests life's impulse '*to restore an earlier state of things*', to follow its own path to death. In the fluctuation between life and death, sexual expenditure and organic conservatism, the organism is thrust forwards and backwards in the play of repetition, resistance and satisfaction: the 'persisting tension' between an impulse to regain complete satisfaction in a recovery of maternal presence that is impossible (because a return is blocked by the resistances governing repression) and the recurrent demand that never goes away, leaving a gap which cannot be filled. Wanting to take a 'backward path', being is none the less impelled forward with 'no alternative but to advance in the direction in which growth is free' (315, original emphasis). This offers a dynamic model of organic existence, 'as though the life of the organism moved with a vacillating rhythm': one group of instincts, Freud continues, 'rushes forward so as to reach the goal of life as swiftly as possible' while 'the other group jerks back to a certain point to make a fresh start and so prolong the journey' (313). In the compulsion to repeat a curious beyond to the pleasure principle appears and disappears in the very movement of departure and return. Mental life, it seems, cannot be reduced to a single overriding principle: another mysterious, daemonic power haunts its economy of pleasure in the vacillating pulse of tension and its release. Rushing forward, jerking back, life exhibits the movements of a child's game. The play of disappearance and return that, earlier in the essay, Freud had left in suspension and behind, itself returns. The game prefigures the overarching pattern of life's compulsion to repeat, of which it is itself a repetition.

That the game involves objects, mirror images and vocalisations, moreover, are facets not lost on subsequent psychoanalytic commentators, Jacques Lacan in particular. His account of the fort-da game emphasises the role of signification, noting a kind of transcendence to the game, a transformation of being from the body to cultural identity: 'in his phonematic opposition, the child transcends, brings onto the symbolic plane, the phenomenon of presence and absence. He renders himself master of the thing, precisely insofar as he destroys it' (Lacan, 1988a: 173). The Thing which the child negates, the biological thing which he is, sees desire established in its empty place, deferred and redirected from the presence/absence of the maternal body to the structure of language and law. Signification hollows out real being to disclose the 'world of negativity' defining human desire and reality: signifiers, not objects, fill the gap and move desire to another level: 'raising desire to a second power' in destroying the object, the child's 'action thus negatives the field of forces of desire in order to become its own object to itself' (1977a: 103). Meaning and identity take their bearing in relation to the desire of the Other, the fluctuating locus of symbolic oppositions of which 'fort' and 'da' (which have no meaning except in their difference, any other term being attributed by the adults who observe the game) constitute early examples. A nascent imaginary sense of wholeness and self-mastery is evinced along with the inscription in the system of desire and signification. As Jacques Derrida glosses: 'he makes himself disappear, he masters himself symbolically, he plays with the dummy, the dead man, as if with himself, and he makes himself reappear henceforth without a mirror, in his disappearance itself, maintaining himself like his mother at the other end of the line'(Derrida, 1987: 319). The line is telephonic, calling up presence at a distance: the chain of signification, in which subjectivity appears without body, becomes like the reel and image, a kind of technology, a tool for self-production and a tool-box that is not one's own. The subject none the less remains split; the gap disclosed and covered over by the compulsion to repeat is never fully overcome, remaining both a space of loss and a space for identity to reassert itself.

Disclosing the gap and the pulse of subjective constitution, the game's repetitive movements demonstrate, moreover, a dependence on objects, on tools, on technology whose non-appearance renders it ghostly and reveals an 'ever-open gap introduced by the absence' and 'remains a cause of a centrifugal tracing' (Lacan, 1977b: 62). The game brings out the priority of alienation not mastery, which 'is difficult to imagine being increased in endless repetition, whereas the endless repetition that is in question reveals the radical vacillation of the subject' (239). And it is repetition that discloses the insistence of something other than the pleasure principle, something demonic, in excess of its own repetitive economy: 'Coming back (*revenant*) – subject to a rhythm – this phantom deserves an analysis of the passages and the procedure, of everything that both makes him come back and conjures him up cadentially'(Derrida, 1987: 269). The rhythm of repetition founding the subject allows an aneconomic excess to

manifest its effects: 'not opposed to' the dominance of the pleasure principle, the death drive 'hollows it out with a testamentary writing "en abyme"
originally, at the origin of origin' (304). Hollowed, it can be filled again.
The subject can symbolically master himself, recall himself to himself, but
only on the condition of self-distancing, a self-sending away by way of
objects and words:

> He speaks to himself telephonically, he calls himself, recalls himself,
> 'spontaneously' affects himself with his presence-absence in the presence-
> absence of his mother. He makes himself *re*-. Always according to the law of
> the PP. In the grand speculation of a PP which (who) never seems to absent
> itself-(himself) from itself-(himself). Or from anyone else. The telephonic
> or telescripted recall provides the "movement" by contracting itself, by signing
> a contract with itself. (319)

The movement appears auto-matic in its return to self. At the same time
repetition calls up a curious (non) return of the demonic: 'the demon is
that very thing which *comes back* [*revient*] without having been called by
the PP. The demon is the *revenance* which repeats its entrance, coming
back [*revenant*] from one knows not where ("early infantile influences,"
says Freud), inherited from one knows not whom, but already persecutory, by means of the simple form of its return, indefatigably repetitive,
independent of every apparent desire, *automatic*' (341). In excess of the
autoaffective structure of the game, another automatism appears: 'this
automaton comes back [*revient*] without coming back to [*revenir à*] anyone, it produces effects of ventriloquism without origin, without emis-
sion, and without addressee ... Tele without telos. Finality without end,
the beauty of the devil' (341). Technology and subjectivity emerge, not as
opposed entities, but as effects entangled in the same rhythms, returning
on the other in a pulse in which a difference is disclosed, a spectral,
phantasmatic gap, in the very repetition that serves as the condition of
their articulation. The rhythm of appearance and return, the loss and recovery of the pleasure principle's dominance depends on the abyss over
which the objects and utterances are projected and recalled.

Though it is in terms of the work of signification that the subjectification
of the fort-da is understood, the oppositional system of language alone is
insufficient to explain the entirety of the process. Something else is at
work:

> Everything begins when several signifiers can present themselves to the subject
> at the same time, in a *Gleichzeitigkeit*. It is at this level *Fort* is the correlative
> of *Da*. *Fort* can only be expressed as an alternative derived from a basic
> synchrony. It is on the basis of this synchrony that something comes to be

organized, the something that the mere play of *Fort* and *Da* could not produce
by itself. (Lacan, 1992: 65)

Beyond the play of repetition, Lacan identifies the effects of the *objet petit
a*, a conception of his own tied to the move from body to language. It is an
object that marks and stands in place of loss, a loss pertaining, not so
much to the mother, but to the narcissistic self-relation wounded by her
disappearance. Of 'secondary importance' is the act of compensation for
mother's disappearance: the reel is not a maternal substitute but 'such part
of the subject that detaches itself from him while still remaining his' and
establishes the place 'where man thinks with his object' and the signifier.
The game, Lacan notes, 'is accompanied by one of the first oppositions to
appear' and 'it is in this object to which the opposition is applied in act,
the reel, that we must designate the subject' (1988b: 62). The object *a*,
then, serves as the locus, the gap, for the institution of the signifier and the
symbolic, the point, not of mastery but of a fundamental alienation, the
splitting in which the subject is subjected to language: 'overcome by the
attenuating game, *fort-da*, which is a *here or there*, and whose aim in its
alternation, is simply that of being the *fort* of a *da*, and the *da* of a *fort*'
(63). The alternating movement, the pulse of fort-da, covering and uncovering a gap in being discloses the place of the unconscious, 'always a
manifested as that which vacillates in a split in the subject' (1977b: 28).
Indeed, it is 'the *pulsative* function of the unconscious' that is manifested
in the movement of the fort/da (43).

Beyond the scaffolding of words and things that circulate with the appearance of the fort-da, a gap and a rhythm come to fore in determining
the movement that may go beyond the pleasure principle. Discussing the
question of a moral law that traverses Freudian thought, Lacan sums up
the process:

> It is a movement which makes him the start with a first opposition between
> reality principle and pleasure principle in order, after a series of vacillations,
> oscillations and imperceptible changes in his references, to conclude at the
> end of the theoretic formulations by positing something beyond that pleasure
> principle that might well leave us wondering how it relates to the first
> opposition. Beyond the pleasure principle we encounter that opaque surface
> which to some has seemed so obscure that it is the antimony of all thought
> – not just biological but scientific in general – the surface that is known as
> the death instinct. (1992: 20–1)

Vacillations, oscillations, imperceptible changes provide the very movement that takes Freud's text beyond the pleasure principle to disclose a
drive in form of a 'law beyond all law, that can only be posited as a final

structure, as a vanishing point of any reality that might be attained' (20–1). Beyond the law of pleasure, a movement within it that exceeds its bounds, the death drive appears in and as vacillation. For Derrida, the 'vacillation' that is more obvious and thematic in 'The Uncanny' manifests a rhythm that is purely 'differantial' in function (Derrida, 1987: 361).

What is important in the subjective formation manifested in the course of the fort-da game is the rhythm, the vacillation and alternation, of the play: the movement itself, a play of oppositions, of sounds, objects, presence and absence, brings the subject into being in relation to the determining gap of the object *a* as that which fills the hollow disclosed by repetition and the death drive: ultimately, *a*, like death, 'reflects our own nothingness' (Lacan, 1977b: 92). The void attendant on the movement towards cultural identity remains, however, as the invisible point anchoring subjective being, returning it to itself, the locus where identity appears and disappears, the mark of a radical alienation in respect of which loss and recuperation define subjectivity. The subject emerging in *Beyond the Pleasure Principle* is no fixed entity, secure in itself and its position, but a being of process, a being structured, establishing and maintaining, and losing, itself through a dynamic movement back and forth over a gap. The subject is an effect of an obscure 'cause' belonging 'to the order of the *non-realised*, thwarted – that is, *it is in itself structured as a gap*, a void insisting indefinitely on its fulfilment.' The death drive forms 'the point of absolute self-contraction which constitutes the subject as the Void of pure self-relating'(Zizek, 1999a: 317, original emphasis); it 'empties the (sacred) Place, creates a Clearing, the Void, the Frame, which is then filled in by the object, "elevated to the dignity of the Thing"' (2000: 30). The death drive, in these terms, remains a 'dimension of radical negativity', a movement of destabilisation in relation to which language, subjectivity and culture takes its bearing: 'all "culture" is in a way a reaction-formation, an attempt to limit, canalize – to *cultivate* this imbalance, this traumatic kernel, this radical antagonism through which man cuts his umbilical cord with nature, with animal homeostasis' (1989: 5). Separated from 'animal homeostasis' by the negativity of the drive, culture and its subject are cast adrift in a tension which can only briefly be returned to the symbolic equilibrium of pleasure.

The death drive, the point of negativity at which culture, repetition and pleasure attempts to institute itself and its signifiers, does not simply represent the return to homeostasis, but marks the movement by which disequilibrium is engendered. It 'must be said to bring about an *increase* of tensions', threatening 'to overload the psychical organization with a wave of unmastered energies' (Boothby, 85). Death, 'in its fundamental *process of unbinding*, of fragmentation, of breaking up, of separation, of bursting', is no longer localised but manifests 'the principle of discord' between every psychical agency: 'it is internalized. It spreads out, it multiplies itself. In changing area, it changes meanings'. As the 'most fundamental form of the "work of the negative"', it is 'a-topia' (Pontalis, 1978: 89–91). Hence psychoanalytical method, in broaching the death drive, 'ana-lyses' and 'dissolves':

> it is governed by the 'zero-principle', setting in motion what Freud, in his way, designated as the 'death drive'; which has nothing to do with biological death, but which, potentially, leads to the dissolution of all formations – psychical, egoic, ideological, symptomatic. But as a counter-balance to this force of unbinding, this liberation of psychic energies, psychoanalysis offers itself as a guarantor of constancy; of containment, as it has been called, of support. (Laplanche, 227)

The 'matrix of desire', the symbolic circulations that the death drive underpins and undermines, can never maintain its constancy however, repeatedly interrupted as it is by the drive, 'that radical force, usually fixed and fixating, which surfaces in a catastrophic or ecstatic incident, at the point where the organic coherence of the subject in his body appears for what it is, unnameable or inexpressible, swoon or ecstasy, shouting its appeal for a word to veil and sustain it' (Laplanche and Leclaire, 142–3). In excess of words, the drive refuses to be fixed or contained. For Guattari, the priority given to the signifier in the Lacanian account of the fort/da is an attempt at 'petrification', of submitting the drive to the frozen stasis of a 'transcendent signifying order', rather than acknowledging the multivalent and heterogeneous energies at work (Guattari, 1995: 74–5).

Julia Kristeva's reading of the death drive is carefully attuned to its multivalent and heterogeneous movements: in ex-pulsions, in the throwings away, the pro- re- and intro-jections, the negativity of the death drive appears constitutive and destructive, a matter of tensions and stases:

> It is at the level of 'concrete operations' that Freud perceives, in the *Fort/Da* of the infant, the movement of repulsion (*Austossung* or *Verwerfung*) which indicates a fundamental biological operation, of division, separation, scission, and at the same time produces a relation of the body (always already in division) to the outside, as a relation of expulsion. It is in this precise, corporeal and biological, but already social space (as a link to others) that a non-symbolized negativity is active, a negativity not arrested by the terms of judgement, nor predicated as a negation internal to judgement. This negativity of expenditure poses an object as separate from the body proper and at the same moment fixes it as absent: a sign. The relation to the sign thus established by expulsion in a dimension which we might call vertical

(speaking subject/outside) will find itself projected, within the signifying system, into a horizontal, linguistic dimension (syntactic subject/predicate). The outside, becomes graspable object, and the function of predication thus appears as points of arrest of negativity or of expulsion, and are indissociable and complicit with one another. Negativity – expulsion – is therefore a functioning only distinguishable across *positions* which absorb and camouflage it: the real, the sign, the predicate, are presented as the differential moments, milestones in the process of expulsion. (Kristeva, 1998: 141)

Drive 'denotes waves of attack against stases, which are themselves constituted by the repetition of these changes'. The absence of identity that results from the movement of drives is associated with the 'semiotic *chora*':

> The death drive is transversal to identity and tends to disperse 'narcissisms' whose constitution ensures the link between structures and, by extension, life. But at the same time and conversely, narcissism and pleasure are only temporary positions from which the death drive blazes new paths. Narcissism and pleasure art therefore inveiglings and realizations of the death drive. The semiotic *chora*, converting drive discharges into stases can be thought of both as a delaying of the death drive and as a possible realization of this drive, which tends to return to a homeostatic state (1984: 241, n. 23)

The drives thus enable signification and break it open: 'in a moment that constitutes a *leap* and a *rupture – separation* and *absence* – the successive shocks of drive activity produce the signifying function' (167). Their negativity 'even as it posits the symbolic and its differentiations', is an 'expenditure' of energies that return 'to shatter difference and introduce, through its play, what silently acts on it: the scissions of matter' (160). Negativity, formless matter and unbinding, destructive energy, introduces a repetition, daemonic perhaps, that refuses pleasure's return to equilibrium and sameness.

Two forms of repetition, repetition doubled, as it were, emerge in the movement beyond the pleasure principle. Deleuze's careful reading of Freud's text distinguishes between the repetition that serves in the process of binding energies and drives within an id that becomes 'a mobile place, a "here and there" of excitations and resolutions' (Deleuze, 1994: 96). Remaining close to Lacan in the first part of his analysis, Deleuze proposes a 'virtual object' integral to the 'automatism' or 'repetition of the same' functioning according to principles of homeostasis and 'subordinated to the requirements of simple representation'. This object, however, is 'cleaved or doubled into two virtual parts' (100). The doubling discloses 'two real series' that are 'coexistent in relation to a virtual object' and redefines repetition as 'constituted not from one present to another', but between the two coexistent series that create these presents in relation to the 'function of the virtual object' (104–5). The function discloses a form of repetition that is primary: 'we do not repeat because we repress, we repress because we repeat' (105). The mother, then, is not a fixed (repressed) point of reference, but 'the displacement of that object=x' (105). Repetition, 'in essence symbolic, spiritual, and intersubjective or monadological', opens on to death as 'the empty form of time' irreducible to symbolic negation and the dissolution of the ego (106; 112–13). An 'other death' emerges which 'refers to the state of free differences when they are no longer subject to the form imposed on them by an I or ego, when they assume a shape which excludes any of their own coherence no less than that of any identity whatsoever'. This form of death is 'insubordinate, multiple'; it 'cannot be "recognised" in the first aspect' (113). It affirms 'everything of the multiple, everything of the different, everything of chance' (115). It is a 'dark precursor', a 'difference in itself or difference in the second degree which relates heterogeneous systems and even completely disparate things, the *disparate*' (120). Like the eternal return, this form of repetition is not a matter of sameness, but is 'derived from a world of pure difference' (125). Repetition, as it turns on a virtual object (*a?*), returns from it, back to sameness, pleasure, signification, difference subordinated to structures of identity. At the same time, unrecognised, inassimilable, it discloses a heterogeneous movement, a death drive in which the '*jouissance* of destruction' is evinced (Kristeva, 1984: 144).

The doubleness of repetition, the scission of pleasure and death, manifests a 'wholly different time-space than that of the repetition of the same' (Lyotard, 1989: 173). Critiquing the manner in which the Lacanian object serves to establish the reflected unity of the subject and the singular equilibrium of the symbolic order, he asks 'why the drives spread about the polymorphic body *must have* an object where they can unite' (176). The answer leads to multiplicity and heterogeneity since, beyond pleasure, beyond the 'repetition of the same', the death drive manifests a 'repetition of the other' which remains unknown, lying 'just outside the regime delimited by the body or whole considered, and therefore it is impossible to discern *what* is returning, when returning with these drives is the intensity of extreme *jouissance* and danger that they carry' (173). Lyotard's model is economic as much as dynamic, taking its bearing from Bataille's distinction between restricted and general economy: pleasure follows the former in circulating productively and returning to meaning, sense and profitable differences. Death manifests the wasteful, excessive and unproductive expenditures of the latter, a consumption, a burning up of goods, meanings and sense in intensities that have no aim outside themselves, 'sterile differences leading nowhere', 'uncompensated losses',

'dissipation of energy' (171). Derrida's account of the an-archival operations of the 'diabolical death drive' similarly offers an economic reading of
Freud's text as it introduces 'this destruction drive in the psychic economy,
or rather the psychic aneconomy, in the accursed share of this pure-loss
expenditure.' 'Mute', the death drive 'never leaves any archives of its own',
destroying in advance its own archive' (Derrida, 1996: 9–10). An accursed,
unproductive expenditure, the death drive introduces aneconomy into the
cycle of production, exchange and conservation, 'aiming to ruin the archive
as accumulation and capitalization of memory of some substrate and in
an exterior place' (12). Though, Derrida notes, in the manner he outlines
for excessive expenditures in *Given Time*, aneconomy can be reinvested in
another symbolic logic, thus keeping economy (re)turning, the devastating consumption of the death drive remains beyond the return to pleasure, circulation, exchange, manifesting the negativity of a play that refuses all reason and profit: pure waste, useless expenditure without re-
serve.

## To infinity and beyond

Play, waste and excess link the fort-da game and Gothic fictions in a repetitive technological and economic rhythm of consumption-destruction,
a rhythm in which an unemployed negativity comes to the fore/fort. The
'o-o-o-o s' of pleasure and desire crash against the 'a-a-a-a s' of 'a': a-ratio-
nal, amoral, an-economic, the game is ateleological. Some Thing keeps
turning and re-turning, a negativity, a locus of excess refusing to serve any
purpose, a site of utter expenditure. Play, as Caillois underlines, 'creates
no wealth or goods': 'nothing has been harvested or manufactured, no
masterpiece has been created, no capital has accrued. Play is an occasion
of pure waste: waste of time, energy, ingenuity, skill, and often of money
for the purchase of gambling equipment or eventually to pay for the establishment (Caillois, 5–6). Videogames follow the same pattern (Buse).
If play participates in the formation of culture, as Huizinga argues, it does
so on the basis of a principle that remains heterogeneous to productive
activity and recuperative norms. Even though culture restores its boundaries with ritual, the underlying negativity of useless, destructive expenditure is never fully assimilated. For all the ceremonies intent on restoring
community and school to itself, the violent events at Columbine remain
difficult to rationalise or explain: 'what Harris and Klebold offered us on
Hitler's birthday was a deadly counter-gift, a performative symbol as fatal
strategy, a contestative transgression that staked itself in the game'. Even as

it offers the occasion 'reparative ritual', play spills over into the community, opening up a violent counter-festive transgression which tears its structure apart. Torn, it must be repaired. In between, a space of excess, of senseless violence, remains to haunt the institution of community:

> a nihilism, evidently, that is mired in reactiveness and can only abstractly negate. The lack of anything to affirm is rendered positive only by becoming an active will to annihilate. At the same time, the lack of an affirmed self with which to affirm is met by identifying (to the point of personification) with the negating impulse itself. It is the hateful negation of a hateful world; destructive rage self-affirmed. Such a spirit – manifest in real and fictional moral monsters, as well as in the audio-visual surround of attack games and industrial music to which Harris and Klebold were supposedly addicted – may be the signature of the times. (Wernick)

Gothic times, perhaps, real and fictional monsters enveloped in the soundtrack of a game.

The excess disclosed by games becomes the rule of a culture given over to consumption: expenditures beyond the restraints of need or use value become the norm, or even the imperative. More, more. A repetition. To excess. The 'zero-sum game' that, for Goux, 'postulates the quantifiable equivalence between what is given and what is returned, becomes the paradigm of all social relations, the sole principle of every bond, what organizes civil society and governs it', depends on a plenitude rendered impossible by its very operations, predicated, as they are, on the fundamental uncertainty of human desire (Goux, 1998: 37). Pac-Man exemplifies the principle: 'he is the pure consumer. With his obsessively gaping maw, he clearly wants only one thing: to feel whole, at peace with himself'. A disk with a slice cut out, always wanting and anxious (he is pursued by flickering ghostly figures), his demand for plenitude remains thwarted by the insufficiency of gratification. More is never enough: Pac-Man 'is doomed forever to metaphysical emptiness' (Poole, 189). Like games themselves, consuming is refused an end: 'no conceivable quantity of dots is enough' (192–3). No game is over that cannot begin again. 'Death', no longer absolute in its expenditure, is merely the occasion for starting again (and again): a little death of orgasmic intensity punctuating the pleasures and anxieties of accelerated performance, a break-flow in circulation. Death, 'the *petit mort* of *Homo Ludens*' is transformed along with life as it becomes 'expendable' and 'iterable' (Poole, 68–9). No more life or death. Just life-death, over and over again, multiple oscillations of little lives and little deaths threatened with the diminishing returns of intensity that exhaust the tension through repetition. Violent little losses, from horror's assaults on the eyes, laying waste to sense, coherence and reason, are exacerbated on the monitor on which games flicker and fade in alternating, rapid rhythm.

The rhythm of the fort-da is taken up by the screens on which games are played, their oversaturation with images dependent on the loss of the locus of phantasmatic projection. Video games have their own 'tempo'; they require 'the ebb and flow of anxiety and satisfaction' (Poole, 200). Their rhythm, however, while traversing the hollow of subjective constitution returns to the pleasure principle only by insinuating a different alien, technological rhythm, increasing the pulse of the fort-da game with a speed no organism can match. The subject is sucked out and resituated at speed, subject to the rhythms of plenitude and absence appearing and disappearing on the screen. Virilio's accounts of the way that new media both overstimulate the organism and demand a passivity bordering on inertia manifest the dual imperatives of technological reconfiguration in a tele-repetition and acceleration without end. Abolishing differences, distinctions and distances, here and there, fort and da, giving way to the technological instant, vision machines 'would make derangement of the senses a permanent state, conscious life becoming an oscillating trip whose only absolute poles would be birth and death' (Virilio, 1991b: 92). The escalating rhythm, allowing no time for thought, speeds up the oscillation: it is no more than the digital pulse of life-death.

No more life. Nor death. No more mother and father: just genetic materialisation and digital recreations of doubles. No more humanity, history, or modernity. Just more and more ghosts gliding across screens. Beyond life and death, but insisting as an alien, daemonic, repetitive rhythm of life-death, machinic pulsations and intensities are curiously cast in Gothic dress: 'cybergothic' names a momentum that tears up rather than returns to the past while the present presses forward to a future divested of familiar trappings. An 'affirmative telecommercial dystopianism', 'cybergothic' describes the effects of economic and biological transformation as systems that have sped out of any control to follow their own rapid, chaotic and immanent logic. Though the terms are drawn from a Gothic modernity, the effects exceed anything it could imagine: 'v(amp)iro finance', a collapsing of biology and economy in an utterly machinic context, devastates the bodies and systems that once seemed to operate in the service of human production and reproduction: 'vampiric transfusional alliance cuts across descensional filiation, spinning lateral webs of haemocommerce. Reproductive order comes apart into bacterial and intergalactic sex, and libidino-economic interchange machinery goes micro-military' (Land, 1998: 80; 86–7). The Gothic of 'cybergothic' is little more than a disguise to describe processes that, despite their evocations of fantasies, desires, horror and thrills, have minimal relation to any precedent: it only signifies an 'archaic revival', a 'postmodern symptom' conjuring up 'the final dream of mankind, crashed into retrospection at the encountered edge of history' (80). The fantastic apocalypticism, with its enthusiasm for destruction, barely veils the proximity of the gaping maw of an alien future assembled from the ruins and wreckage of the present. Negativity, machinic and inhuman, pulses beneath the fantasy. Gothic images only serve as a disguise, a retrospective gloss on a terrifyingly prospective gaze, a blank staring ahead. They provide the camouflage, the hallucinatory and vain comfort in a history and modernity that already lies in ruins: 'the future of runaway processes derides all precedent, even when deploying it as camouflage, and seeming to unfold within its parameters' (1993: 476). Machinic desire

> Rips up political cultures, deletes traditions, dissolves subjectivities, and hacks through security apparatuses, tracking a soulless tropism to zero control. This is because what appears to humanity as the history of capitalism is an invasion from the future by an artificial intelligent space that must assemble itself entirely from its enemy's resources. (479)

The process has no human hand at the helm. It is driven by a headless and immanent drive – 'synthanatos' – an artificial death drive (as if the drive were ever natural) which manifests 'the terminal productive outcome of human history as machinic process' (474). In the pulses of machinic process, it seems, a final, and futile, 'fort!' is uttered. As if all was not already gone, disappearing in a flight across an undead atopia of screens. Game over and over again.

# References

Adams, Parveen (1996) *The Emptiness of the Image: Psychoanalysis and Sexual Difference*, London and New York: Routledge.

Addison, Joseph (1970) *Critical Essays from the Spectator*, ed. Donald F. Bond, London: Oxford University Press.

Anon. (1796) 'Review of *The Monk*', *British Critic*, 7 (June), 677.

Anon. (1797a) 'Terrorist novel writing', *Spirit of the Public Journals*, 1, 227–9.

Anon. (1797b) 'Review of *The Italian*', *Monthly Mirror*, 3 (March), 155–8.

Anon. (1797c) 'Review of *The Monk*', *Critical Review* (2nd series), 19 (Feb.), 194.

Ariès, Philippe (1981) *The Hour of Our Death*, trans. Helen Weaver, London: Penguin.

Attali, Jacques (1985) *Noise*, Manchester: Manchester University Press.

Ayers, Robert (1999) 'Serene and happy and distant: An interview with Orlan', *Body and Society*, 5: 2/3, 171–84.

Baldick, Chris (ed.) (1992) *The Oxford Book of Gothic Tales*, Oxford: Oxford University Press.

Banks, Iain (1990) *The Wasp Factory*, London: Abacus.

Barker, Clive (1985) 'The forbidden', *Books of Blood: Vol V*, London: Sphere Books.

Barthes, Roland (1976) *The Pleasure of the Text*, trans. Richard Miller, London: Jonathan Cape.

Barthes, Roland (1984) *Camera Lucida*, trans. Richard Howard, London: Fontana.

Bataille, Georges (1955) *Lascaux*, trans. Austryn Wainhouse, Geneva: Skira Books.

Bataille, Georges (1971) 'L'abjection et les formes miserables', *Oeuvres Completes II*, Paris: Gallimard, 218–221.

Bataille, Georges (1987) *Eroticism*, trans. Mary Dalwood, London and New York: Marion Boyars.

Bataille, Georges (1991) *The Accursed Share*, Vols II and III, trans. Robert Hurley, New York: Zone Books.

Bataille, Georges (1997) 'Base materialism and gnosticism', in Fred Botting and Scott Wilson (eds), *The Bataille Reader*, Oxford: Blackwell.

Baudrillard, Jean (1983) *Simulations*, New York: Semiotexte.

Baudrillard, Jean (1990a) *Fatal Strategies*, trans. Philip Beitchman and W.G.J. Niesluchowski, London: Pluto Press.

Baudrillard, Jean (1990b) *Seduction*, Basingstoke and London: Macmillan.

Baudrillard, Jean (1993a) *Symbolic Exchange and Death*, trans. Iain Hamilton Grant,

London: Sage.

Baudrillard, Jean (1993b) *The Transparency of Evil*, trans. James Benedict, London: Verso.

Baudrillard, Jean (1994) *The Illusion of the End*, trans. Chris Turner, London: Polity.

Baudrillard, Jean (1995) 'Plastic surgery for the Other', *CTheory*, 22 November, www.ctheory.com/a33-plastic_surgery.html.

Baudrillard, Jean (1996) *The Perfect Crime*, trans. Chris Turner, New York and London: Verso.

Baudrillard, Jean (2002) *Screened Out*, trans. Chris Turner, London and New York: Verso.

Benjamin, Walter (1973) *Illuminations*, trans. Harry Zohn, London: Fontana.

Benjamin, Walter (1983) *Charles Baudelaire: A Lyric Poet in the Era of High Capitalism*, trans. Harry Zohn, London and New York: Verso.

Benjamin, Walter (1999) *The Arcades Project*, trans. Howard Eiland and Kevin McLaughlin, Cambridge, MA and London: Belknap Press.

Benshoff, Harry M. (1997) *Monsters in the Closet: Homosexuality and the Horror Film*, Manchester: Manchester University Press.

Benson, E.F. (1992) 'Negotium perambulans', in Richard Dalby (ed.), *The Collected Ghost Stories of E.F. Benson*, London: Robinson Publishing.

Berry, Adrian (1977) *The Iron Sun: Crossing the Universe through Black Holes*, London: Book Club Associates.

Birkhead, Edith (1921) *The Tale of Terror: A Study of the Gothic Romance*, London: Constable.

Boothby, Richard (1991) *Death and Desire*, London and New York: Routledge.

Boscough, John (1984) *Beyond the Black Hole*, London: Fontana/Collins.

Boss, Pete (1986) 'Vile bodies and bad medicine', *Screen*, 27:1, 14–24.

Briefel, Aviva and Ngai, Sianne (1996) '"How much did you pay for this place?" Fear, entitlement, and urban space in Bernard Rose's *Candyman*', *Camera Obscura*, 37, 70–91.

Bronfen, Elisabeth (1992), *Over Her Dead Body*, Manchester: Manchester University Press.

Brophy, Philip (1986) 'Horrality: The textuality of contemporary horror films', *Screen*, 27:1, 2–13.

Broughton, John (1996) 'The bomb's-eye view: Smart weapons and military TV', in Stanley Aronowitz, Barbara Martinson and Michael Menser (eds), *Technoscience and Cyberculture*, New York and London: Routledge.

Bruhm, Steven (2000) 'Picture this: Stephen King's queer gothic', in David Punter (ed.), *A Companion to the Gothic*, Oxford: Blackwell.

Burke, Edmund (1990) *A Philosophical Enquiry into our Ideas of the Sublime and the Beautiful*, ed. Adam Phillips, Oxford: Oxford University Press.

Buse, Peter (1996) 'Nintendo and telos: Will you ever reach the end?' *Cultural Critique*, Fall, 163–84.

Caillois, Roger (1962) *Mind, Play, and Games*, trans. Meyer Barash, London: Thames.

Carter, Angela (1974) *Fireworks*, London: Quartet Books.

Carter, Angela (1981) *The Bloody Chamber*, Harmondsworth: Penguin.

Castle, Terry (1995) *The Female Thermometer: Eighteenth-century Culture and the Invention of the Uncanny*, New York and Oxford: Oxford University Press.

Charnas, Suzy McKee (1997) 'Meditation in Red', in Jan Gordon and Veronica Hollinger (eds), *Blood Read*, Philadelphia, PA: University of Pennsylvania Press.

Cixous, Hélène (1976) 'Fiction and its phantoms: A reading of Freud's *Das Unheimliche* (The "uncanny")', *New Literary History*, 7, 525–48.

Clarke, Julie (2002) 'The human/not human in the work of Orlan and Stelarc', in Joanna Zylinska (ed.), *The Cyborg Experiments*, London and New York: Continuum.

Clery, E.J. (1995) *The Rise of Supernatural Fiction 1762–1800*, Cambridge: Cambridge University Press.

Clover, Carol (1989) 'Her body, himself: Gender in the slasher film', in James Donald (ed.), *Fantasy and Cinema*, London: BFI Publishing.

Coleridge, S.T. (1794) 'Review of *The Mysteries of Udolpho*', *Critical Review* (2nd series), 11 (Aug.), 361–72.

Coleridge, S.T. (1798) 'Review of *The Italian*', *Critical Review* (2nd series), 23, (June), 166–9.

Coleridge, S.T. (1975) *Biographia Literaria* (1817), ed. George Watson, London: Dent.

Coles, Joanna (1998) 'Southern comfort eating', *Guardian*, 26 March, 17.

Connolly, Kate (2002) 'Dracula terror park', *Guardian*, 23 March, 19.

Copjec, Joan (1994), *Read My Desire: Lacan Against the Historicists*, Cambridge, MA and London: MIT Press.

Copjec, Joan (2000) 'The strut of vision: Seeing's corporeal support', in Carolyn Bailey Gill (ed.), *Time and the Image*, Manchester: Manchester University Press.

Creed, Barbara (1989) 'Horror and the monstrous-feminine: An imaginary abjection', in James Donald (ed.), *Fantasy and Cinema*, London: BFI Publishing.

Dadoun, Roger (1989) 'Fetishism in the horror film', in James Donald (ed.), *Fantasy and the Cinema*, London: BFI Publishing.

de Bolla, Peter (1989) *The Discourse of the Sublime*, Oxford: Blackwell.

de Certeau, Michel (1984) *The Practice of Everyday Life*, trans. Steven F. Rendall, Berkeley, CA: University of California Press.

de Lauretis, Teresa (1984) *Alice Doesn't: Feminism, Semiotics, Cinema*, London and Basingstoke: Macmillan.

de Rougemont, Denis (1993) *Love in the Western World*, trans. M. Belgion, Princeton, NJ: Princeton University Press.

Deleuze, Gilles (1990) *Logic of Sense*, trans. Mark Lester, London: Athlone.

Deleuze, Gilles (1994) *Difference and Reptition*, trans. Paul Patton, London: Athlone Press.

Deleuze, Gilles and Guattari, Felix (1983) *Anti-Oedipus: Capitalism and Schizophrenia*, trans. Robert Hurley, Mark Seem and Helen Lane, Minneapolis, MN: University of Minnesota Press.

Deleuze, Gilles and Guattari, Felix (1988) *A Thousand Plateaus*, trans. Brian Massumi, London: Athlone Press.

Derrida, Jacques (1981) *Dissemination*, trans. Barbara Johnson, London: Athlone Press.

Derrida, Jacques (1987) *The Post Card*, trans. Alan Bass, Chicago: University of Chicago Press.

Derrida, Jacques (1990) 'Some statements and truisms about neologisms, newisms, postisms, parasitisms, and other small seismisms', in David Carroll (ed.), *The States of 'Theory'*, Stanford, CA: Stanford University Press.

Derrida, Jacques (1992a) 'Passages – from traumatism to promise', trans. Peggy Kamuf et al., Elisabeth Weber (ed.), *Points ...: Interviews, 1974–1994*, Stanford, CA: Stanford University Press.

Derrida, Jacques (1992b) *Given Time*, trans. Peggy Kamuf, Chicago and London: University of Chicago Press.

Derrida, Jacques (1996) *Archive Fever*, trans. Eric Prenowitz, Chicago: University of Chicago

Press.

Descartes, René (1981) *A Discourse on Method*, trans. John Veitch, London: Dent.

Dickens, Charles (1982) *Dombey and Son*, ed. Peter Fairclough, Harmondsworth: Penguin.

Dickens, Charles (1985) *Selected Letters*, ed. David Paroissien, Basingstoke and London: Macmillan.

Dika, Vera (1996) 'From Dracula – with love', in Barry Keith Grant (ed.), *The Dread of Difference*, Austin, TX: University of Texas Press.

Doane, Mary Ann (1990) 'Information, crisis, catastrophe', in Patricia Mellencamp (ed.), *Logics of Television: Essays in Cultural Criticism*, London, Bloomington and Indianapolis: BFI and Indiana University Press.

Doane, Mary Ann (1996) 'Temporality, storage, legibility: Freud, Marey, and the cinema', *Critical Inquiry*, 22, 313–43.

Dolar, Mladen (1991) '"I shall be with you on your wedding-night": Lacan and the Uncanny', *October*, 58, 5–23.

Dolar, Mladen (1994), 'La femme-machine', *New Formations*, 23, 43–54.

Donald, James (1989), 'The fantastic, the sublime and the popular Or, what's at stake in vampire films?', in James Donald (ed.), *Fantasy and Cinema*, London: BFI Publishing.

Ferguson, Frances (1984) 'The nuclear sublime', *diacritics*, 14, 4–10.

Ferguson, Frances (1992) *Solitude and the Sublime*, New York and London: Routledge.

Fielding, Henry (1955) *The History of Tom Jones*, London: Dent.

Fletcher, John (1995) 'Primal scenes and female gothic: *Rebecca* and *Gaslight*', *Screen*, 36:4, 341–70.

Forrester, Viviane (1999) *The Economic Horror*, Cambridge: Polity Press.

Forry, Steven (1990) *Hideous Progenies*, Philadelphia, PA: University of Pennsylvania Press.

Foster, Hal (1996) *The Return of the Real*, Ann Arbor, MI: MIT Press.

Foucault, Michel (1970) *The Order of Things*, London: Tavistock.

Foucault, Michel (1977) *Language, Counter-Memory, Practice*, trans. Donald F. Bouchard and Sherry Simon, Ithaca, NY: Cornell University Press.

Foucault, Michel (1981) *The History of Sexuality: Vol. I An Introduction*, trans. Robert Hurley, Harmondsworth: Penguin.

Foucault, Michel (1982) *This is Not a Pipe*, trans. James Harkness, Berkeley and Los Angeles: University of California Press.

Foucault, Michel (1987) *The Use of Pleasure*, trans. Robert Hurley, London: Penguin.

Freud, Sigmund (1955a) 'The "uncanny"', *The Standard Edition of the Complete Psychological Works*, Vol. XVII, trans. James Strachey, London: Hogarth Press.

Freud, Sigmund (1955b) *Civilization and its Discontents*, in *The Standard Edition of the Complete Psychological Works*, Vol. XXI, trans. James Strachey, London: Hogarth Press.

Freud, Sigmund (1955c) *The Ego and the Id*, in *The Standard Edition of the Complete Psychological Works*, Vol. XIX, trans. James Strachey, London: Hogarth Press.

Freud, Sigmund (1984) *On Metapsychology*, trans. James Strachey, Harmondsworth, Penguin.

Gibson, William (1984) *Neuromancer*, London: HarperCollins.

Gibson, William (1996) *Idoru*, London: Penguin.

Gordon, Joan (1997) 'Sharper than a serpent's tooth: The vampire in search of its mother', in Jan Gordon and Veronica Hollinger (eds), *Blood Read: the Vampire as Metaphor in*

*Contemporary Culture*, Philadelphia, PA: University of Pennsylvania Press.

Goux, Jean-Joseph (1990a) *Symbolic Economies: After Marx and Freud*, trans. Jennifer Curtiss Gage, Ithaca, NY: Cornell University Press.

Goux, Jean-Joseph (1990b) 'General economics and postmodern polemics', *Yale French Studies*, 78, 206–24.

Goux, Jean-Joseph (1998) 'Subversion and Consensus: Proletarians, Women, Artists', in Jean-Joseph Goux and Philip R. Wood (eds), *Terror and Consensus: Vicissitudes of French Thought*, Stanford, CA: Stanford University Press.

Gray, Chris Hables, Mentor, Steven and Figueroa-Sarriera, Heidi J. (1995) 'Cyborgology', in Chris Hables Gray (ed.), *The Cyborg Handbook*, New York and London: Routledge, 1–14.

Gribbin, John (1983) *Spacewarps*, Harmondsworth: Penguin.

Grixti, Joseph (1989) *Terrors of Uncertainty: The Cultural Contexts of Horror Fiction*, London: Routledge.

Grosse, Carl (1968) *Horrid Mysteries*, trans. Peter Will, London: Folio Press.

Guattari, Félix (1995) *Chaosmosis*, trans. Paul Bains and Julian Pefanis, Sydney: Power Publications.

Gunning, Tom (1989) 'An aesthetic of astonishment: Early film and the (in)credulous spectator', *Art and Text*, 34, 31–45.

Halberstam, Judith (1995) *Skin Shows*, Durham, NC and London: Duke University Press.

Hale, Terry (ed.) (1992) *Tales of the Dead*, Chislehurst: The Gothic Society.

Hamilton, Robert (1997) 'Virtual idols and digital girls: Artifice and sexuality in Anime, Kisekae and Kyoko Date', *Bad Subjects*, 35 (November), http://bad.server.org/issues/1997/35/hamilton.html.

Haraway, Donna (1990) 'A Manifesto for cyborgs: science, technology and socialist feminism in the 1980s', in Linda J. Nicholson (ed.), *Feminism/Postmodernism*, New York and London: Routledge.

Haraway, Donna (1997) *Modest_Witness@Second_Millenium,* London and New York: Routledge.

Hawking, Stephen (1988) *A Brief History of Time*, London and New York: Bantam Press.

Hawthorne, Nathaniel (1958) *The Marble Faun*, New York: Pocket Books.

Hayles, N. Katherine (1999) *How We Became Posthuman*, Chicago and London: University of Chicago Press.

Heath, Stephen (1982) *The Sexual Fix*, London and Basingstoke: Macmillan.

Heiman, J.D. (2000) 'Lollipop ladies', *Marie Claire* (July), 64–8.

Henderson, Andrea (1994) '"An embarassing subject": Use value and exchange value in early gothic characterization', in Mary Favret and Nicola J. Watson (eds), *At the Limits of Romanticism*, Bloomington and Indianapolis, IN: Indiana University Press.

Hertz, Neil (1985) *The End of the Line: Essays on Psychoanalysis and the Sublime*, New York: Columbia University Press.

Hirschhorn, Michelle (1996) 'Orlan artist in the post-human age of mechanical reincarnation: Body as ready (to be re-)made', in Griselda Pollock (ed.), *Generations and Geographies in the Visual Arts*, New York and London: Routledge.

Hobsbawn, Eric (1994) *The Age of Extremes*, London: Penguin.

Hogle, Jerrold E. (1994) 'The ghost of the counterfeit in the genesis of the gothic', in Allan Lloyd Smith and Victor Sage (eds), *Gothick Origins and Innovations*, Amsterdam: Rodopi.

Hogle, Jerrold E. (1998a) '*Frankenstein* as neo-gothic: From the ghost of the counterfeit to the monster of abjection', in Tillotama Rajan and Julia M. Wright (eds), *Romanticism, History and the Possibilities of Genre*, Cambridge: Cambridge University Press.

Hogle, Jerrold E. (1998b) 'Stoker's counterfeit gothic: *Dracula* and theatricality at the dawn of simulation', in William Hughes and Andrew Smith (eds), *Bram Stoker: History, Psychoanalysis and the Gothic*, Basingstoke and London: Macmillan.

Hogle, Jerrold E. (2002) *The Undergrounds of* The Phantom of the Opera, Basingstoke: Palgrave.

Huizinga, Johann (1944) *Homo Ludens*, London: Routledge and Kegan Paul.

Hurley, Kelly (1996) *The Gothic Body*, Cambridge: Cambridge University Press.

Hutchings, Peter (1996) 'Tearing your soul apart: Horror's new monsters', in Victor and Alan Lloyd Smith (eds), *Modern Gothic: A Reader*, Manchester: Manchester University Press.

Irigaray, Luce (1985) *This Sex Which is Not One*, trans. Catherine Porter with Carolyn Burke, New York: Columbia University Press.

Jameson, Fredric (1984) 'Postmodernism, or the Cultural Logic of Late Capitalism', *New Left Review*, 146: 53-92.

Jancovich, Mark (1996) *Rational Fears: American Horror in the 1950s*, Manchester: Manchester University Press.

Jeffries, Stuart (2002) 'But is it art?', *Guardian G2*, 19 March, 2-3.

Jentsch, Ernst (1995 [1906]) 'On the Psychology of the Uncanny', trans. Roy Sellars, *Angelaki*, 2:1, 7-16.

Johnson, Fred (1996), 'Cyberpunks in the White House', in Jon Dovey (ed.), *Fractal Dreams: New media and social context*, London: Lawrence and Wishart.

Kafka, Franz (1959) *Letters to Milena*, ed. Willy Haas, trans. Tania and James Stern, New York: Schocken Books.

Kant, Immanuel (1952) *The Aesthetic of Judgement*, ed. James Creed Meredith, Oxford: Oxford University Press.

Keegan, Paul (1999) 'In the line of fire', *Guardian*, 1 June, 2-3.

Kermode, Mark (2000) 'Horror will eat itself', *Independent on Sunday*, 29 Oct., 1.

King, Maureen (1993) 'Contemporary Women Writers and the "New Evil": The Vampires of Anne Rice and Suzy McKee Charnas', *Journal of the Fantastic in the Arts*, 5.3, 75-84.

Kittler, Friedrich (1990) *Discourse Networks 1800/1900*, trans. M. Metteer with C. Cullens, Stanford, CA: Stanford University Press.

Kittler, Friedrich (1997) *Essays: Literature media information systems*, ed. John Johnston, The Netherlands: G+B Arts International.

Kittler, Friedrich (1999) *Gramophone, Film, Typewriter*, trans. Geoffrey Winthrop-Young and Michael Wutz, Stanford, CA: Stanford University Press.

Kofman, Sarah (1991) *Freud and Fiction*, trans. Sarah Wykes, Cambridge: Polity Press.

Kristeva, Julia (1982) *Powers of Horror: An Essay in Abjection*, trans. Leon S. Roudiez, New York: Columbia University Press.

Kristeva, Julia (1984) *Revolution in Poetic Language*, trans. Leon S. Roudiez, New York: Columbia University Press.

Kristeva, Julia (1986) 'Ellipsis on dread and the specular seduction', in Philip Rosen (ed.), *Narrative, Apparatus, Ideology*, New York: Columbia University Press.

Kristeva, Julia (1998) 'The subject in process', in Patrick ffrench and Roland-Francois Lack (eds), *The Tel Quel Reader*, London and New York: Routledge.

La Mettrie, Julien Offray de (1994) *Man a Machine* and *Man a Plant*, trans. Richard Watson A. and Maya Rybalka, Indianapolis, IN and Cambridge: Hackett Publishing.

Lacan, Jacques (1977a) *Ecrits*, trans. Alan Sheridan, London: Tavistock.

Lacan, Jacques (1977b) *The Four Fundamental Concepts of Psychoanalysis*, trans. Alan Sheridan, London: Penguin.

Lacan, Jacques (1977c) 'Desire and the interpretation of desire in *Hamlet*', *Yale French Studies*, 55/56, 11–52.

Lacan, Jacques (1988a) *The Seminar of Jacques Lacan Book I: Freud's Papers on Technique 1953–1954*, ed. Jacques-Alain Miller, trans. John Forrester, Cambridge: Cambridge University Press.

Lacan, Jacques (1988b) *The Seminar of Jacques Lacan Book II: The Ego in Freud's Theory and in the Technique of Psychoanalysis 1954–1955*, ed. Jacques Alain Miller, trans. Sylvana Tomaselli, Cambridge: Cambridge University Press.

Lacan, Jacques (1992) *The Ethics of Psychoanalysis*, trans. Dennis Porter, London: Routledge.

Lacan, Jacques (1993), *The Psychoses: The Seminar of Jacques Lacan Book III: 1955-56*, trans. Russell Grigg, London: Routledge.

Lacan, Jacques (1998) *The Seminar of Jacques Lacan Book XX Encore 1972–1973*, ed. Jacques-Alain Miller, trans. Bruce Fink, New York and London: Norton.

Land, Nick (1993) 'Machinic Desire', *Textual Practice*, 7:3, 471–82.

Land, Nick (1998) 'Cybergothic', in Joan Broadhurst Dixon and Eric J. Cassidy (eds), *Virtual Futures*, New York and London: Routledge.

Laplanche, Jean (1976) *Life and Death in Psychoanalysis*, trans. Jeffrey Mehlman, Baltimore, MD and London: Johns Hopkins University Press.

Laplanche, Jean and Leclaire, Serge (1972) 'The Unconscious: A Psychoanalytic Study', *Yale French Studies*, 48, 118–75.

Latham, Rob (1997) 'Consuming youth: The lost boys cruise mallworld', in Joan Gordon and Veronica Hollinger (eds), *Blood Read: The Vampire as Metaphor in Contemporary Culture*, Philadelphia, PA: University of Pennsylvania Press.

Leclaire, Serge (1998) *A Child is Being Killed*, trans. Marie-Claude Hays, Stanford, CA: Stanford University Press.

Lévy, Maurice (2004) 'FAQ: What is gothic?', *Anglophonia*, 15, 23–37.

Lieberman, Rhonda (1993) 'Shopping disorders', in Brian Massumi (ed.), *The Politics of Everyday Fear*, Minneapolis, MN: University of Minnesota Press.

Lotringer, Sylvère (1988) *Overexposed*, London: Paladin.

Lovelace, Carey (1995) 'ORLAN: Offensive acts', *Performing Arts Journal*, 49, 13-25.

Lyotard, Jean-Francois (1984) *The Postmodern Condition*, trans. Geoff Bennington and Brian Massumi, Manchester: Manchester University Press.

Lyotard, Jean-Francois (1989) 'Acinema', in Andrew Benjamin (ed.), *The Lyotard Reader*, Oxford: Blackwell.

Lyotard, Jean-Francois (1991) *The Inhuman*, trans. Geoff Bennington and Rachel Bowlby, Oxford: Polity Press.

Lyotard, Jean-Francois (1994) *Lessons on the Analytic of the Sublime*, trans. Eric Rottenberg, Stanford, CA: Stanford University Press.

Macaulay, Thomas (1848) *'Horace Walpole' (1833)*, *Critical and Historical Essays*, Vol. II, London: Longman.

McCabe, Colin (1993) 'More things in heaven and earth', *Sight and Sound*, 3:3, 22–4.

MacCannell, Juliet Flower (1998) 'Perversion in public places', *new formations*, 35, 43–59.

McConnell, Kathleen (2000) 'Chaos at the mouth of hell', *Gothic Studies*, 2:1, 119–35.

McGowan, Patrick 'We killed a man, drank his blood and made love in a coffin says "vampire"', *Evening Standard*, 17 January 2002, 5.

Machen, Arthur (1894) *The Great God Pan*, London: John Lane.

Machen, Arthur (1977) 'The Novel of the White Powder', in Charles Fowkes (ed.), *The Best Ghost Stories*, London: Hamlyn.

MacKenzie, Adrian (2000) 'Losing time at the Playstation: Realtime individuation and the *whatever* body', *Cultural Values*, 4:3, 257–78.

McNutt, Dan J. (1975) *The Eighteenth-century Gothic Novel: An Annotated Bibliography of Criticism and Selected Texts*, New York: Garland.

Mandeville, Bernard (1970) *The Fable of the Bees*, ed. Phillip Harth, Harmondsworth: Penguin.

Marcus, Laura (2000) 'Oedipus express: Trains, trauma and detective fiction', *new formations*, 41, 173–88.

Marx, Karl (1973) *Grundrisse*, trans. Martin Nicolaus, Harmondsworth: Penguin.

Marx, Karl (1976) *Capital*, Vol. I, trans. Ben Fowkes, Harmondsworth: Penguin.

Marx, Karl and Engels, Friedrich (1985) *The Communist Manifesto*, London: Penguin.

Masse, Michelle (2000) 'Psychoanalysis and the gothic', in David Punter (ed.), *A Companion to the Gothic*, Oxford: Blackwell.

Matthias, T.J. (1805) *The Pursuits of Literature*, 13th edn, London: Thomas Becket.

Mellencamp, Patricia (1990) 'TV time and catastrophe, or beyond the pleasure principle of television', in Patricia Mellencamp (ed.), *Logics of Television: Essays in Cultural Criticism*, London, Bloomington, IN and Indianapolis: BFI Publishing/Indiana University Press.

Michasiw, Kim Ian (1998) 'Some stations of suburban gothic', in Robert K. Martin and Eric Savoy (eds), *American Gothic: New Interventions in National Perspective*, Iowa City, IA: University of Iowa Press.

Miles, Robert (1993) *Gothic Writing 1750–1820*, London and New York: Routledge.

Miller, Jacques-Alain (1988) 'Extimité', *Prose Studies*, 11:3, 121–31.

Modleski, Tania (1986) 'The terror of pleasure: The contemporary horror film and postmodern theory', in Tania Modleski (ed.), *Studies in Entertainment: Critical Approaches to Mass Culture*, Bloomington, IN: Indiana University Press.

Morrison, Blake (1997) 'Murderous innocence', *Guardian Weekend*, 1 February, 12–18.

Mulholland, Garry (2002) *This is Uncool: The 500 Greatest Singles since Punk*, London: Cassell Illustrated.

Mulvey, Laura (1975) 'Visual pleasure and narrative cinema', *Screen*, 16:3, 6–87.

Munsterberg, Hugo (1970) *The Film: A Psychological Study*, New York: Dover Publications.

Neumeier, Beate (1996) 'Postmodern gothic: Angela Carter's writing', in Victor Sage and Alan Lloyd Smith (eds), *Modern Gothic*, Manchester: Manchester University Press.

Newman, Kim (1993) 'Candyman', *Sight and Sound*, 3:3, 39.

Nixon, Nicola (1998) 'Making monsters, or serializing killers', in Robert K. Martin and Eric Savoy (eds), *American Gothic: New Interventions in National Perspective*, Iowa City, IA: University of Iowa Press.

Onfray, Michel (1996) 'Surgical aesthetics', in Duncan McCorquodale (ed.), *This is my body … This is my Software*, London: Black Dog Publishing.

Orlan (1996) 'Conference', in Duncan McCorquodale (ed.), *This is my body … This is my*

*Software*, London: Black Dog Publishing.

Penley, Constance (1986) 'Time travel, primal scene, and the critical dystopia', *Camera Obscura*, 15, 67–84.

Plant, Sadie (1995) 'The future looms: Weaving women and cybernetics', in Mike Featherstone and Rob Burrows (eds), *Cyberspace/Cyberbodies/Cyberpunk: Cultures of Technological Embodiment*, London: Sage.

Polan, Dana (1986) 'Brief encounters: Mass culture and the evacuation of sense', in Tania Modleski (ed.), *Studies in Entertainment: Critical Approaches to Mass Culture*, Bloomington, IN: Indiana University Press.

Pontalis, Jean-Bertrand (1978) 'On death-work in Freud, in the self, in culture', in Alan Roland (ed.), *Psychoanalysis, Creativity, and Literature*, New York: Columbia University Press.

Pontalis, Jean-Bertrand (1981) *Frontiers in Psychoanalysis: Between the Dream and Psychic Pain*, trans. Catherine Cullen and Philip Cullen, London: Hogarth Press.

Poole, Steven (2000) *Trigger Happy: The Inner Life of Videogames*, London: Fourth Estate.

Poovey, Mary (1979) 'Ideology and *The Mysteries of Udolpho*', *Criticism*, 21:4, 307–30.

Poster, Mark (2002) 'High-tech Frankenstein, or Heidegger meets Stelarc', in Joanna Zylinska (ed.), *The Cyborg Experiments*, London: Continuum.

Punter, David (1998) *Gothic Pathologies*, Basingstoke: Macmillan.

Radcliffe, Ann (1826) 'On the supernatural in poetry', *New Monthly Magazine*, 16, 145–52.

Radcliffe, Ann (1980) *The Mysteries of Udolpho*, eds Bonamy Dobrée and Frederick Garber, Oxford: Oxford University Press.

Ragland, Ellie (1995), *Essays on the Pleasures of Death*, New York and London: Routledge.

Rank, Otto (1971) *The Double: A Psychoanalytical Study*, trans. Harry Tucker Jr., Chapel Hill, NC: University of North Carolina Press.

Reeve, Clara (1977) *The Old English Baron: A Gothic Story* (1777), ed. James Trainer, Oxford: Oxford University Press.

Reynolds, Simon (2005) *Rip it Up: Postpunk 1978–1984*, London: Faber and Faber.

Rice, Anne (1977) *Interview with the Vampire*, London: Futura Publications.

Rice, Anne (1995) *The Vampire Lestat*, New York: Warner Books.

Richardson, Samuel (1964) *Selected Letters of Samuel Richardson*, ed. John Carroll, Oxford: Clarendon.

Ronell, Avital (1992) *Crack Wars: Literature, Addiction, Mania*, Lincoln, NE and London: University of Nebraska Press.

Roof, Judith (1996) *Reproductions of Reproduction: Imaging Symbolic Change*, London: Routledge.

Rose, Barbara (1993) 'Is it art? Orlan and the Transgressive act', *Art in America*, 81:2 (Feb.), 82–7.

Rose, Jacqueline (1993) *Why War? Psychoanalysis, Politics, and the Return of Melanie Klein*, Oxford: Blackwell.

Rucker, Rudy (1994) *Wetware*, in *Live Robots*, New York: Avon Books.

Russ, Joanna (1995) *To Write Like a Woman: Essays in Feminism and Science Fiction*, Bloomington, IN and London: Indiana University Press.

Sade, D.A.F., Marquis de (1989) 'Reflections on the novel', in *One Hundred and Twenty Days of Sodom*, trans. Austryn Wainhouse and Richard Seaver, London: Arrow Books.

Sage, Victor (1988) *Horror Fiction in the Protestant Tradition*, London and Basingstoke: Macmillan.

Salecl, Renata (1998) 'Cut in the body: From clitoridectomy to body art', *new formations*, 35, 28–42.

Scarborough, Dorothy (1917) *The Supernatural in Modern English Fiction*, New York and London: Knickerbocker Press.

Schivelbusch, Wolfgang (1979) *The Railway Journey*, trans. Anselm Hollo, New York: Urizen Books.

Schnapp, Jeffrey T. (1999) 'Crash (speed as engine of individuation)', *Modernism/Modernity*, 6:1, 1–49.

Scott, Walter (1824) 'Mrs Ann Radcliffe', *Lives of Eminent Novelists and Dramatists*, London: Frederick Warne.

Scott, Walter (1881) 'Novels of Ernest Theodore Hoffman', *The Miscellaneous Works*, Vol. XVIII, Edinburgh: Adam and Charles Black.

Seltzer, Mark (1993) 'Serial killers (1)', *differences*, 5:1, 92–128.

Seltzer, Mark (1995) 'Serial killers (II)', *Critical Inquiry*, 22, 122–49.

Seltzer, Mark (1998) *Serial Killers*, New York and London: Routledge.

SHaH (2003), 'How It Feels', in Jane Arthurs and Iain Grant (eds), *Crash Cultures*, Bristol and Portland, OR: Intellect.

Shelley, Mary (1969) *Frankenstein; Or, the Modern Prometheus* (1831), ed. M.K. Joseph, Oxford: Oxford University Press.

Shelley, Mary (1994) *The Last Man*, ed. Morton Paley, Oxford: Oxford University Press.

Sobchack, Vivian (1987) *Screening Space*, 2nd edn, New Brunswick and London: Rutgers University Press.

Sobchack, Vivian (1996) 'Bringing it all back home: Family economy and generic exchange', in Barry Keith Grant (ed.), *The Dread of Difference*, Austin, TX: University of Texas Press.

Sontag, Susan (1974) 'The imagination of disaster', in Gerald Mast and Marshall Cohen, *Film Theory and Criticism*, New York and London: Oxford University Press.

Sponsler, Claire (1993) 'Beyond the ruins: The geopolitics of urban decay and cybernetic play', *Science Fiction Studies*, 20:2, 251–65.

Stelarc (1997) 'From psycho to cyber strategies', *Cultural Values*, 1:2, 241–9.

Stelarc (1999) 'Parasite Visions: alternate, intimate and involuntary experiences', *Body and Society*, 5: 2/3, 117–27.

Sterling, Bruce (1991) 'CyberView 91', *Well Gopher*, 3, 3–4.

Sterling, Bruce (1998) 'Cyberpunk in the Nineties', www.streettech.com/bcp/BCPtext/Manifestos/CPInThe90s.html.

Stevenson, Robert Louis (1979) *The Strange Case of Dr Jekyll and Mr Hyde and Other Stories*, ed. Jenni Calder, Harmondsworth: Penguin.

Stieg, Michael (1971) '*Dombey and Son* and the railway panic of 1845', *The Dickensian*, 67:3, 145–8.

Stiegler, Bernard (1998) *Time and Technics, 1: The fault of Epimetheus*, trans. Richard Beardsworth and George Collins, Stanford, CA: Stanford University Press.

Stoker, Bram (1993) *Dracula*, ed. Maurice Hindle, Harmondsworth: Penguin.

Stone, A.R. (1995) *The War of Desire and Technology at the Close of the Mechanical Age*, Cambridge, MA and London: MIT Press.

Summers, Montague (1964) *The Gothic Quest: A History of the Gothic Novel* (1938), New York: Russell and Russell.

Tarantino, Quentin (1994) *Reservoir Dogs*, London: Faber and Faber.

Tarantino, Quentin (1995) *Natural Born Killers*, London: Faber and Faber.

Tarantino, Quentin (1996) *From Dusk Till Dawn*, London: Faber and Faber.

Tomc, Sandra (1997) 'Dieting and Damnation: Anne Rice's *Interview with the Vampire*', in Jan Gordon and Veronica Hollinger (eds), *Blood Read*, Philadelphia, PA: University of Pennsylvania Press.

Twitchell, James (1988) 'The Vampire Myth', in Margaret L. Carter (ed.), *Dracula: The Vampire and the Critics*, Ann Arbor, MI and London: UMI Research Press.

Virilio, Paul (1991a) *Lost Dimension*, trans. Daniel Moshenberg, New York: Semiotexte.

Virilio, Paul (1991b) *The Aesthetics of Disappearance*, trans. Philip Beitchman, New York: Semiotexte.

Virilio, Paul (1994) *The Vision Machine*, trans. Julie Rose, Bloomington, IN: Indiana University Press.

Virilio, Paul (1995a) *The Art of the Motor*, trans. Julie Rose, Minneapolis, MN: University of Minnesota Press.

Virilio, Paul (1995b), 'Speed and information: Cyberspace alarm!', *CTHEORY*, www.aec.at/ctheory/a30-cyberspace_alarm.html.

Virilio, Paul (1997) *Open Sky*, trans. Julie Rose, London: Verso.

Virilio, Paul (1998) *The Virilio Reader*, ed. James Der Derian, Oxford: Blackwell.

Virilio, Paul (2000) *A Landscape of Events*, trans. Julie Rose, Cambridge, MA and London: MIT Press.

Virilio, Paul (2003) *Art and Fear*, trans. Julie Rose, London: Continuum.

Voller, Jack (1993) 'Neuromanticism: Cyberspace and the sublime', *Extrapolation*, 34:1, 18–29.

Walpole, Horace (1982) *The Castle of Otranto: A Gothic Story*, ed. W.S. Lewis, Oxford: Oxford University Press.

Wells, H.G. (1993) *The Island of Dr Moreau*, London: Everyman.

Wernick, Andrew (1999) 'Bataille's Columbine: The sacred space of hate', *CTheory*, http://gd.tuwien.ac.at/soc/ctheory/articles/Bataille's_Columbine:_The_Sacred_Space_Of_Hate_byAndrew_Wernick_.html.

Wicke, Jennifer (1992) 'Vampiric typewriting: Dracula and its media', *English Literary History*, 59, 467–93.

Will, Peter (1968) *Horrid Mysteries*, London: Folio Press.

Williams, Anne (1995) *Art of Darkness*, Chicago: University of Chicago Press.

Williams, Ioan (ed.) (1970), *Novel and Romance 1700–1800: A Documentary Record*, London: Routledge.

Williams, Tony (1996) 'Trying to survive on the darker side: 1980s family horror', in Barry Keith Grant (ed.), *The Dread of Difference*, Austin, TX: University of Texas Press.

Wilson, John (1876) *Noctes Ambrosianae*, Vol. I, Edinburgh: William Blackwood.

Wilt, Judith (1980) *Ghosts of the Gothic*, Princeton: Princeton University Press.

Wood, Gaby (2002) *Living Dolls: A Magical History of the Quest for Mechanical Life*, London: Faber and Faber.

Wood, Robin (1996) 'Burying the undead: the use and obsolescence of Count Dracula', in Barry Keith Grant (ed.), *The Dread of Difference*, Austin: University of Texas Press.

Wordsworth, William (1920) Preface to 'Lyrical Ballads' (1802), *The Poetical Works*, ed. Thomas Hutchinson, London: Oxford University Press.

York, Peter and Jennings, Charles (1995) *Peter York's Eighties*, London: BBC Books.

Zizek, Slavoj (1989) *The Sublime Object of Ideology*, London and New York: Verso.

Zizek, Slavoj (1991a) *For They Know Not What They Do*, London and New York: Verso.

Zizek, Slavoj (1991b) *Looking Awry*, Cambridge, MA and London: MIT Press.

Zizek, Slavoj (1992) *Enjoy Your Symptom*, London and New York: Routledge.

Zizek, Slavoj (1993) *Tarrying with the Negative*, Durham, NC: Duke University Press.

Zizek, Slavoj (1994) *The Metastases of Enjoyment*, New York and London: Verso.

Zizek, Slavoj (1996) *The Indivisible Remainder*, New York and London: Verso.

Zizek, Slavoj (1997) *The Plague of Fantasies*, London and New York: Verso.

Zizek, Slavoj (1999a) *The Zizek Reader*, eds Elizabeth Wright and Edmond Wright, Oxford: Blackwell.

Zizek, Slavoj (1999b) *The Ticklish Subject*, London and New York: Verso.

Zizek, Slavoj (2000) *The Fragile Absolute*, London and New York: Verso.

# Index

CPSIA information can be obtained
at www.ICGtesting.com
Printed in the USA
JSHW022357300321
13049JS00004B/138